MEASUREMENT AS A POWERFUL SOFTWARE MANAGEMENT TOOL

THE McGRAW-HILL INTERNATIONAL SOFTWARE QUALITY ASSURANCE SERIES

Consulting Editor

Professor D. Ince
The Open University

Other titles in this series

Practical Implementation of Software Metrics	Goodman
Software Testing	Roper
Software Metrics for Product Assessment	Bache and Bazzana

Related titles on software engineering are published in an accompanying series:
The International Software Engineering Series, also edited by Professor Darrel Ince.

MEASUREMENT AS A POWERFUL SOFTWARE MANAGEMENT TOOL

Nicholas Ashley

McGRAW-HILL BOOK COMPANY

London · New York · St Louis · San Francisco · Auckland · Bogotá
Caracas · Lisbon · Madrid · Mexico ·Milan · Montreal
New Delhi · Panama · Paris · San Juan · São Paulo · Singapore
Sydney · Tokyo · Toronto

Published by
McGRAW-HILL Book Company Europe
Shoppenhangers Road · Maidenhead · Berkshire · SL6 2QL · England
Telephone 0628 23432
Fax 0628 770224

British Library Cataloguing in Publication Data

Ashley, Nicholas
Measurement as a Powerful Software
Management Tool. – (McGraw-Hill
International Software Quality Assurance Series)
I. Title II. Series
005.1068

ISBN 0-07-707902-7

Library of Congress Cataloging-in-Publication Data
Ashley, Nicholas
    Measurement as a powerful software management tool / Nicholas
Ashley
        p.   cm. – (The McGraw-Hill international software quality
    assurance series)
    Includes bibliographical references and index.
    ISBN 0-07-707902-7 (U.S.)
    1. Computer software–Quality control.   I. title.   II. Series.
QA76.76.Q35A85   1995   94–27967
005. 1′4–dc20   CIP

12345 CL 98765

Typeset by TecSet Ltd, Wallington, Surrey
and printed and bound in Great Britain by Clays Ltd, St Ives plc

CONTENTS

PREFACE

Not everything that counts can be counted and not everything that can be counted counts.

Albert Einstein

In the 1990s information services (IS) departments are under threat as never before. Just witness the phenomenal growth in the number of IS departments that are being outsourced, rightsized, re-engineered and anything else that happens to be the flavour of the month. The pace of change sweeping through IS departments shows no sign of abating. To survive, IS departments need to change. Measurement is the driving force behind change. For without measurement we cannot objectively identify where changes are needed and we cannot objectively assess the impact of changes.

This book is about how measurement can be used as a powerful tool to support management in decision making — not just to deliver information for management in a timely manner but also to provide them with value. In other words, to provide managers with information that will help them to be more effective.

Today, the main problems facing IS departments are:

- Poor management, especially the management of change
- Lack of visibility of the development process
- Lack of communications both internally in the IS department and between the IS department and its customers.

This book shows software managers how measurement can help to tackle these problems. As a manager responsible for developing and maintaining software systems, you want answers to questions such as:

- How much will it cost to develop?
- Will it be ready on time?
- How effective is our test strategy at finding defects?

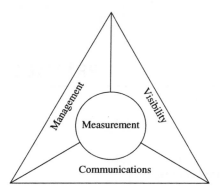

The main problems facing IS departments.

- What is the trend in effort spent on rework?
- What impact are the changes having on our productivity?
- How do we compare with the competition?

But what confidence can you place in the answers you are given? In order to help you manage you need answers that are based on quantifiable information rather than wishful thinking. You need to collect measures that are related to your business goals, measures that talk to you rather than measures that don't say much and when they do still don't say much.

MAIN GOAL

This book is aimed at software managers who want to take the first steps towards treating software development as a process that can be measured, controlled and improved.

The main goal of this book is to provide a step-by-step guide on how to use measurement as a powerful management tool to help to:

- Understand, control and then improve software development.

The book is based upon a case study of an IS department in a major financial institution whose short-term goal was to set up a Measurement Programme to support a process improvement programme. Having shown how to set up such a programme, the book then shows how it can be expanded to meet the following long-term goals of the IS department, namely:

- Derive a set of measures that can be used to specify and measure the quality of a software system.
- Develop a Measurement Programme to enable defects to be used as a process improvement tool.
- Develop a Measurement Programme to support an estimation process.

APPROACH

This book has harmonized the best practices of leading companies in Europe, USA and Japan who successfully run Measurement Programmes to control and optimize their software development processes. It has also taken on board the lessons learnt by those organizations who have failed in their initial attempts to run Measurement Programmes. Case studies are used to illustrate how organizations have used measurement as a management tool. The emphasis is on techniques that can be implemented easily by a project or department without causing undue disruption to their work environment. An evolutionary approach rather than a revolutionary approach is advocated.

Many of the ideas presented in this book were formulated while I was involved in METKIT (Ashley, 1993; Ashley and Bush, 1993). METKIT was a project partially funded by the Commission of the European Communities under ESPRIT (European Strategic Programme of Research in Information Technology). One of the main goals of METKIT was to develop a set of training courses on software engineering measurement that can be used by an organization to enable them to provide in-house training to managers and project teams. METKIT was born out of a need for building a bridge between the best practices of leading IS departments and the rest of the software development community. METKIT is now a commercially available product.

STRUCTURE OF THE BOOK

Each section is self-contained and can be studied independently.

Section 1 provides a comprehensive blueprint for setting up a Measurement Programme to support a process improvement programme, based on a case study for a major international insurance company. In particular, it answers the following questions:

- What are the main problems associated with setting up a Measurement Programme?
- Why is it necessary to appoint an executive sponsor?
- What are the responsibilities of the executive sponsor?
- How do you derive the goals of the Measurement Programme?
- How do you derive the measures to be used?
- What needs to be done to help ensure that there is a common and consistent approach to data collection?
- How do you measure the success of the Measurement Programme?
- How do you develop a feedback mechanism to support the Measurement Programme?

Section 2 shows how to use statistical process control (SPC) as a tool to help managers determine when to act on the data generated by a Measurement Programme. In particular, it answers the following questions:

- What is SPC?
- What is a control chart?
- How can SPC be used to provide an objective means of improving the effectiveness and quality of a software development process?

Section 3 shows how to expand the Measurement Programme developed in Section 1, to support the long-term goal of devising a set of measures to help specify and measure certain aspects of software quality. First, it defines a generic set of qualitative requirements that are common to all software systems. It then defines a set of measures, together with example benchmarks, that can be used to express each generic qualitative requirement in quantifiable terms. In particular, it answers the following questions:

- What is software quality?
- How is it possible to transform a qualitative requirement into a quantitative requirement?
- How can we define a set of indicators to help gauge the quality of a software development process?
- How can we define a set of indicators to help gauge the quality of a software system?

Section 4 shows how to expand the Measurement Programme developed in Section 1, to support the long-term goal of using defect analysis as a software process improvement tool. In particular, it answers the following questions:

- What is a defect?
- How do you develop a defect classification scheme?
- How do you use defect analysis as an improvement tool?
- How can you use defect analysis to help determine which testing techniques are most effective at detecting a particular type of defect?
- How can you use defect analysis to help determine when to stop testing and declare the software system reliable?
- How can you use defect analysis to estimate the defect density for a system on release to the user?
- How can you use defect analysis to help determine which processes are in most urgent need of improvement?
- How can you use defect analysis to help determine which are the most defect-prone modules?

Section 5 shows how to expand the Measurement Programme developed in Section 1, to support the long-term goal of developing a Measurement Programme to support an estimation process. In particular, it answers the following questions:

- What should be the format of an estimate?
- What are the main principles of estimating?
- What properties should an estimate possess?
- What are the main steps involved in performing an estimate?
- What information needs to be recorded in order to assess the plausibility of an estimate?
- How is it possible to detect unrealistic timescales?

Finally, the appendices contain the following:

- Glossary of abbreviations

- A set of analysis tools to support a Measurement Programme
- An overview of function point analysis (FPA)
- An introduction to the Software Engineering Institute (SEI) Capability Maturity Model (CMM)
- Example set of data collection forms associated with a Measurement Programme to support a process improvement programme
- Answers to typical questions that are likely to be asked by a team given the task of setting up and running a Measurement Programme
- A bibliography.

Nicholas Ashley
Brameur Ltd

ACKNOWLEDGEMENTS

I would like to thank the following friends and colleagues for helping to shape my thoughts and ideas and to improve this book, namely:

Anne Algar	David Hufton
Mike Berwick	Mike Kelly
Martin Burke	Thandi Moyo
Martin Bush	John Nunn
Norman Fenton	Meg Russell
Paul Goodman	Evans Woherem
Jim Hemsley	

I would also like to thank the following professionals whose books I have enjoyed reading and whose ideas have influenced my thinking:

Fred Brooks
Tom DeMarco
W. Edwards Deming
Watts Humphrey
Gerald Weinberg

The Quality Forum is pleased to publish jointly with McGraw-Hill this book which covers topics pertinent to software quality assurance.

The aim of the organization is 'to help the member organizations improve the quality of their products and services through the exchange of information between members and with other organizations with similar interests'.

The Quality Forum has over 200 members, including organizations from all sectors of industry and commerce, as well as local and national government. While these organizations are predominantly based in the UK, this includes a growing number from other countries in Europe.

This series of books aims to provide an opportunity for authors to publish works which are both practical and state-of-the-art. In this way Quality Forum members and other organizations will benefit from the exchange of information and the development of new ideas which will further the cause of quality in Information Technology (IT).

The Quality Forum publishes these books with the aim of stimulating discussion in the software community so that the industry as a whole will move forward to improved products and services. It is proud to be associated with the series while not endorsing every single point of view in every book.

If you would like to know more about the Quality Forum, please contact:

Quality Forum
17 St Catherine's Rd
Ruislip
Middlesex HA4 7RX
UK
Tel: +44 (0) 895 635222
Fax: +44 (0) 895 679178

Section 1

Blueprint For A Measurement Programme

You don't have to do this —
survival is not compulsory.

W. Edwards Deming

This section provides a blueprint for setting up a Measurement Programme to support a process improvement programme through the use of a case study. It should be noted that the principles put forward in this section are applicable to all types of measurement programmes.

1

BACKGROUND

Are the goals of the Measurement Programme aligned to our business goals and stated in quantifiable terms? Have we put into place all the infrastructure to support the Measurement Programme? Do the staff know why we are running the Measurement Programme and do they know what is expected of them? What type of training should our staff be given? Are we able to measure the success of the Measurement Programme? These questions, and others like them, are all too often asked by most teams faced with the challenge of setting up and running a software Measurement Programme.

In 1993 the IS division of a major international insurance company was faced with just such a challenge when it decided to set up a Measurement Programme as part of its strategy to improve its overall software development process. Many of its development processes were unstable in the sense that their future performance was not predictable. For example, estimating more often than not was based on guesses rather than on quantifiable historical data. Although some quality standards and procedures existed, there was little checking done to determine whether they were being followed. However, management had reached the stage where they wanted to treat software development as a process that can be controlled, measured and improved. They had just embarked on a set of process improvement initiatives to:

- Improve productivity
- Reduce rework
- Improve the accuracy of estimates of effort and timescales

and had introduced the following changes:

- Establishment of a quality group
- Appointment of process managers responsible for process improvement initiatives

- Formal reviews for each project deliverable
- Formal approach to risk assessment
- Independent project health checks
- Use of a repeatable and auditable estimation process that quantifies risk
- Production of a database of system test scripts
- Use of checklists to support each development process
- Use of a standard work breakdown structure.

The IS divisional manager wanted to know how well the changes were working. He also wanted to identify and prioritize where improvements were needed together with the changes needed to bring about the improvements. But first he wanted answers to five fundamental questions:

- Where are we?
- Where do we want to go?
- How do we get there?
- Have we got to where we want to go?
- How do we compare with the competition?

In particular he wanted to know what the current position was regarding:

- The productivity of development teams
- The effort spent correcting defects
- The effectiveness of reviews and system testing
- The accuracy of estimates of effort and timescales for projects.

The job of implementing a Measurement Programme to generate this information consisted of eight phases which are depicted in Fig. 1.1.

TIMESCALES

The IS divisional manager wanted to get the Measurement Programme up and running in three months and see tangible benefits within six to twelve months. Furthermore, since the measurement team were going to adopt an evolutionary approach to using measurement as a management tool, the Measurement Programme would not be piloted but rolled out to the whole department all at once.

Since the implementation was going to be based on tailoring METKIT materials (Ashley, 1993), rather than reinventing the wheel, it was felt that this timescale was achievable. In general, the time needed to set up and run a Measurement Programme will depend on the size of the IS department and the scope of the programme.

MEASUREMENT TEAM

The measurement team consisted of two people working full time:

- An external consultant who had set up a number of Measurement Programmes to support process improvement initiatives
- A member of staff from the IS department who had extensive experience of working on

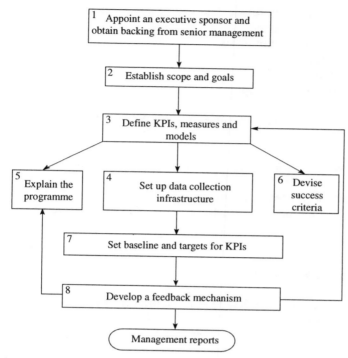

Figure 1.1 Process for setting up a Measurement Programme.

software projects and who was enthusiastic to learn how to use measurement as a management tool.

As well as heading the team and designing and implementing the programme, the external consultant was also required to train the other member of the team to take over when the consultant left.

Skills and responsibilities

What skills do the members of the measurement team need? It is no good giving the job to someone simply because there is nothing else for them to do. Apart from the obvious reasons, this type of approach sends the wrong signal to the project teams. A measurement team need a variety of skills in order to carry out the following responsibilities:

- Plan, design and implement the Measurement Programme
- Analyse the data collected
- Publicize the results of the Measurement Programme through graphs on noticeboards, monthly newsletter, etc.
- Provide feedback on a monthly basis to management on the results of information collected
- Hold meetings with project managers and team leaders on a monthly basis to discuss

data collection issues, to determine when future data will be generated and to provide feedback on results of information collected

- Liaise with the quality group on a monthly basis
- Take part in end-of-project reviews
- Document the measurement process
- Refine and expand the Measurement Programme.

The main skills needed by a measurement team to carry out these responsibilities are as follows:

- Ability to build relationships with project managers and project leaders to help ensure their cooperation
- Ability to persuade reluctant project teams to provide data
- Confidence to ask awkward questions relating to the data supplied by the project teams.

COLLECTION AND ANALYSIS OF DATA

It was going to be the responsibility of the project teams to collect the data generated on their projects. The measurement team would then be responsible for collating, analysing and reporting on the data relating to all of these projects.

PROBLEMS TO AVOID

From the outset the measurement team wanted to make sure that they adopted the 'best practices' of those IS departments that successfully use measurement as a management tool. In particular, they did not want to end up in the situation where a new initiative is launched without a captain, and wanders aimlessly, before floundering and sinking without trace. Therefore, they wanted to avoid the problems that had beset other organizations when they had tried to set up a Measurement Programme, such as:

- Not appointing an executive sponsor who would have overall responsibility for the Measurement Programme
- Not determining precisely who the customers of the Measurement Programme were and what they wanted from it
- Lack of management commitment
- Lack of commitment from project teams because they had not been told why the Measurement Programme was important and what it meant to them
- Not appointing an executive sponsor who would have overall responsibility for the Measurement Programme
- Imprecise objectives with no clear direction or timescales
- Not deriving the goals of the Measurement Programme from the needs of management and the business goals
- Collecting data for its own sake rather than deriving the measures from the goals of the Measurement Programme

- Not matching the measures to the capability of the software development process
- Management having unrealistic expectations of the benefits
- Being too ambitious by trying to do too much at once rather than using an evolutionary approach
- Not treating the implementation as a project and not providing sufficient resources
- Not implementing a standard work breakdown structure that was used consistently across all projects
- Management failing to act upon the information generated by the Measurement Programme
- Not defining objective criteria to assess whether the Measurement Programme was providing tangible benefits
- Not providing feedback to the project teams who were supplying data and being measured
- Making inappropriate use of the information, for example to assess the performance of an individual
- Management failing to instigate a culture change where project teams viewed measurement as an integral part of a continuous process improvement programme.

Taking on board these lessons, the measurement team adopted an evolutionary approach because they recognized that they were not going to get everything *right first time*. Furthermore, trying to solve everyone's problems at once was a recipe for disaster.

OVERVIEW OF APPROACH

The approach used to set up and run the Measurement Programme consisted of eight phases. Figure 1.2 provides a high-level overview of these phases. The remaining chapters in this section describe these phases in detail.

Phase	Objectives of phase	Main outputs
1	Appoint an executive sponsor Establish who the customers will be Obtain backing and commitment from senior management	Responsibilities for executive sponsor Responsibilities for measurement team List of customers Plan to implement the programme
2	Establish the scope and goals of the Measurement Programme Validate scope and goals against budget, timescales and requirements of the customers	Concerns of managers Management goals Questions to be answered Goals and scope of programme
3	Define the key performance indicators (KPIs) Derive a set of measures to monitor performance against the KPIs Define models relating measures to KPIs	Set of KPIs Set of measures Set of models relating measures to KPIs
4	Set up a data collection infrastructure	Data collection plan Procedures and guidelines Set of checklists Data collection forms Work breakdown structure Database (spreadsheet)
5	Explain the Measurement Programme to managers and project teams Train the staff involved in data collection Instigate a culture change to support the programme	Workshop for managers Workshop for project teams Plan for culture change
6	Devise a set of objective criteria to assess the success of the Measurement Programme	Set of objective criteria
7	Define baselines and targets for the KPIs Identify data to be produced by projects over the year	Baselines for KPIs Targets for KPIs Table of data to be generated by projects during the year
8	Implement a feedback mechanism to: provide managers and project teams with the results of analysing the data collected; provide feedback to data collectors; help improve the Measurement Programme Devise templates and guidelines for presenting the results of analysing the data collected	Feedback mechanism to support communications Feedback mechanism to support process improvements for the Measurement Programme

Figure 1.2 High-level overview of phases.

2

PHASE 1 — APPOINT AN EXECUTIVE SPONSOR

This phase consisted of appointing an executive sponsor for the Measurement Programme and obtaining commitment and backing from senior management.

The appointment of an executive sponsor was seen as a vital activity. It sent a clear signal to everybody concerned that the Measurement Programme was going to be implemented seriously.

The executive sponsor should be at least one level higher than project managers.

RESPONSIBILITIES OF THE EXECUTIVE SPONSOR

The responsibilities of the executive sponsor were as follows:

- Determining who the customers were; in other words, who was going to be provided with information
- Gaining management commitment and backing for the Measurement Programme
- Acting as a focal point for the Measurement Programme
- Providing direction to the measurement team
- Defining the responsibilities of the measurement team
- Representing the aims of management
- Ensuring the Measurement Programme was aligned to the needs of the business
- Ensuring that the goals of the Measurement Programme were communicated to and understood by all the IS department and signed off by the customers
- Formulating a vision statement for the Measurement Programme
- Ensuring management did not have unrealistic expectations of the benefits
- Getting the template for the annual report on the performance of the IS department against the key performance indicators signed off by the customers

- Ensuring project managers were committed to the programme, especially as most of the benefits would not be realized in the first six to twelve months. It would be unrealistic to expect project managers to commit resources without support from senior managers
- Liaising with process managers
- Ensuring that the information generated by the Measurement Programme was acted upon by management
- Demonstrating to project teams the commitment of management to the Measurement Programme so that staff did not get the opinion that it was yet another half-hearted initiative from management
- Instigating a culture change to support the Measurement Programme.

WHO ARE THE CUSTOMERS?

One of the first jobs of the executive sponsor is to determine who the customers of the Measurement Programme are. In general, there will be more than one customer and each will have different needs.

The key customers for this Measurement Programme were as follows:

- Manager of the IS department
- Senior managers directly under the manager of the IS department
- Software project managers
- Software quality assurance group.

OBTAINING MANAGEMENT SUPPORT AND COMMITMENT

The executive sponsor needs to get the support and commitment from senior management otherwise you might as well not begin. To obtain long-term commitment and funding from senior management it was necessary to demonstrate the benefits of using measurement. Management needed to be convinced that measurement would improve their business, in other words improve the 'bottom line'. Managers wanted answers to two questions:

- What are the benefits?
- How much will it cost?

The high-level benefits were going to be:

- The generation of quantifiable information to help in decision-making
- An ability to determine the impact of changes
- An ability to help identify where changes were needed
- A more effective development environment.

The specific benefits would depend on the goals of the Measurement Programme which would be generated from the needs of the customers, for example the need to produce accurate estimates of effort and timescales.

The question of how much will it cost to implement and run a Measurement Programme should be rephrased as:

- How much will it cost our organization if we don't use measurement?

Japanese IS departments, such as those in Hitachi, Fujitsu and NEC, are not too concerned with how much it costs to implement and run a Measurement Programme. They believe it is something that must be done irrespective of cost because it is vital for survival.

Few IS departments have indicated exactly what they have spent on setting up and running a Measurement Programme, but the proportion seems to be from two to five per cent of the overall running costs of the IS department, depending on the scope of the programme. The costs will include:

- Effort spent by measurement team
- Effort spent on consultancy
- Effort spent on training staff
- Effort spent by project teams collecting data
- Tools such as spreadsheets and databases.

Having decided to set up a Measurement Programme where should the funding come from? There is no hard and fast rule on how the Measurement Programme should be funded. An organization should decide what funding mechanism is appropriate for itself. A general guideline based on the experience of organizations which have successfully run a Measurement Programme would be to divide the costs between the project and central funds. That way the project can be seen to pay for the immediate benefits of information with which to monitor and control the project and the organization contribution is justified in the form of improvements spread across other projects and general improvement of its competitive position in the marketplace.

HOW TO SUSTAIN MANAGEMENT COMMITMENT

We now provide some guidelines on how to sustain management commitment:

- Be realistic: don't promise what you cannot deliver.
- Manage the expectations of the customers.
- Hold monthly meetings to discuss the information generated by the Measurement Programme.
- Refine the Measurement Programme to meet the changing needs and priorities of management. Remember they are the customers.

3

PHASE 2 — ESTABLISH SCOPE AND GOALS

This phase consisted of establishing the scope and goals of the Measurement Programme and then validating them.

APPROACH

In order to determine the scope and goals of the Measurement Programme, the measurement team first observed its key customers in their environment to help to understand what their jobs involved. For example:

- The type of long-term strategic decisions that needed to be made by the manager of the IS department
- The type of information that needed to be provided to the business
- The type of reports that needed to be produced by the manager of the IS department
- The type of day-to-day decisions that needed to be made by project managers
- The type of reviews that were conducted by the project teams on project deliverables, such as project plans, specifications, code, etc.

Next the measurement team held meetings with the following staff to determine their problems and what they wanted from the Measurement Programme to help them do their job more effectively:

- Manager of the IS department
- Cross-section of managers reporting to the manager of the IS department
- Project managers
- QA manager
- Senior software engineers working on projects.

To help ensure that the meetings were structured, the measurement team developed a set of questionnaires around which the meetings were based. For example, managers were asked the following questions:

- Which phases of the development process are in most urgent need of improvement?
- What are the main problems affecting projects?
  - effort overruns
  - late delivery
  - excessive rework
  - non-conformance to requirements
  - not using an evolutionary approach to developing systems
  - not providing value to the customer
  - etc.
- What are the main causes of the problems affecting projects?
  - managerial
  - poor communications
  - lack of visibility
  - not focusing in on key issues
  - technical
  - inappropriate tools and methods
  - etc.
- What do you want from a Measurement Programme?
  - help in estimating effort and timescales
  - help in decision making
  - help in improving communications across the IS department
  - more visibility of the development process
  - identifying trends in productivity and effort spent on rework
  - identifying where changes are needed
  - etc.
- What data is currently collected to support managers?
- Are critical decisions based on quantifiable information?
- Is there a mechanism used to identify and apply lessons learnt from each project for new projects?

The meetings served a dual purpose. First, to elicit information so that the shape and scope of the Measurement Programme could be formulated. In particular to find out where management had problems and the information they needed to help them manage. Secondly, to inform managers and project teams what the measurement team were doing and to help ensure that they felt an integral part of it. The outputs from the meetings were:

- A prioritized list of management goals
- A set of questions that required quantifiable answers
- The main concerns of managers and project teams.

MANAGEMENT GOALS

The long-term qualitative goal of management was to:

- Re-engineer their software development process to enable project teams to work more effectively.

The main short-term qualitative goals of management were as follows:

- Improve the productivity of the development teams
- Reduce effort spent on rework by finding defects earlier
- Identify and improve the most defect-prone processes
- Reduce the time spent detecting and correcting defects
- Improve the effectiveness of system testing
- Improve the accuracy of estimates of effort and timescales.

Not surprisingly these goals were no different from the goals of managers in most companies across all sectors of industry. These goals were then used to derive the scope and goals of the Measurement Programme.

QUESTIONS

The main questions management wanted answers to were as follows:

- What is the current productivity of project teams?
- What needs to be done to improve productivity?
- Is it more cost-effective to tailor a packaged-based solution rather than do all the development in-house?
- What is the average time spent correcting a defect during development?
- How much effort is spent on rework?
- What needs to be done to reduce rework?
- What percentage of defects are caused by bad fixes?
- What is the effectiveness of reviews of project deliverables?
- How can reviews be improved?
- What is the effectiveness of system testing?
- How can system testing be improved?
- How can we specify and measure software quality?
- What is the accuracy of estimates of effort and timescales?
- How can the accuracy of estimates be improved?
- What are the most time-consuming development activities?

Many IS departments do not know which of their development activities are the most time-consuming. A major computer manufacturer was concerned that they were spending too much of their software development effort on rework. They intuitively believed that correcting defects was their most time-consuming activity. Therefore, they set up a Measurement Programme to confirm their beliefs. It came as no surprise to management that the most time-consuming activity was indeed correcting defects. However, what surprised them was that their second most time-consuming activity was attending meetings. Even more of a surprise was the fact that their third most time-consuming activity was travelling to meetings. These findings were used as a catalyst to re-engineer their development process.

CONCERNS

The main concerns of project managers and project teams were:

- Lack of a formal estimation process
- Open-ended requirements
- Uncontrolled change
- Arbitrary timescales
- Insufficient time to test new systems
- Inefficient system test strategy
- Inadequate training in the use of tools and methods
- Unmanaged system standards
- No mechanism to assess the impact of changes.

SCOPE

The scope of a Measurement Programme can cover three main areas, namely:

- Supporting managers in estimating and planning projects
- Supporting managers in monitoring and controlling the progress of projects
- Supporting process improvement initiatives.

The scope of this Measurement Programme was to:

- Support managers in estimating and planning projects
- Assess the impact of process improvement initiatives.

The scope did not cover monitoring and controlling software projects against plans as this was already being performed as a separate activity. It should be noted that one of the long-term objectives of the Measurement Programme would be to integrate this activity into the main Measurement Programme.

Having defined the scope in terms of areas to be covered, the next step was to define the scope in terms of projects to be covered. Essentially, there were two choices:

- Pilot-based approach
- Blanket approach covering all projects.

It was decided to adopt a blanket approach using an evolutionary strategy. The main reason for this decision was that management wanted to identify trends in productivity and rework across the whole department as quickly as possible. The evolutionary strategy would tackle the highest priority problems first and would enable the Measurement Programme to grow with respect to the capability of the development environment.

It should be noted that projects refer to enhancing and developing software systems and do not cover corrective maintenance.

The main role of the Measurement Programme was to:

- Define a set of key performance indicators for productivity, quality and accuracy of estimates in order to assess the performance of the IS department
- Determine baselines and targets for the key performance indicators
- Determine the impact of changes introduced by the process improvement programme by monitoring the trend in the key performance indicators
- Identify where changes were needed to improve the software development process in order to meet the targets for the key performance indicators.

GOALS OF THE MEASUREMENT PROGRAMME

The goals of the Measurement Programme were derived from the goals of management and the questions that management wanted answers to. The goals were determined in terms of:

- What is wanted
- Who wants it
- Why it is wanted
- When it is wanted.

The goals were then divided up into short-term and long-term goals.

It should be noted that the Measurement Programme was not intended to be used to get staff to work harder. Neither was it to assess the productivity of individuals. Its primary goal was to assess the impact of changes on productivity and rework.

PRODUCTIVITY GOALS OF THE MEASUREMENT PROGRAMME

The short-term goals of the Measurement Programme to support the process improvement initiative concerning productivity were as illustrated in Fig. 3.1.

QUALITY GOALS OF THE MEASUREMENT PROGRAMME

The short-term goals of the Measurement Programme to support the process improvement initiative concerning quality were as illustrated in Fig. 3.2.

The long-term goals of the Measurement Programme to support the process improvement initiative concerning quality were as illustrated in Fig. 3.3.

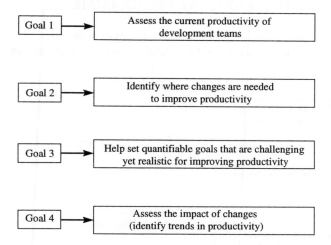

Figure 3.1   Productivity goals of the Measurement Programme.

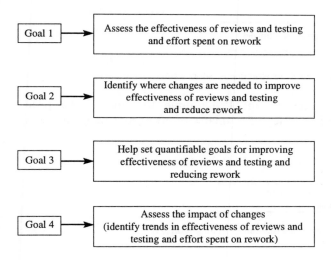

Figure 3.2   Quality goals of the Measurement Programme — short term.

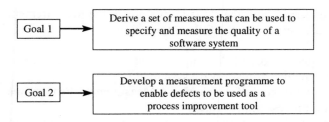

Figure 3.3   Quality goals of the Measurement Programme — long term.

ESTIMATING GOALS OF THE MEASUREMENT PROGRAMME

The short-term goals of the Measurement Programme to support the process improvement initiative concerning accuracy of estimates of effort and timescales were as illustrated in Fig. 3.4.

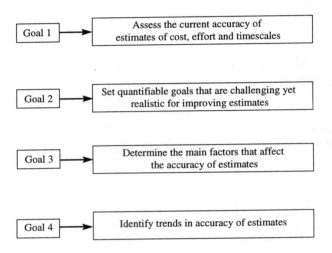

Figure 3.4   Estimating goals of the Measurement Programme — short term.

The long-term goal of the Measurement Programme to support the process improvement initiative concerning accuracy of estimates of effort and timescales was as illustrated in Fig. 3.5.

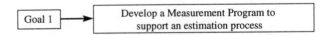

Figure 3.5   Estimating goals of the Measurement Programme — long term.

NOTE

The remainder of this section is concerned with the short-term goals of the Measurement Programme. The long-term goals are covered in the following sections:

- Section 3 covers the long-term quality goal of deriving a set of measures that can be used to specify and measure the quality of a software system.
- Section 4 covers the long-term quality goal of developing a Measurement Programme to enable defects to be used as a process improvement tool.
- Section 5 covers the long-term goal of developing a Measurement Programme to support an estimation process.

VALIDATION OF GOALS

Having defined the scope and the goals of the Measurement Programme, they were then validated to ensure consistency between:

- The goals and business objectives of the organization
- The goals and the measurement budget, to ensure that the measurement team was being realistic and not trying to do too much
- The goals and the timescales
- The goals and the capability of the software development process
- Each goal.

4

PHASE 3 — DEFINE KPIs, MEASURES AND MODELS

This phase consisted of defining the key performance indicators (KPIs) (Fig. 4.1) for the Measurement Programme and then deriving a set of measures to monitor the performance of the IS department against these KPIs.

The KPIs were derived from the short-term goals of the Measurement Programme and the questions that management wanted answers to, which were generated in Phase 2. We now provide an overview of these KPIs.

KEY PERFORMANCE INDICATOR FOR PRODUCTIVITY

The classic equation for measuring productivity is:

$$\frac{\text{output}}{\text{effort}}$$

In order to apply this equation to software development we need to define an objective measure for the 'output' of a software project. Such a measure needs to reflect the impact of changes to the development process. For example, any change to the development process that reduces the effort needed to develop or enhance a software system should be reflected in an increase in productivity.

Function point analysis (Appendix C) was chosen to measure the output of a software project because it provides a measure of the output that is independent of the programming language used. Essentially Function Point Analysis measures the functionality that the system provides to the user and emphasizes the user's view rather than the implementation used to satisfy the requirements. Function Point Analysis produces a unitless measure known as a Function Point Count (FPC).

Productivity	Function Point Count per person month
	Cost per Function Point Count
Quality	Percentage of effort spent on rework
	Percentage of effort spent on reviews
	Effectiveness of reviews
	Effectiveness of system testing
	Average effort in hours to correct a defect found during development
	Percentage of bad fixes during development
Estimates	Variance between estimated and actual effort
	Variance between estimated and actual timescale

Figure 4.1   Key performance indicators.

The two main key performance indicators for productivity for a project were defined as:

$$\frac{\text{Function Point Count on handover to customer}}{\substack{\text{project effort} + \text{effort spent on correcting defects found} \\ \text{and corrected during first two months of operational use}}}$$

$$\frac{\text{development cost of the project}}{\text{Function Point Count on handover to the customer}}$$

The main points concerning these productivity indicators are as follows:

- The Function Point Count per person month takes into account the quality of the delivered project.
- The Function Point Count per person month can be used to establish productivity trends for 'similar' projects. For example, similar may mean enhancement projects relating to a particular system. In general, projects will need to be split into categories to help ensure that like is compared with like. New systems based on packaged-based solutions, will, in general, be more productive than non-packaged-based solutions. The following is a list of typical categories:
  - mainframe new systems that are packaged-based
  - mainframe new systems that are non-packaged-based
  - mainframe enhancements that are packaged-based
  - mainframe enhancements that are non-packaged-based
  - PC new systems that are packaged-based
  - PC new systems that are non-packaged-based
  - PC enhancements that are packaged-based
  - PC enhancements that are non-packaged-based.
- Not all defects will be detected during the first two months of operational use. The two month timescale is a pragmatic approach in order to get the Measurement Programme up and running. Furthermore, it should be noted that it may be the case that not all defects detected during the first two months of operational use will be corrected in the first two months. Chapter 25 discusses the problem of deciding when a defect is regarded as a defect with respect to the Measurement Programme.

- Project effort is defined to be the total effort expended by each project team member who worked on the project during the elapsed time for the project from the start of the project to handover to the customer.
- Development cost is defined to be the cost of each person who worked on the project, plus the cost of maintenance staff who performed corrective maintenance during the first two months of operational use, plus the cost of support tools, plus the cost of package solutions.

KEY PERFORMANCE INDICATORS FOR QUALITY

The six main key performance indicators for Quality, were defined as:

$$\text{Percentage of effort spent on rework} = \frac{\text{effort spent correcting defects}}{\text{project effort}}$$

$$\text{Percentage of effort spent on reviews} = \frac{\text{effort spent on reviews}}{\text{project effort}}$$

$$\text{Effectiveness of reviews} = \frac{\text{defects detected}}{\text{defects present}}$$

$$\text{Effectiveness of system testing} = \frac{\text{defects detected}}{\text{defects present}}$$

$$\text{Average effort in hours to correct a defect} = \frac{\text{effort spent correcting defects}}{\text{number of defects corrected}}$$

$$\text{Percentage of bad fixes} = \frac{\text{defects caused by bad fixes}}{\text{defects detected}}$$

The main points concerning these quality indicators are as follows:

- The effort spent on reviews consists of the effort spent preparing for the review and the effort spent conducting the review. It does not include the effort spent correcting the defects/issues raised in the review.
- Effort spent on correcting defects covers all defects found during development, and defects corrected during the first two months of operational use.
- The effectiveness of reviews refers to reviews of each deliverable from the project, namely the project plan, quality plan, requirements specification, design specification, test plan, etc.
- The defects present during a phase of development is defined as the defects introduced during the phase and those defects that were introduced during an earlier phase but were not detected. This raises the question of how to calculate the defects present. The following approach was used. The number of defects detected during development and the number of defects detected during the first two months of operational use should be

used to approximate the total number of defects introduced. These defects should then be allocated to the phases of development that they were introduced in. It should be recognized that it may not be possible to determine this information for all the defects (see Section 4). Thus when a defect is detected, the phase of development where it was introduced needs to be recorded. Thus the effectiveness of a review cannot be calculated until the system has been in operational use for two months. However, it is possible to determine the partial efficiency of reviews after testing by using the number of defects detected during development as a coarse approximation for the total number of defects introduced.

- Defects caused by bad fixes are defined as defects caused by correcting a defect. For example, consider a defect found during a review or test which is corrected. On a subsequent review or test (which may be in a different phase of development) a defect was found which was not there on the original review or test and can be attributable to the correction made.

KEY PERFORMANCE INDICATOR FOR ESTIMATING

The key performance indicator for estimating was defined as the variation between the actual effort and estimated effort and the actual timescale and estimated timescale. The variations were calculated using the following formula:

$$\frac{(\text{actual} - \text{estimate})}{\text{estimate}}$$

The main points concerning this estimating indicator are as follows:

- A negative variation implies the actual effort/timescale was under budget and a positive variation implies the actual effort/timescale was over budget.
- It can be used to establish estimating trends.
- It can be used across all projects.
- The variation was based on the estimate without contingency added. The rationale for this decision is as follows. The formal definition of an estimate of effort/timescale is a prediction that is equally likely to be above or below the actual effort/timescale. To produce such a prediction requires assessing all the major risk factors and incorporating their potential impact into the estimate. Having produced an estimate it is then a management decision of whether they want to increase or decrease the estimate to increase or decrease the chance that the estimate will have an equal chance of being above or below the actual value. For example, since an estimate has the property that there is a 50 per cent chance that the actual will be above or below the estimate, management may want to reduce the chance that the actual is above the estimate. In such cases a contingency may be added to the estimate. In general, the contingency is a subjective decision by management that will be influenced by their experience and also influenced by political decisions, etc. In the light of these comments, the variance between the actual and estimate should be based on the estimate without contingency.

MEASURES

The measurement team derived a set of measures to monitor the performance of the IS department against the KPIs. A two-step approach was used which consisted of:

- Refining the goals of the Measurement Programme into a set of related questions
- Refining the questions into a set of measures that help to answer the questions.

This approach was based on the GQM (goal–question–metric) approach of Basili and Rombach (1988).

QUESTIONS RELATED TO GOALS

The goals of the Measurement Programme were refined into two high-level questions, namely:

Q1   What are the current baselines for the KPIs?
Q2   Where are improvements needed?

These two questions were then refined into the following sixteen specific questions:

Q1.1   What is the productivity of the project teams?
Q1.2   What is the cost of productivity?
Q1.3   What percentage of effort is spent on rework?
Q1.4   What percentage of effort is spent on reviews?
Q1.5   How effective are reviews?
Q1.6   How effective is system testing?
Q1.7   What is the average effort to correct a defect found in development?
Q1.8   What is the percentage of bad fixes during development?
Q1.9   What is the accuracy of the estimates of effort for projects?
Q1.10   What is the accuracy of the estimates of timescales for projects?
Q2.1   What are the most defect-prone development phases?
Q2.2   What percentage of defects found during development are corrected?
Q2.3   Which modules are the cause of most operational failures?
Q2.4   What is the breakdown of effort across the phases of development?
Q2.5   What factors affect productivity?
Q2.6   What factors affect the accuracy of estimates?

MEASURES RELATED TO GOALS

The twenty measures listed in Fig. 4.2 were derived to help answer these sixteen questions.

	Description of measure	Related questions
M1	Function Point Count (FPC)	Q1.1
		Q1.2
M2	Development cost	Q1.2
M3	Actual effort for the project	Q1.1
		Q1.3
		Q1.4
		Q1.9
		Q2.4
M4	Estimated effort for the project	Q1.9
M5	Actual phase effort	Q1.9
		Q2.4
M6	Estimated phase effort	Q1.9
M7	Actual elapsed time for the project	Q1.10
M8	Estimated elapsed time for the project	Q1.10
M9	Effort spent correcting defects during development	Q1.3
		Q1.7
M10	Effort spent on reviews	Q1.4
M11	Effort expended during the first two months of operational use correcting defects caused by a project	Q1.1
		Q1.3
		Q1.9
M12	Number of defects introduced during a phase of development	Q1.5
		Q2.1
M13	Number of defects detected during a review	Q1.5
M14	Number of defects detected during a phase of development	Q1.6
		Q2.2
M15	Number of defects present during a review but introduced during an earlier phase	Q1.5
M16	Number of defects corrected during a phase of development	Q1.7
		Q1.8
		Q2.2
M17	Number of defects caused by bad fixes during development	Q1.8
M18	Number of defects in a module which led to an operational failure over a set period of time	Q2.3
M19	Number of operational faults found over a set period of time that are attributable to a project	Q1.6
M20	Size of a module measured in lines of code	Q2.3

Figure 4.2   Measures related to goals.

MODELS

We now describe the models relating the sixteen questions to the twenty measures (Fig. 4.3).

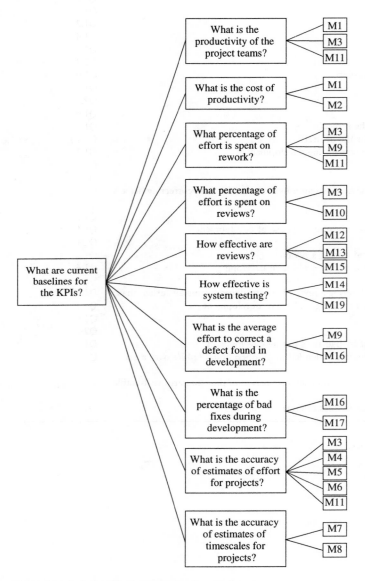

Figure 4.3   Relationship between questions and measures.

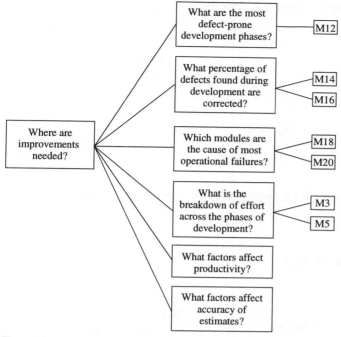

Figure 4.3 (*continued*)

Q1.1 What is the productivity of the project teams?

The following model was used:

$$\text{Productivity} = \frac{M1}{M3 + M11}$$

Q1.2 What is the cost of productivity?

The following model was used:

$$\text{Cost of productivity} = \frac{M2}{M1}$$

Q1.3 What percentage of effort is spent on rework?

The following model was used:

$$\% \text{ project rework} = \frac{M9 + M11}{M3}$$

Q1.4 What percentage of effort is spent on reviews?

The following model was used:

$$\% \text{ of project effort spent on reviews} = \frac{M10}{M3}$$

Q1.5 How effective are reviews?

The following model was used:

$$\text{Effectiveness of a review for a phase of development} = \frac{M13}{M12 + M15}$$

Q1.6 How effective is system testing?

The following model was used:

$$\text{Effectiveness of system testing} = \frac{M14'}{M14' + M14'' + M14''' + M19}$$

where:

M14′ refers to the number of defects found during system testing
M14″ refers to the number of defects found during acceptance testing
M14‴ refers to the number of defects found during regression testing.

Q1.7 What is the average effort to correct a defect found in development?

The following model was used:

$$\text{Average effort to correct a defect} = \frac{M9}{\sum M16}$$

where $\sum M16$ denotes summation over all development phases.

Q1.8 What is the percentage of bad fixes during development?

The following model was used:

$$\text{Defect propagation ratio} = \frac{M17}{\sum M16}$$

where $\sum M16$ denotes summation over all development phases.

Q1.9 What is the accuracy of estimates of effort for projects?

The following models were used:

$$\text{Effort variation} = \left[\frac{\text{M3} + \text{M11} - \text{M4}}{\text{M4}}\right] \times 100$$

$$\text{Phase effort variation} = \left[\frac{\text{M5} - \text{M6}}{\text{M6}}\right] \times 100$$

where $[y]$ denotes the absolute value of a number. For example, $[-2] = 2$ and $[2] = 2$.
Note that if the absolute value is not used, that is the effort variation is allowed to be a negative number, then the average variation for a number of projects may turn out to be low simply because high negative variations are nullified by high positive variations.

Q1.10 What is the accuracy of the estimates of elapsed timescales for projects?

The following model was used:

$$\text{Timescale variation} = \left[\frac{\text{M7} - \text{M8}}{\text{M8}}\right] \times 100$$

where $[y]$ denotes the absolute value of a number.

Q2.1 What are the most defect-prone development phases?

The following model was used:

$$\text{Percentage of defects per phase} = \frac{\text{M12}}{\sum \text{M12}}$$

where $\sum \text{M12}$ denotes summation over all development phases.

Q2.2 What percentage of defects found during development are corrected?

The following model was used:

$$\text{Percentage of defects corrected} = \frac{\sum \text{M16}}{\sum \text{M14}}$$

where $\sum \text{M14}$ denotes summation over all development phases
and $\sum \text{M16}$ denotes summation over all development phases.

Q2.3 Which modules cause the most operational failures?

The following model was used:

$$\text{Defect-prone module ratio} = \frac{M18}{M20}$$

Q2.4 What is the breakdown of effort across the phases of development?

The following model was used:

$$\% \text{ effort per phase} = \frac{M5}{M3} \times 100$$

Q2.5 What factors affect productivity?

A model is not applicable. However, from the results of applying the models associated with questions 1.1 to 2.4, the following factors were identified as having a detrimental effect on productivity:

- Project timescales
- Amount of rework
- Inaccurate estimate of project size
- Complexity of project
- Time spent system testing
- Time spent on analysis and design
- Unplanned changes to requirements
- Novelty of project
- Size of project team
- Experience of project team
- Experience of project manager
- Premature loss of key staff
- Use of new methods/tools.

Q2.6 What factors affect accuracy of estimates?

A model is not applicable. However, from the results of applying the models associated with questions 1.1 through to 2.4, the following factors were identified as having a detrimental affect on the accuracy of estimates:

- Project timescales
- Productivity rate of project team
- Amount of rework
- Estimated size of project
- Complexity of project

- Time spent system testing
- Premature loss of key staff
- Misunderstanding of requirements
- Unplanned changes to requirements
- Miscalculation of risks
- Novelty of project
- Size of project team
- Experience of project team
- Experience of project manager
- Use of new methods/tools
- Strategic/political decision
- Experience of estimator
- Incorrect formula/assumptions.

5

PHASE 4 — SET UP A DATA COLLECTION INFRASTRUCTURE

This phase consisted of setting up a data collection infrastructure to help ensure a common and consistent approach to data collection. In particular, it covered:

- Data collection plan
- Procedures, guidelines and checklists
- Definitions
- Process to validate data collected
- Data collection forms
- Quick reference measurement card
- Standard work breakdown structure
- Database.

We now provide an overview of these topics.

DATA COLLECTION PLAN

The data collection infrastructure contained a data collection plan which identified:

- What data was to be collected
- Bounds for each data item
- When the data was to be collected
- Frequency of data collection
- Where the data was to be collected from
- Who would collect, validate, store, interpret and present the data
- How the data was to be collected, validated, recorded and stored

- Where the data was to be stored.

PROCEDURES, GUIDELINES AND CHECKLISTS

The data collection infrastructure contained a set of procedures, guidelines and checklists on how to collect, record, validate, store, interpret and present data. In particular it contained:

- A procedure on data collection for project teams
- A procedure for storing the data that has been collected
- Guidelines for analysing and interpreting the data collected
- Guidelines for presenting the results
- A checklist for setting up a data collection infrastructure
- A checklist for producing a data collection plan
- A checklist to support the process of validating data
- A checklist for determining the type of defects to be recorded.

DEFINITIONS

The data collection infrastructure contained a set of definitions for all the terms used, including the measures.

PROCESS TO VALIDATE DATA COLLECTED

The data collection infrastructure contained a process to assess the accuracy of the data collected. The objectives of a validation process are to help answer the following set of questions:

- What data items need to be validated?
- What can be done to determine whether the data is within a standard deviation of the norm?
- What data can be ignored?
- What can be done to help to ensure that standard units of measure have been used and used consistently?
- What can be done to help to ensure the data is of the right type?
- What can be done to help to ensure that the data is traceable and complete?
- Can historical data be used to validate data?
- How is it possible to ensure that data collectors have collected what was wanted?

Step 1 — Data to be validated

Data validation should be performed on all data collected, before it is stored and analysed, to help ensure its accuracy.

Step 2 — Check bounds for each data type

In order to determine whether the data items collected are within a standard deviation of the norm, check that when data is collected, it is within its bounds. For example, the bounds relating to the hours worked by an individual in a single day, on a particular activity, may be between zero and ten hours. If the data is outside its bounds, determine reasons why and, if necessary, take action to rectify the situation.

Step 3 — Implausible values

Outlier detection, using box plots, should be used to detect implausible values. An explanation of this technique is provided in Appendix B.

Step 4 — Use standards

In order to ensure consistency and commonality in the units of measures used by different project teams, check to see that a common set of standard measures have been used.

Step 5 — Type of data

Wherever possible check that the type of data is correct. For example, ensure that integers are given where integers are required, hours are given where hours are required, etc. For example, it may be the case that an individual has recorded that they have worked 40 days in one week. This would suggest that the person has recorded hours instead of days.

Step 6 — Traceable and complete

To help ensure that the data is traceable and complete, the following should be done:

- Ensure that all data is recorded on standard data collection forms.
- Confirm that all relevant data has been recorded on the data collection form.

Step 7 — Historical data

Wherever possible, compare data with similar validated historical data.

Step 8 — Data collectors

To help ensure that data collectors conscientiously collect what is required, the following points should be adhered to:

- Managers should motivate project teams to keep accurate records.
- Data collectors and data recorders should be told why the data is being collected and how it is going to be used.
- Data collectors should have received training in data collection.
- Feedback should be provided to data collectors.
- Standards, procedures, guidelines and checklists should be used by data collectors.

DATA COLLECTION FORMS

The data collection infrastructure contained a set of data collection forms having the following properties:

- They were self-explanatory, except for common technical terms which were defined elsewhere.
- They were based on quantifiable answers to questions.
- They stated the units of measure and bounds for each data item that was collected.
- Choices were provided where variable information was required.
- Each form was contained on one side of A4 paper.

Appendix E provides examples of the data collection forms.

QUICK REFERENCE MEASUREMENT CARD

The data collection infrastructure contained a quick reference measurement card for project teams, which contained the following information:

- List of KPIs together with their baselines and targets
- List of data to be collected together with instructions on when it is to be collected and where it is to be recorded
- List of supporting documentation.

STANDARD WORK BREAKDOWN STRUCTURE

The data collection infrastructure contained a standard work breakdown structure (WBS) which was used by all projects to help ensure consistency in data collection. A WBS is a methodical way of defining all the work to be carried out on a project. A standard WBS gives projects a predefined checklist of activities for them to consider including in the scope of their project. Collecting software measures against these predefined standard activities enables the measures to be compared with those from other projects. Individual projects can select a subset of the standard WBS to meet its needs without compromising those aspects that ensure commonality across projects.

A WBS breaks the totality of the work needed to be carried out to achieve the objectives of the project into a hierarchy of defined activities. At any level in the hierarchy the totality of activities at that level will produce the complete project/system. At the next level down from a particular activity, the activities emanating from it refine it into sub-activities which in their entirety form that activity.

A WBS is a system for subdividing a project into manageable work packages to provide a common framework for:

- Scope
- Cost
- Schedule
- Coordinating the work

- Communications
- Allocation of responsibility
- Monitoring
- Management.

The definition of each activity needs to be detailed enough so that there is no misunderstanding as to what is and is not included in an activity.

A WBS can be represented and documented using a tree structure (Fig. 5.1).

The topmost node, Level 0, represents all the activities that need to be carried out to achieve the project. The total work is then broken down into a number of Level 1 activities. These Level 1 activities together cover all the work that the node at Level 0 encompassed. Similarly, each Level 1 activity is broken down into Level 2 activities, etc. The level to which the work needs to be broken down depends on the nature of the work. The lowest level should be sufficient to monitor and control the work.

Typical Level 1 activities related to developing a software system should include:

- Defining the business case
- Performing a feasibility study
- Setting up infrastructure to support the project
- Project management
- Configuration management
- Quality assurance
- Requirements specification
- Procurement
- High-level design
- Detailed design
- Code and unit testing
- Performing system testing and acceptance testing
- Data conversion
- Defining infrastructure to support the system during operational use

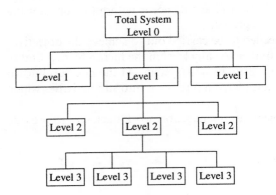

Figure 5.1 Representation of a WBS.

- Installation
- Operational maintenance.

Checklist

For each activity identified by the WBS, a checklist was produced which defined:

- Its objective
- Criteria for triggering the activity
- Who was responsible for the activity
- Groups/departments involved in the activity
- Which phase(s) of the lifecycle the activity was to be performed in
- List of sub-activities
- Dependencies with respect to other activities
- Inputs to activity
- Outputs from activity
- Criteria and method for assessing the quality of the outputs
- Support materials (standards, etc.)
- Tips to help perform the activity.

Coverage

A standard WBS should identify all activities that can be carried out on any project and can thus act as a checklist of work to be carried out on any new project. These activities are grouped for commonality of subject matter through the tree structure. There should also be a cross-reference, in the form of a two-dimensional matrix, between the deliverables produced during the project lifecycle and the activities associated with the WBS.

Relationship between WBS and lifecycle

A WBS differs from a lifecycle in that a lifecycle defines the sequence in which the activities are carried out whereas the WBS is unordered in terms of time. As activities within different lifecycles have much in common in terms of their outputs, one WBS can accommodate many lifecycles.

DATABASE

The data collection infrastructure contained a database which was set up in the form of a spreadsheet running on a PC, to record and manipulate the data, which allowed:

- The worksheet schema to be modified easily
- Totals to be generated automatically
- Graphics to be created automatically.

6

PHASE 5 — EXPLAIN THE PROGRAMME

This phase consisted of:

- Explaining the Measurement Programme to both managers and project teams
- Training the staff involved in data collection and analysis
- Instigating a culture change to support the Measurement Programme.

The measurement team needed to explain to managers and project teams what was going on and to get their cooperation. Gaining the commitment and involvement of the staff who would contribute to the measurement and analysis process, or be affected by it, was as important as gaining support from management. Otherwise, data may be distorted, morale may drop, and changes may not be implemented.

The main messages of this phase were that:

- Management needed to understand that measurement by itself does not bring about improvement. Measurement is a management tool that can be used to provide visibility of the software development process, assist in decision making and focus on what is important.
- Management needed to understand that measurement if used in an *ad hoc* fashion without clear objectives can have a negative effect.
- Project teams needed to understand what the Measurement Programme could do for them.
- Project teams needed to be convinced that management would not misuse the information generated from the Measurement Programme.

The primary objective of this task was to run workshops to communicate the goals of the Measurement Programme to all the IS department and to explain to managers and project team members the following:

- The benefits and limitations of the Measurement Programme
- What data they were to collect
- What the data was to be used for
- Contents of the data collection plan
- How to fill in data forms
- How to validate data
- How to store data
- How to analyse the data that was collected
- What should be included in the analysis report
- How to use standards, procedures and checklists
- The feedback mechanism
- Potential problems with data collection and how to avoid them.

WORKSHOP FOR MANAGERS

In order to get management buy-in to the Measurement Programme they wanted answers to two questions, namely:

- What will it do for me? (What are the benefits?)
- How much will it cost?

The objectives of the workshop for managers were to:

- Explain what information was going to be generated by the Measurement Programme
- Explain how the information should be used, emphasizing that it needed to be acted upon
- Explain when to act and when not to act on the information; for example, if a measure was between a certain bound what action needed to be taken
- Help ensure that management did not use the data inappropriately; for example, trying to get data to confirm wrong beliefs rather than evaluating data and investigating why it is in conflict with their beliefs
- Gain their approval and commitment to the Measurement Programme.

Examples were used to highlight various situations.

It was important to avoid using technical terms that managers were not familiar with. In general, senior managers are not interested in the number of function points achieved per month by a project team. Rather, they are interested in productivity trends. Is productivity increasing or decreasing and what are the reasons?

WORKSHOP FOR PROJECT TEAMS

The objectives of the workshop for project teams were to:

- Explain the importance of measurement in the context of software engineering
- Explain the objectives of the Measurement Programme
- Explain the benefits of the Measurement Programme, in particular, that the Measurement Programme is not just for managers but for the whole of the IS

department. It is important to explain what is in it for the project teams, namely:
- less hassle
- better work environment to help them work more effectively
- better communications
- more realistic estimates of effort and timescales
- a tool to help them solve their own problems
- Explain what project teams need to do to support the Measurement Programme
- Allow project teams to comment on the:
  - proposed data to be collected
  - procedures to support data collection
  - proposed presentation of the data.

TIPS FOR WORKSHOPS

Visibility of management commitment

To help show project teams the commitment of management to the Measurement Programme the following was done. The executive sponsor of the Measurement Programme spent ten minutes at the beginning of the workshop setting the scene and explaining the importance management attach to the Measurement Programme.

States of transition

In general, people try to resist change but adapt very quickly once they are convinced of the benefits of the change. When introducing a Measurement Programme there are four main states that people go through (Fig. 6.1).

First, understanding why the measurement programme is necessary and what are its associated benefits. For example, project teams can use the information generated by the Measurement Programme to support their protests to management when saddled with unrealistic effort and timescales. Secondly, accepting that the Measurement Programme is necessary and that it has been shown to work for other organizations. Thirdly, providing support, whether this is:

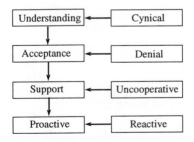

Figure 6.1 States of transition.

- Total support in the sense of staff accepting responsibility and ownership and making suggestions for improvements
- Partial support in the sense of: 'I'll provide initial support, to enable you to convince me that it works.'

Finally, the fourth state is where managers and project teams become proactive. For example, a project team may ask the measurement team to help them quantify the quality of the test scripts and the risk of reducing the time spent on system testing.

It is important to recognize that these states exist and to cover each of them in the workshops for managers and project teams.

During the first three stages you will inevitably encounter:

- Denial that there is a problem
- Resistance from cynics who are either openly hostile or are unconvinced by the benefits.

You need to identify who the cynics are before commencing the workshops. One of the ways of dealing with cynics is to mix up the workshops so that they are matched against staff who do see the benefits and are openly supportive of the Measurement Programme. Then hopefully the believers will try to win over the sceptics. Of course, if all else fails, then tell them that the bottom line is that if the IS department does not use measurement then they may not have a job next year. More and more IS departments are now looking towards outsourcing as a more cost-effective provider of services. It is up to the IS department to convince the business that the changes being introduced are improving productivity and making them cost-effective. But this can only be demonstrated by the use of measurement.

Concerns of project teams

The main concern expressed by the project teams was that senior managers were going to misuse the data; for example, comparing across projects and departments without taking into account the differences between projects, such as the complexity of the requirements, skill of development teams, availability and use of automated tools, quality of the supporting documentation, etc. This issue was addressed by explaining to the project teams that management had attended a workshop where it was explained to them what could and could not be done with the data.

Size of workshops

Each workshop should consist of fifteen to twenty people. Attendees at a workshop for project teams should not all be from the same project team. The attendees should be from a cross-section of project teams to help promote communications across the department.

TRAINING

The measurement team recognized that training is a key factor in introducing changes. Therefore, they ran a variety of training courses for managers and project teams covering the following topics:

- Role of measurement in software engineering
- Function point analysis
- Validation of data
- Analysis of data
- Presentation of data
- When to act and when not to act on the information generated
- Estimating techniques.

These training courses were based on the METKIT materials (Ashley, 1993).

The measurement team also held meetings with project team members who were going to be responsible for collecting and analysing the data in order to explain in detail:

- What data needed to be collected
- When the data needed to be collected
- How to complete the data collection forms
- How to analyse the data
- How to use the checklists to support data collection and analysis
- Potential problems, such as:
  - misinterpreting data
  - apportioning project effort across the phases of development
  - making predictions based on historical data that has not been validated.

To support this activity the measurement team produced a booklet containing a set of typical questions that may be raised by project teams concerning data collection and analysis, together with a set of answers.

It was going to be the responsibility of the project managers and project leaders to ensure that the instructions on data collection should cascade through the project teams.

INSTIGATE A CULTURE CHANGE

Having explained the programme, management then embarked on a culture change to support the Measurement Programme to one where measurement became an integral part of the development culture.

The main message was that management needed to ensure that project teams had a positive attitude towards both measurement and the more broader goal of continuous process improvement. In other words, project teams viewed measurement as an integral part of a continuous process improvement programme which was the responsibility of all the staff (Figure 6.2 illustrates the problem!).

Figure 6.2   There's never time to do it right but there's always time to correct it.

Management needed to change the culture to one where:

- Project teams are convinced that management is committed to moving away from a culture of sacrificing quality to meet deadlines to one of ensuring that productivity gains are not achieved at the expense of quality. For example, there is no point in producing unreliable systems faster. However, it should be recognized that this type of culture cannot happen overnight. But management should ensure that the IS department is moving in the right direction.
- Project teams report problems early to enable corrective action to be taken before it is too late.
- Defects are seen as a valuable source of information that can be used to improve processes. For example, analysing defects can help to determine the most defect-prone phases of development, the effectiveness of reviews and test strategies, etc. Changing people's attitudes to one where it is encouraged to identify and analyse the cause of defects is not always easy as the western culture teaches children from an early age that mistakes are bad and children are punished for making mistakes. Furthermore, slogans such as 'Get it right first time' don't help either.
- Shift the culture from testing to inspections.

SUSTAINING THE CULTURE CHANGE

The greatest challenge with introducing a culture change is not getting it accepted, but sustaining momentum to support the culture change after the initial wave of enthusiasm has worn off. This then leads onto the question of how you hold onto gains that are made and build on these gains to become even better.

Consider drink–driving campaigns on the television at Christmas. Initially, the impact is very effective and accidents caused by alcohol fall dramatically. However, a couple of months after the adverts have stopped, the number of accidents caused by alcohol returns to its normal level. Of course if the adverts were not taken off, people would become bored with them and they would eventually lose their impact unless they were updated in an imaginative way. It is the same with trying to sustain a culture change in an organization. Too much continuous selling will eventually have a negative impact. The solution is to learn from organizations that have successfully achieved one or more culture changes.

To further illustrate the concept of sustaining a culture change in an IS department we turn to the world of golf. Asking a golf fan who were the greatest golfers, they will invariably choose players who not only reached the top of their profession but remained there year after year: people like Ben Hogan, Jack Nicklaus, Arnold Palmer and Gary Player. Few people remember the golfer who won a major championship but did little else. What makes a winner want to carry on winning? Some say success breeds success, but it is much more than this. It is not only a will to win which is very important, or a fundamental belief in themselves, but also the dedication to perfecting their skills to stay one step ahead of the rest. Hours spent on the practice ground and hours spent watching videos of golfers who they regard as the greatest. Nick Faldo is widely regarded as the best golfer of the 1990s but it wasn't always like this. Back in the early 1980s Faldo was a good golfer and made a comfortable living from playing a game he liked. But he had an ambition to become not only the best of his generation but the best of the best. So he sought out the best teacher and began the long and sometimes painful process of changing his swing and whole attitude to the game. Success didn't come overnight but it came and now he is the best golfer of his era. But he is still striving to improve to become the best of the best.

The point here is that whatever profession you are in there is no magic formula to becoming the best and remaining there. Instead there are fundamental principles that need to be continuously adhered to. The keys to helping to meet the challenge of sustaining a culture change to support both an improvement programme and its associated Measurement Programme are as follows:

- Choosing a leader who is committed to the culture change and has the dynamic drive to sustain the improvement programme and motivate project teams
- Setting challenging targets that are attainable and not so unrealistic as to be demotivating
- Providing feedback to employees to show them what they have achieved
- Providing incentive to the workforce and providing recognition of achievement
- Providing training to the workforce to help them become more effective
- Ensuring that improvements are not just helping profits but benefiting all the employees by creating a better working environment that enables them to work more effectively
- Creating a company culture where process improvement is at the forefront of every employee's perception of the company and where employees are:
  - given the opportunity to suggest improvements
  - listened to when they give advice on how they think something can be improved.

Finally, what happens when you achieve your ultimate goal of becoming the best of the best? You will then have companies benchmarking against you, trying to oust you from your number one position. Sweet dreams are made of this.

7

PHASE 6 — DEVISE SUCCESS CRITERIA

This phase consisted of devising a set of evaluation criteria to assess the success of the Measurement Programme after it had been running for 12 months. In other words, what was the customer's return on their investment? The primary objective of the Measurement Programme was to provide information to help managers and projects in:

- Decision making
- Providing better communications, both internally in the IS department and between the IS department and the business
- Understanding, controlling and improving the software development process
- Setting quantifiable goals
- Setting baselines and targets for the key performance indicators
- Determining if goals were being met
- Identifying where changes were needed
- Assessing the performance of the IS department.

The main objectives of the evaluation criteria were to:

- Assess the success of the Measurement Programme after it had been running for 12 months in terms of the value it provides to its customers;
- Manage the expectations of the customers of the Measurement Programme
- State in quantifiable terms what is going to be delivered to whom and when.

QUESTIONS RELATED TO EVALUATION CRITERIA

The criteria for judging a Measurement Programme must not only assess whether the right information is being generated but also needs to take into account the quality of the information being generated. Judging the success of the Measurement Programme was based on the answers to the following questions:

- *Is the right information being generated?*
  The answer to this question was determined in relation to the objectives of the Measurement Programme.
- *Is the information being generated in a timely manner?*
  The answer to this question was determined in relation to management needs, that is, when they need data to help them in decision making, producing reports, etc.
- *What is the quality of the information being generated?*
  The answer to this question was determined in terms of the extent to which the Measurement Programme had identified where changes were needed to improve processes. One way to assess the quality of the measurement information is to see what impact the subsequent changes had. In other words, had the Measurement Programme identified the right areas? However, if the changes are not implemented effectively, then this should not reflect adversely on the assessment of the Measurement Programme.
- *To what extent has the Measurement Programme generated data to enable baselines and targets to be set for each key performance indicator?*
  The answer to this question was determined in relation to the percentage of baselines and targets that had been set for the KPIs. The quality of the targets was assessed in terms of whether they:
  - were challenging
  - were achievable
  - took into account the process improvement changes
  - were validated against the capability of development process
  - were validated against timescales.
- *To what extent has the Measurement Programme provided reasons for discrepancies where actual values for key performance indicators fall outside target values?*
  For example, when evaluating the accuracy of estimates of effort it is not sufficient to simply determine the variance between estimates and actuals. Other factors need to be taken into consideration such as the productivity achieved. Otherwise it may be the case that the variation looks good simply because large contingencies were added to the estimates, which resulted in low productivity.
- *To what extent has the Measurement Programme provided management with increased visibility of the software development process?*
  The answer to this question was determined in terms of how well the Measurement Programme alerted management to potential problems and enabled them to act in a problem prevention mode rather than a problem recovery mode.
- *To what extent has the Measurement Programme provided managers with quantifiable information to support process improvements?*
  The answer to this question was determined in terms of:
  - identifying which processes need to be improved
  - identifying which methods used by a project are proving beneficial.
- *Have management acted on the information to improve the software development process?*
  The answer to this question was determined in terms of the changes that had been implemented, decisions made, etc.
- *Do management understand when they should and should not act on the information?*

The answer to this question was determined in terms of whether management understood the different states a process can be in (see Section 2), namely:
- capable and stable
- capable but unstable
- stable but not capable
- unstable and not capable.

- *Are graphs used to present data and are the graphs self-explanatory?*
  The answer to this question was determined by getting managers and project teams to complete a questionnaire.
- *Are the project teams supportive of the Measurement Programme?*
  The answer to this question was determined by getting managers and project teams to complete a questionnaire.
- *Do the project teams understand the purpose of the Measurement Programme?*
  The answer to this question was determined by getting managers and project teams to complete a questionnaire.
- *Do the project teams know what is expected of them in terms of collecting and analysing data?*
  The answer to this question was determined by getting managers and project teams to complete a questionnaire.
- *To what extent has feedback been provided to the project teams?*
  The answer to this question was determined by getting managers and project teams to complete a questionnaire.
- *What state are the project teams at in terms of accepting measurement?*
  When introducing a Measurement Programme there are four main states that people go through. First, understanding why the Measurement Programme is necessary and its associated benefits. Secondly, accepting that the Measurement Programme is necessary and that it has been shown to work for other organizations. Thirdly, providing support. Finally, the fourth state is where managers and project teams become proactive. The answer to this question should be categorized as either:
  - understanding
  - accepting
  - supportive
  - proactive.
- *What is the coverage and quality of the infrastructure to support the Measurement Programme?*
  The answer to this question was determined by examining the level of supporting documentation (procedures, guidelines and checklists) to support data collectors and data analysts and the extent to which the responsibilities of the measurement team had been documented.
- *To what extent are projects providing data?*
  The answer to this question was determined in terms of the percentage of projects that were supplying data for each KPI.
- *What has been done to help ensure that the Measurement Programme does not just slowly fade away and die?*
  The answer to this question was determined in terms of:
  - the feedback provided to managers and project teams
  - the dynamic drive of the leader of the measurement team

- whether targets were attainable and not so unrealistic as to be demotivating
- incentives to the workforce
- recognition of achievement
- training of the workforce to help them become more effective
- ensuring that improvements were not just helping profits but benefiting project teams by creating a better working environment that enabled them to work more effectively
- the extent to which process improvement and measurement were at the forefront of project teams' perception of the company
- extent to which project teams were given the opportunity to suggest improvements and listened to when they made suggestions.

8

PHASE 7 — SET BASELINES AND TARGETS FOR KPIs

This phase consisted of setting baselines and targets for the key performance indicators. In order to do this it was necessary to produce a table of when projects would be providing data.

Baselines and targets for projects should be established annually and should be derived from the quantifiable information generated by the Measurement Programme. Then performance can be judged against these baselines and targets on a yearly basis.

SETTING BASELINES

Data generated during the first three to six months of running the Measurement Programme was used to set the initial baselines.

Once the initial baselines had been set, subsequent baselines were defined as follows:

Baseline for productivity = average productivity of projects that were completed during the previous year

Baseline for effort spent on rework = average rework of those projects that were completed during the previous year

Baseline for variance of estimates of effort/timescales = average accuracy of estimates of effort/timescales of those projects that were completed during the previous year

In certain cases abnormal data values were excluded from these calculations using box plots (see Appendix B).

PRINCIPLES OF TARGET SETTING

The main principles for setting targets are that they should be:

- Stated in measurable terms
- Related to time
- Challenging yet achievable
- Validated against budget, timescales, capability of the development process and the process improvement programme
- Communicated to everyone involved
- Revised as more information becomes available or targets are met.

The two main ways of setting targets are as follows:

- Base the targets on the achievements of organizations who have embarked on a similar process improvement programme. Ideally, these organizations should be in the same business sector.
- Use the data generated by the Measurement Programme to plot trends in the KPIs. Then generate base targets using the slope of the trend line. Then adjust these base targets to take account of:
  - the capability of the process improvement programme
  - how well changes have been implemented.
  Note that if as a result of the changes, processes are approaching their optimal level and project teams are working very effectively, then you can only expect 'small' productivity improvements.

A combination of these two methods was used to generate the initial targets for the KPIs. For example, the following targets were produced, where timescales commenced when the initial baselines had been established:

- Within 12 months increase the average productivity of projects by 20 per cent.
- Within 6 months decrease the effort spent on rework for the department by 35 per cent.
- Within 12 months produce estimates of effort and timescales from the high level design that are within 20 per cent of the actual effort in 85 per cent of the cases.

These targets were based on the assumption that the following changes were introduced:

- Formal reviews for each project deliverable
- Formal approach to risk assessment
- Analysis of defects to help identify and improve the processes that caused the defects
- Use of a repeatable and auditable estimation process that quantifies risk
- Production of a database of system test scripts
- Use of checklists to support each development process
- Use of a standard work breakdown structure.

9

PHASE 8 – DEVELOP A FEEDBACK MECHANISM

This phase consisted of developing a feedback mechanism and devising the following guidelines and templates for presenting the results of analysing the data collected:

- Guidelines for presenting data
- Guidelines for producing graphs
- Guidelines for sustaining a Measurement Programme
- Template for the report on the evaluation of the Measurement Programme
- Template for the monthly report on the performance of the IS department against the KPIs
- Template for the annual report on the performance of the IS department against the KPIs.

Feedback starts with the workshops for managers and project teams to explain the importance of the Measurement Programme to the IS department.

The main roles of the feedback mechanism (Fig. 9.1) were to:

- Help ensure that management acted on the information generated by the Measurement Programme
- Help ensure that the Measurement Programme was still operational after the initial motivation had waned
- Help improve the software development process
- Help improve the Measurement Programme, for example by sending out a questionnaire to project teams to elicit their comments and ideas
- Provide feedback to the data collectors
- Provide managers with the results of analysing the data collected
- Use the information generated by the Measurement Programme to motivate managers and project teams to develop higher quality software.

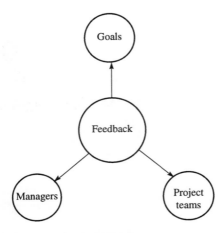

Figure 9.1 Feedback mechanism.

It was important to learn from the results and to refine the Measurement Programme in the light of the findings.

GUIDELINES FOR PRESENTING DATA

The following guidelines should be used to present the results of analysing the data collected:

- Different customers want different information; for example, as the information passes up through the management structure, less detail is needed.
- Reports should be self-explanatory and results should not require the reader to interpret them.
- Reports should be aligned with the quantifiable goals against which the data has been collected.
- Trends should be shown visually as graphs or charts.
- Choose a graph that meets your requirements; for example, Kiviat diagrams, pie charts, bar charts and histograms have different uses.
- Comparisons should be made against baselines and targets.
- Reasons should be given when the variation between targets and actuals for the KPIs exceeds 15 per cent.
- Where targets have failed to be met, state what has been done to rectify the situation.
- Summaries of results should be presented as the first page of the report with the details in subsequent sections.
- Standardize reports by using a common format, especially for graphs and charts.
- Ensure that for any figures in the report it is a simple matter to determine if the figure is above average, average, below average or an exception; if necessary label figures using one of these categories.
- Ensure that the report is disseminated.

GUIDELINES FOR PRODUCING GRAPHS

A graph should fit on one side of A4 paper and contain:

- Title of graph
- Graph
- A brief description of the purpose of the graph
- The goals which the graph relates to
- The calculations used to produce the graph
- Additional information, such as unusual information on the graph, what can be concluded from the graph, techniques used to smooth the graph, etc.

GUIDELINES FOR SUSTAINING A MEASUREMENT PROGRAMME

We now discuss how feedback can be used to sustain a Measurement Programme through motivation and communication.

Display graphs

One way to help ensure that managers and project teams continue to be motivated to contribute to the Measurement Programme and have a positive attitude towards measurement is as follows. When the Measurement Programme has generated sufficient data to plot trends in productivity, rework and accuracy of estimates, represent the trends using coloured graphs. Then display the graphs in prominent places in the work environment so that everyone can see how their contributions are having an effect on the performance of the IS department. Remember it is the simple things that are usually the most effective.

Measurement user group

To help sustain a measurement programme you should form a Measurement User Group (MUG) consisting of one representative from each strategic project. The MUG should meet once a month for one hour. The first half-hour should be a discussion, where members share experiences relating to measurement. The second half-hour should consist of a presentation by one of the MUG members on a chosen technique that could be introduced into the development process to help make improvements. For example, a member could be asked to talk on how some of the techniques used in the Space Shuttle software testing strategy could be incorporated into their testing strategy.

Newsletter

To support the feedback process the measurement team should produce a monthly newsletter covering such items as:

- Trends in KPIs
- Support the measurement team provides to project teams

- Training courses available to support measurement activities
- New or updated documents to support measurement activities, such as procedures, guidelines and checklists.

The newsletter should consist of no more than two sides of A4 paper and should be distributed to all members of the IS department.

Meetings

Use the data generated by the Measurement Programme in staff meetings, presentations to management, etc. to help ensure that measurement becomes part of the culture of the IS department.

TEMPLATE FOR EVALUATION REPORT

The purpose of this report was to record the finding from the evaluation of the Measurement Programme after it had been running for 12 months. The report consisted of answers to the questions relating to the evaluation criteria as defined in Phase 6 of the Measurement Programme. This report was distributed to managers and project teams.

TEMPLATE FOR MONTHLY PERFORMANCE REPORT

The purpose of this report was to present the trends in the KPIs on a monthly basis. Essentially, for each KPI, the report contained a graph depicting the monthly trend in the KPI on a 12-month rolling cycle, together with reasons whenever the graph depicted exceptional behaviour. This report was distributed to managers and project teams.

TEMPLATE FOR ANNUAL PERFORMANCE REPORT

The remainder of this chapter provides an example of an annual report on the performance of an IS department against its key performance indicators. For simplicity, it is assumed that as far as productivity is concerned there is only one category of project. In practice, there will be more than one type of category (to help ensure that you are comparing like with like) and the annual report should report individually on each category in terms of baselines, targets and trends.

Example

Annual Report On Performance Against KPIs

ABSTRACT

This document reports on the performance of the IS department against the key performance indicators.

Author	Measurement Team
Date	January 1994
Reference	AR.KPI/Issue 1

TABLE OF CONTENTS

56

EXECUTIVE SUMMARY

This document reports on the performance of the IS department during the year 1993 in terms of the following key performance indicators (KPIs) for productivity, quality and accuracy of estimates, namely:

- Productivity (FPC per person month)
- Cost per FPC
- Effort spent on rework
- Effort spent on reviews
- Effectiveness of reviews
- Effectiveness of system testing
- Average effort spent correcting a defect
- Percentage of bad fixes
- Accuracy of estimates of effort
- Accuracy of estimates of timescales.

STATUS OF PROJECTS

During the year two new systems were completed and 87 enhancements were made to three operational systems.

CHANGES IMPLEMENTED

The following changes were implemented during the year:

- Formal reviews for each deliverable from each phase of development
- Analysis of defects to help identify and improve the processes that caused the defects

- Introduction of a standard work breakdown structure that was used consistently by all projects
- Introduction of checklists to support each development process and each activity in the work breakdown structure
- Use of a traceable and auditable estimation process incorporating a quantifiable risk assessment technique
- Appointment of process managers who were responsible for carrying out improvements to the development processes
- Independent project health checks
- Production of a database of system test scripts.

IMPACT OF CHANGES

The overall impact of the changes introduced during the year had a positive effect on the IS department (Fig. 1 and Table 1).

The impact of some changes took longer to filter through than others. In particular, the efficiency of design reviews took six months to show a positive impact in reducing the effort spent on rework.

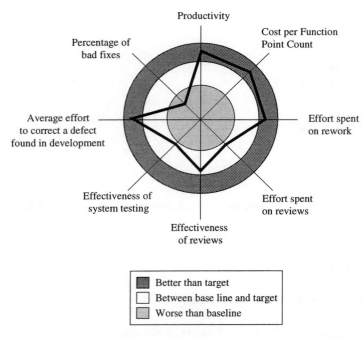

Figure 1 Overview of performance against productivity and quality KPIs.

Table 1   Table of performance against KPIs

KPI	Baseline	Target	Actual
FPC per person month	5	6	7
Cost in £ per FPC	950	800	780
Percentage of effort spent on rework	30	19	18
Percentage of effort spent on reviews	4	6	5
Effectiveness of reviews	80	90	88
Effectiveness of system testing	70	85	84
Average effort in hours to correct a defect found during development	12	10	9
Percentage of bad fixes	5	4	5.5
Variance between estimated and actual effort	40	20	17.5
Variance between estimated and actual timescales	30	20	18

FINDINGS

The information generated by the Measurement Programme indicates that:

- Project teams collected 96 per cent of the data items they were required to record.
- Formal inspections and reviews of the project deliverables are starting to have a positive impact on reducing the effort spent on rework. The effort to find and correct a defect during an inspection was 1.18 hours. This compares with 10.9 hours to find and correct a defect during testing. It is estimated that inspections and reviews saved over £80,000 during 1993.
- Insufficient effort was spent on unit testing, which had a detrimental effect on the effectiveness of system testing.
- There is more room for improving the efficiency of system testing.
- The difficulty in assessing the knock-on effect of implementing changes to older systems is contributing to the increase in defects that are created when correcting defects.
- The variations in estimates of effort and timescales started to decrease towards the end of the year. This improvement was not achieved at the expense of productivity. In other words, the reduction of variation was not achieved by inflating the estimates.

RECOMMENDATIONS

The measurement team propose the following recommendations:

- More effort should be spent in the analysis phase in order to reduce the amount of rework in later development phases.
- At the end of each review, five minutes should be spent on exploring ways to improve the review process.
- More effort should be spent on unit testing to help reduce the effort spent on system testing. Project managers should ensure that teams cease to adopt the practice of letting system testing perform the work of unit testing.
- The test strategy should target defect-prone modules.

OVERVIEW OF PERFORMANCE AGAINST KPIs

PRODUCTIVITY
✓ target exceeded

The overall trend in productivity is *increasing*, but not at the expense of increasing the amount of rework associated with correcting operational failures.

> *The average productivity for the 89 projects completed during the year is **up** 40% on last year from 5 FPC per person month to 7 FPC per person month.*
>
> *The highest productivity achieved on a project was 17 FPC per person month.*
>
> *The lowest productivity achieved on a project was 3 FPC per person month.*

The main reason for the overall increase in productivity is due to the positive impact formal reviews are having in reducing the effort spent on rework.

COST PER FPC
✓ target exceeded

The overall trend in the cost per FPC is *decreasing*.

> *The average cost per FPC for the 89 projects completed during the year is **down** 17% on last year from £950 per FPC to £780 per FPC.*
>
> *The highest cost per FPC on a project was £1200 per FPC.*
>
> *The lowest cost per FPC on a project was £520 per FPC.*

The main reason for the decrease in cost per FPC is due to the positive impact formal reviews are having in reducing the effort spent on rework.

EFFORT SPENT ON REWORK
✓ *target exceeded*

The overall trend in effort spent on rework is *decreasing*.

> *The average percentage of effort spent on rework for the 89 projects completed during the year is **down** 40% on last year from 30% to 18%.*

> *The highest percentage effort spent on rework for a project was 27%. The lowest percentage of effort spent on rework on a project was 12%.*

> *Most rework was performed in the design phase. 30% of the overall rework was performed in the design phase. 28% of the overall rework was performed in the testing phase.*

The main reason for the decrease in effort spent on rework is the introduction of reviews for each deliverable from each phase of development.

EFFORT SPENT ON REVIEWS
–- *improved on baseline but **failed** to meet target*

The overall trend in effort spent on reviews is *increasing*.

> *The average percentage of effort spent on reviews for the 89 projects completed during the year is **up** 25% on last year from 4% to 5%.*

> *The highest percentage effort spent on reviews for a project was 8%. The lowest percentage of effort spent on reviews for a project was 3%.*

97% of deliverables were formally reviewed.

The main reason for the increase in effort spent on reviews is the introduction of reviews for each deliverable from each phase of development.

EFFECTIVENESS OF REVIEWS
— *improved on baseline but **failed** to meet target*

The overall trend in the effectiveness of reviews is *increasing*.

> *The average effectiveness of reviews for the 89 projects completed during the year is **up** 10% on last year from 80% to 88%.*

> *The highest effectiveness for a review was 98%.*

The lowest effectiveness for a review was 61%.

The main reason for the improvement in the effectiveness of reviews is that:

• Reviews are being conducted on a more formal basis and staff training in review techniques is beginning to have a positive impact.

EFFECTIVENESS OF SYSTEM TESTING
— *improved on baseline but **failed** to meet target*

The overall trend in the effectiveness of system testing is *increasing.*

> *The average effectiveness of system testing for the 89 projects completed during the year is **up** 20% on last year from 70% to 84%.*
>
> *The highest effectiveness for system testing for a project was 96%.*
>
> *The lowest effectiveness for system testing for a project was 54%.*

The main reasons for the improvement in the effectiveness of system testing are that system testing is now:

• Prioritizing where to direct testing effort by using historical data to determine which modules have the highest probability of containing defects and then spending more effort testing these modules
• Making use of a database of test scripts.

AVERAGE EFFORT TO CORRECT A DEFECT
✓ *target exceeded*

The overall trend in the average effort to correct a defect found during development is *decreasing.*

> *The average effort spent correcting a defect found during development for the 89 projects completed during the year is **down** 25% on last year from 12 hours to 9 hours.*
>
> *The highest average effort to correct a defect for a project was 16 hours.*
>
> *The lowest average effort to correct a defect for a project was 5 hours.*

The main reasons for the improvement in the average effort to correct a defect is that defects are being detected earlier through the use of formal reviews.

PERCENTAGE OF BAD FIXES
✗ *failed* to meet target

The overall trend in bad fixes (defects caused by correcting defects) is *increasing*.

> *The average percentage of bad fixes for the 89 projects completed during the year is* **up** *1% on last year from 5% to 5.5%.*

> *The highest percentage of bad fixes for a project was 11%.*

> *The lowest percentage of bad fixes for a project was 1%.*

The reasons for the increase in bad fixes were due to a variety of causes, the main ones being:

- The inexperience of the staff who carried out the corrections
- Allowing design activities to commence before analysis is complete.

ACCURACY OF ESTIMATES OF EFFORT
✓ target exceeded

The overall trend in the variation between actual and estimated effort is *decreasing*.

> *The average variation between actual effort and estimated effort from the high-level design for the 89 projects completed during the year is* **down** *56% on last year from 40% to 17.5%.*

> *The highest variation between the actual effort and the estimated effort from the high-level design was 59%.*

> *The lowest variation between the actual effort and the estimated effort from the high-level design was 3%.*

> *47% of projects underestimated the amount of effort required.*

The histogram in Fig. 2 provides a breakdown of the variation of effort.

The main reason for the reduction in the variation between the actual effort and estimated effort is the introduction of a formal estimation process that incorporates a process to quantify risk.

ACCURACY OF ESTIMATES OF TIMESCALE
✓ *target exceeded*

The overall trend in the variation between actual and estimated timescales is *decreasing*.

Number of projects

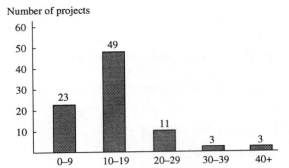

Percentage variation between estimate of effort and actual effort

Figure 2 Histogram showing breakdown of the variation of effort.

*The average variation between actual timescale and estimated timescale from the high-level design for the 89 projects completed during the year is **down** 40% on last year from 30% to 18%.*

The highest variation between the actual timescale and the estimated timescale from the high-level design was 36%.

The lowest variation between the actual timescale and the estimated timescale from the high-level design was 8%.

56% of projects underestimated the amount of time required.

Table 2 provides a breakdown of the variation of timescales. In particular, it shows that 89% of the projects produced estimates of timescales from the high-level design that were within 20% of the actual timescale.

Table 2 Breakdown of the variation of timescales

Variation of timescales	Percentage of projects
Less than 10%	26
Between 10% and 19%	63
Between 20% and 29%	8
Between 30% and 39%	2
Greater than 39%	1

The main reason for the reduction in the variation between the actual timescale and estimated timescale is the introduction of a formal estimation process that incorporates a process to quantify risk.

WHERE ARE IMPROVEMENTS NEEDED?

The following questions are now addressed:

- What are the most defect-prone development phases?
- Where are defects found during development?
- What percentage of defects found in development are corrected?
- What is the average time to detect and correct a defect?
- What is the effort to detect and correct defects found in inspections?
- What is the failure density of each operational system?
- Which modules are the cause of most operational failures?
- What is the breakdown of effort across the phases of development?
- What factors affect productivity?
- What factors affect the accuracy of estimates?

DEFECT-PRONE DEVELOPMENT PHASES

Table 3 provides a breakdown of where defects were introduced for those projects that were completed in 1993. Defects introduced refers to those defects detected during development up to and including user acceptance testing.

DEFECTS FOUND DURING DEVELOPMENT

Table 4 identifies the percentage of defects relating to a particular phase of development that were found during each phase of development, for projects completed during 1993.

Table 3   Defects found during development

Phase	Percentage of defects introduced per phase	
	1993	1992
Analysis	35	40
Design	20	26
Code	43	31
Test	2	3

Table 4   Percentage of defects relating to a particular phase of development that were found during each phase of development

Introduced	% Found			
	Requirements	Design	Code	Test
Requirements	60	18	10	12
Design	–	65	22	13
Code	–	–	89	11
Test	–	–	–	92

Note that the number of defects introduced during a phase refers to those defects that were found during development, up to and including user acceptance testing, that can be attributable to that phase of development. For example, suppose 270 defects were detected during development and 100 of these were introduced during the design phase. Then according to the table, 65 design defects were detected during the design review, 22 design defects were detected during the coding phase and 13 design defects were detected during testing.

CORRECTION OF DEFECTS FOUND DURING DEVELOPMENT

For projects completed during 1993 we have the following statistics:

- 95% of defects detected during development were corrected before the system went into operational use. This compares to 87% last year.
- 65% of defects found during development were detected and corrected before system testing. This compares to 51% last year.

AVERAGE EFFORT TO DETECT AND CORRECT A DEFECT

Table 5 depicts the average effort to detect and correct a defect found during development. For example, the average time to detect a defect found during the requirements phase was 0.2 hours and the average time to correct a defect found during the requirements phase was 0.5 hours. (The effort to detect defects using reviews consists of the preparation for the review and the review itself.)

Table 5 **Average effort to detect and correct a defect found during development**

	Average effort to detect a defect (hours)	Average effort to correct a defect (hours)
Requirements	0.2	0.5
Design	1.4	0.7
Code	0.8	2.1
Test	7.5	3.4

OVERVIEW OF INSPECTIONS

Table 6 depicts an overview of the inspections performed in 1993.

Table 6 **Overview of inspections**

Number of inspections during 1993	42
Effort spent on inspections	503
Number of issues raised	1659
Number of issues which were defects	856
Average effort in hours to detect a defect during an inspection	0.58
Average effort in hours to correct a defect found in an inspection	0.6

FAILURE DENSITY OF OPERATIONAL SYSTEMS

Table 7 depicts the failure density (operational failures per KLOC) for each operational system during 1993.

Table 7 **Failure density of operational systems**

	Failure density during 1993	Failure density during 1992
System A	2.3 failures per KLOC	4.6 failures per KLOC
System B	1.4 failures per KLOC	2.2 failures per KLOC
System C	3.5 failures per KLOC	3.9 failures per KLOC

FAULT-PRONE MODULES

Table 8 identifies the three most fault-prone modules for each system in operational use. Note that the fault density of a module is defined as the number of defects per hundred lines of code and the number of defects refers to the defects that led to an operational failure during a set period of time.

Table 8   The three most fault-prone modules for each system in operational use

	Most fault-prone modules		
System A	Module A1 Fault density = 2.3	Module A2 Fault density = 2.1	Module A3 Fault density = 1.9
System B	Module B1 Fault density = 1.9	Module B2 Fault density = 1.7	Module B3 Fault density = 1.4
System C	Module C1 Fault density = 2.5	Module C2 Fault density = 2.4	Module C3 Fault density = 1.9

GRAPH OF BREAKDOWN OF EFFORT ACROSS THE PHASES OF DEVELOPMENT

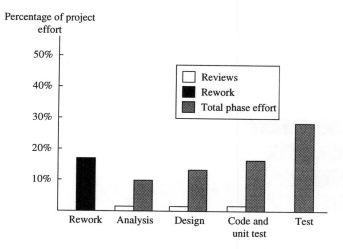

Figure 3 Graph of breakdown of effort across the phases of development.

Purpose

Figure 3 depicts the breakdown of effort for all projects that were completed during 1993.

Related goals

Figure 3 relates to the following goals:

- Collect measures to support an estimation process.
- Assess effort spent on rework.

Calculation

The calculation used to construct Fig. 3 was as follows. For each phase of development sum the effort expended on that phase over all the projects that were completed. For example, the graph shows that 10% of the total effort was spent on analysis.

Additional information

None.

GRAPH OF FACTORS AFFECTING PRODUCTIVITY

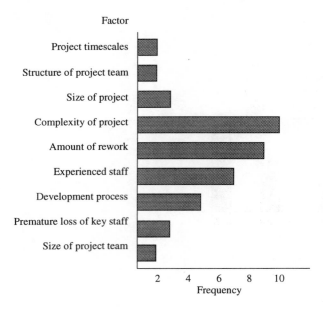

Figure 4 Graph of factors affecting productivity.

Purpose

The purpose of this histogram is to depict the frequencies of the factors that were cited by projects as reasons why productivity targets were not met.

Related goals

This graph relates to the goal:

- Identify where changes are needed to improve productivity.

Calculation

The calculation used to construct this graph was to sum the reasons cited for why productivity targets were not met over all projects completed during 1993.

Additional information

None.

GRAPH OF FACTORS AFFECTING THE ACCURACY OF ESTIMATES

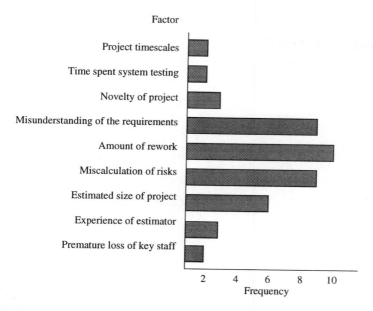

Figure 5   Graph of factors affecting the accuracy of estimates.

Purpose

The purpose of this histogram is to depict the frequencies of the factors that were cited by projects as reasons why the targets for variance between estimates of effort and actual effort were not met.

Related goals

This graph relates to the goal:

- Determine the main factors that affect the accuracy of estimates.

Calculation

The calculation used to construct this graph was to sum the reasons cited for variation over all projects completed during 1993.

Additional information

None.

DEFECT DETECTION PROFILE

Purpose

This graph provides a comparison between the defects present and the defects detected during each phase of development in order to help identify which reviews are in most need of improvement in order to increase the number of defects identified.

Related goals

This graph relates to the goal:

• Assess effectiveness of reviews and testing.

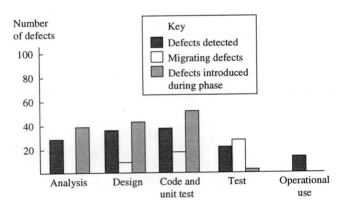

Figure 6 Defect detection profile.

Calculation

We have defined the number of defects that were present to be the number of defects detected during development plus the number of defects detected during the first two months of operational use. These defects were then allocated to the phases of development that they were introduced.

Additional information

The column representing defects detected in a phase of development refers to defects that were detected which were either introduced during that phase or introduced at an earlier phase but not detected at earlier phases.

TREND ANALYSIS

This section presents the trends in the KPIs as a series of graphs depicting the following trends:

- Trend in productivity
- Trend in rework
- Trend in rework versus reviews
- Trend in effectiveness of design reviews
- Trend in effectiveness of system testing
- Trend in the average effort to correct a defect
- Trend in variance of estimates of effort.

GRAPH OF TREND IN PRODUCTIVITY

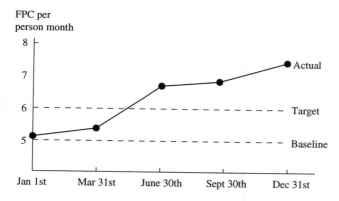

Figure 7 Graph of trend in productivity.

Purpose

This graph shows the trend in the productivity for projects during 1993.

Related goals

This graph relates to the goal:

• Identify trends in productivity.

Calculation

The calculation used to construct this graph was as follows. For each three-month period, we have plotted the average productivity of projects that were completed during the period.

Additional information

The overall trend in productivity is increasing when the curve is smoothed out using the moving average technique. The dip in productivity in the third quarter was caused by two long-term projects that were completed but the bulk of whose work was carried out before the improvement programme was introduced.

GRAPH OF TREND IN REWORK

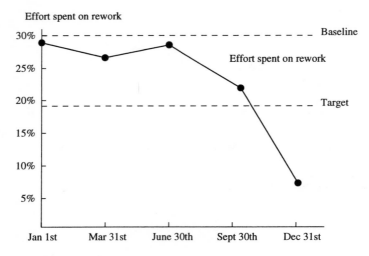

Figure 8 Graph of trend in rework.

Purpose

This graph shows the trend in effort spent on rework for projects during 1993.

Related goals

This graph relates to the goal:

• Identify trends in effort spent on rework.

Calculation

The calculation used to construct this graph was as follows. For each three-month period, we have plotted the average effort spent on rework on all projects that were completed during the period.

Additional information

The overall trend in effort spent on rework is decreasing when the curve is smoothed out using the moving average technique. The blip in the effort spent on rework in the second quarter was caused by two long-term projects that were completed, but the bulk of whose work was carried out before formal reviews for each phase deliverable were introduced.

GRAPH OF TREND IN REWORK VERSUS REVIEWS

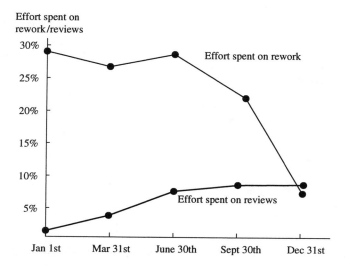

Figure 9   Graph of trend in rework versus reviews.

Purpose

This graph compares the effort spent on rework against the effort spent on reviews during 1993.

Related goals

This graph relates to the goal:

• Identify trends in effectiveness of reviews and testing and effort spent on rework.

Calculation

The calculation used to construct this graph was as follows. For each three-month period we have plotted the effort spent on rework against the effort spent on reviews on all projects that were completed during the period.

Additional information

None.

GRAPH OF TREND IN EFFECTIVENESS OF DESIGN REVIEWS

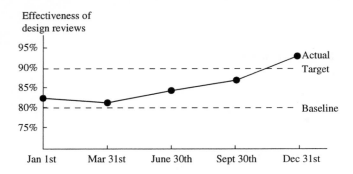

Figure 10 Graph of trend in effectiveness of design reviews.

Purpose

This graph depicts the trend in the effectiveness of design reviews across the whole of the IS department during 1993.

Related goals

This graph relates to the goal:

• Identify trends of effectiveness of reviews.

Calculation

The calculation used to construct this graph was as follows. For each three-month period, we have plotted the average effectiveness of the design reviews on all projects that were completed during the period.

Additional information

The overall trend in the effectiveness of design reviews is increasing when the curve is smoothed out using the moving average technique. The blip in the effectiveness of design reviews in the first quarter was caused by the learning curve when introducing formal reviews.

GRAPH OF TREND IN EFFECTIVENESS OF SYSTEM TESTING

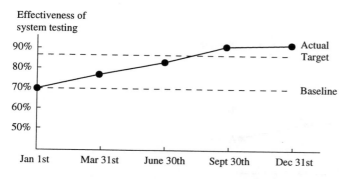

Figure 11   Graph of trend in effectiveness of system testing.

Purpose

This graph depicts the trend in the effectiveness of system across the whole of the IS department during 1993.

Related goals

This graph relates to the goal:

• Identify trends of effectiveness of system testing.

Calculation

The calculation used to construct this graph was as follows. For each three-month period, we have plotted the average effectiveness of system testing on all projects that were completed during the period.

Additional information

None.

GRAPH OF TREND IN THE AVERAGE EFFORT TO CORRECT A DEFECT

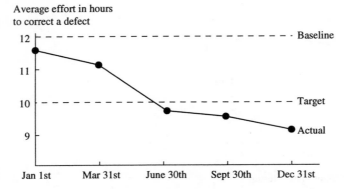

Figure 12 Graph of trend in the average effort to correct a defect.

Purpose

The purpose of this graph is to depict the trend in the average effort to correct a defect found and corrected in development during 1993.

Related goals

This graph relates to the goal:

• Identify trends in effort spent on rework.

Calculation

The calculation used to construct this graph was as follows. For each three-month period, we determined the average effort to correct a defect for those projects that were completed during the period.

Additional information

The trend in the average effort to correct a defect is decreasing due to the fact that reviews are finding defects earlier.

GRAPH OF TREND IN THE VARIANCE OF ESTIMATES OF EFFORT

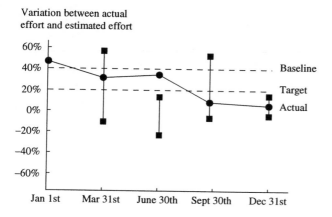

Figure 13   Graph of trend in the variance of estimates of effort.

Purpose

The purpose of this graph is to depict the trend in the accuracy of estimates of effort for all projects that were completed during 1993.

Related goals

This graph relates to the goal:

- Identify trends in the accuracy of estimates of effort.

Calculation

The calculation used to construct this graph is as follows. For each period, determine the average accuracy of estimates of effort for those projects that were completed during the period. The variance of an individual estimate is defined as the absolute value of (actual effort minus estimated effort) divided by the estimated effort.

Additional information

Note that if the variance had not been defined as an absolute value, then it is possible, for a particular period, to have an average variance of zero and yet none of the projects have an actual effort which is within say 40% of the estimated effort. In addition to the trend line, the range in variance for each three-month period is depicted as a high–low bar. Where there is no data for a period, this will be stated above the period as *no data*.

HEALTH OF SYSTEMS

This section provides an overview of the health of the key operational system during 1993 in terms of:

- Failure density (number of operational failures per KLOC)
- Breakdown ratio (BDR) defined as the percentage of defects that cause a total system failure
- Availability ratio
- Mean time to repair (MTTR) defined as average effort in hours to correct a defect
- Number of change requests implemented
- Outstanding fault reports
- Defect propagation rate (bad fixes)
- Percentage of overall effort spent on rework
- Percentage of modules that contain defects.

HEALTH OF A SYSTEM

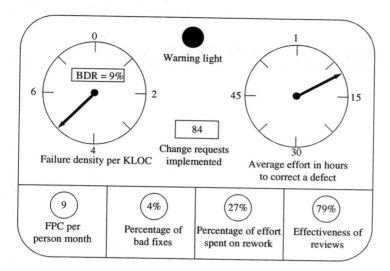

Figure 14   Health of a system.

REVISED BASELINES AND TARGETS FOR 1994

Table 9   Revised baselines and targets for 1994.

KPI	Baseline	Target
FPC per person month	7	8
Cost in £ per FPC	780	700
Percentage of effort spent on rework	18	15
Percentage of effort spent on reviews	5	6
Effectiveness of reviews	88	93
Effectiveness of system testing	84	92
Average effort in hours to correct a defect found during development	9	7
Percentage of bad fixes	5.5	4
Variance between estimated and actual effort	17.5	15
Variance between estimated and actual timescales	18	15

10

SUMMARY

Measurement is not an exact science. It should be used as a tool that provides an indication that further investigation is required. There is no magic solution to setting up a Measurement Programme that delivers timely quantifiable information to support managers in decision making. Measurement is about common sense, but sadly common sense is not always common practice in IS departments. The key principles to setting up and running a successful Measurement Programme are as follows:

1st principle — Learn from others

Don't reinvent the wheel: learn from successful companies and, in particular, learn from their mistakes.

2nd principle — Appoint an executive sponsor

Appoint an executive sponsor who will act as a focal point for the Measurement Programme.

3rd principle — Establish ownership

Establish who the customers are and find out what they want.

4th principle — Use an evolutionary approach and treat it as a project

Use an evolutionary approach rather than a revolutionary approach. Don't try to do everything at one. Prioritize your problems and tackle them one at a time. Leading Japanese companies such as Hitachi and NEC concentrate on using measurement to support initiatives to improve reliability before productivity. Their philosophy is best summed up by a Japanese IT manager who stated:

There is no point in producing unreliable software more quickly.

The implementation should be treated as a project having a plan, resources and commitment and financial backing from senior management.

5th principle — Define the goals of the Measurement Programme

The goals of the Measurement Programme should be:

- Driven by the business goals
- Validated against the budget, timescales and capability of the process
- Communicated to and understood by all concerned
- Signed off by the customers.

6th principle — Derive objective measures from the goals

Measures should be derived from the goals of the Measurement Programme and should be defined objectively. That is, the result of the measurement process must be independent of the person carrying it out. The purpose of the measures will be dependent on the goals (Fig. 10.1). For example, the purpose of the measures may be to help:

- Set baselines and targets for the key performance indicators
- Help determine where changes are needed to meet the business goals
- Determine the impact of changes.

The measures should match the capability of the development process. For example, it is a waste of time collecting detailed information on the experience of project staff in order to measure productivity if the development process is unstable and does not enable staff to work effectively.

Deriving the measures is a two-step process. The first step consists of refining the goals of the Measurement Programme into a set of questions that require quantifiable answers. The second step consists of refining these questions into a set of measures which attempt to answer the questions.

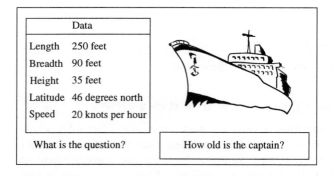

Data	
Length	250 feet
Breadth	90 feet
Height	35 feet
Latitude	46 degrees north
Speed	20 knots per hour

What is the question? | How old is the captain?

Figure 10.1 Measures must be related to goals.

7th principle — Use a standard work breakdown structure

Use a standard work breakdown structure to help ensure a consistent and common approach to data collection across all projects.

8th principle — Explain the Measurement Programme

Do not fall into the trap of trying to impose the Measurement Programme on project teams without explaining its purpose. Run workshops to explain to managers and project teams the reason why a Measurement Programme is being introduced and to explain its benefits and limitations.

9th principle — Devise success criteria

Define criteria for assessing the success of the Measurement Programme after it has been running for twelve months. Without such criteria, management will not be able to form an objective opinion as to whether the Measurement Programme has been a success.

10th principle — Instigate a culture change

Change the culture to help ensure that the Measurement Programme does not just slowly fade away and die.

11th principle — Don't interpret information in isolation

Interpreting information in isolation without regard to its context is a recipe for trouble. For example, consider the following quote from Groucho Marx:

I once shot an elephant in my pyjamas.
How it got in them I'll never know.

The first part of the sentence suggests Groucho shot an elephant while Groucho was wearing his pyjamas. However, on reading the second part of the sentence the meaning becomes less clear. For instance, was the elephant wearing Groucho's pyjamas or was Groucho wearing his pyjamas and there was an elephant inside them with him?

In general, a Measurement Programme generates information that indicates whether further investigation is needed. Data should not be interpreted in isolation: it needs to be interpreted in the context of its environment. For example, consider the situation where the number of defects found during the design phase of development was excessively high. There are a variety of reasons that could apply, such as:

- The quality of the work performed in the design phase was very poor.
- The review of the requirements was very poor and many defects introduced during the specification of the requirements migrated into the design phase.
- The design review was unusually thorough.

At one level the information generated by the Measurement Programme indicates an abnormality. Further information is needed to identify the reason for this abnormality.

12th principle — Provide feedback

Provide feedback to:

- Help ensure that management act on the information generated by the Measurement Programme
- Improve communications by informing project teams about what is being done with the data they supply
- Help improve the Measurement Programme, for example revising the goals, data collection forms, procedures, etc.

Most problems with software development stem from poor management methods where managers operate in a problem recovery mode rather than a problem prevention mode. The key aspects to achieving improvements are measurement and change. First, measure what you are doing to understand what is happening and to identify areas for improvements. Next, make changes and then use measurement to see what impact the changes have made.

FURTHER READING

Two good accounts of how to set up a Measurement Programme are contained in Grady and Caswell (1987) and Goodman (1993).

Section 2

When Should We Act?

The use of the scientific approach — not opinion or emotion — is the best way forward for improving processes. Statistical data-based techniques help managers to focus their attention on the process rather than on individuals, and take decisions based on facts and unprejudiced information and not on subjective 'gut-feelings' or unrealistic expectations.

W. Edwards Deming

This section provides an introduction to statistical process control and shows how to use it to determine when to act on the information generated by a Measurement Programme. In particular it:

- Provides an introduction to control charts, the basic tool for detecting whether a process is out of control.
- Shows how statistical process control can be used to provide an objective means of improving efficiency and quality by providing feedback on processes to minimize variability.
- Provides examples of applying statistical process control to software development.

11

INTRODUCTION

The pioneering work on statistical process control (SPC) was carried out by Dr Walter Shewart in the 1920s while he was working at Bell Laboratories in the USA. His work was geared towards process improvement and the recognition that process improvement is a continuous activity.

We now provide an extract from a presentation by Dr W. Edwards Deming which he made in Versailles on 6th July 1989 (British Deming Association, 1989) on how Walter Shewart came to develop his pioneering thoughts on SPC:

I went to work for Western Electric in Chicago during part of 1925 and 1926. Part of Western Electric's business involved making equipment for telephone systems. The aim was, of course, reliability: to make things alike so that people could depend on them. Western Electric had the ambition to be able to advertise using the phrase: 'as alike as two telephones'. But they found that, the harder they tried to achieve consistency and uniformity, the worse were the effects. The more they tried to shrink variation, the larger it got. When any kind of error, mistake, or accident occurred, they went to work on it to try to correct it. It was a noble aim. There was only one little trouble. Things got worse.

Eventually the problem went to Dr Walter Shewart at the Bell Laboratories in New York. Dr Shewart had worked at Western Electric for 18 months before going to Bell. He worked on the problem. He became aware of two kinds of mistakes:

1. Treating a fault, complaint, mistake, accident, as if it came from a special cause when in fact there was nothing special at all, i.e. when it came from random variation due to common causes.
2. Treating a fault, complaint, mistake, accident, as if it came from common causes when in fact it was due to a special cause.

What difference does it make? All the difference between failure and success.

Dr Shewart decided that this was the root of Western Electric's problems — they were failing to understand the difference between common causes and special causes, and that mixing them up makes things worse. It is pretty important that we understand those two kinds of mistakes. Sure we don't like mistakes, complaints from customers, accidents — but if we weigh in at them without understanding then we make things worse.

CHOICE OF GOALS

Software managers have a choice of goals, namely:

- Developing software systems that conform to requirements; or
- Striving towards process consistency through continual process improvement.

In the past software developers have been concerned with directing their efforts towards conformance to requirements. This has led to much wasted effort being expended in trying to test conformance into a software system.

12

WHAT IS STATISTICAL PROCESS CONTROL?

In this chapter we define what is meant by SPC by answering the following questions:

- What is an informal definition of SPC?
- What is a process?
- What is controlled and uncontrolled variation?
- Why is it important to know which type of variation is present?
- How much time should be spent looking for special causes?
- Is SPC only concerned with process monitoring?
- What is process capability?
- What states can a process be in?
- Is entropy an important consideration in SPC?
- What are the key points concerning SPC?
- What are the principles of SPC?

WHAT IS AN INFORMAL DEFINITION OF SPC?

SPC can be summed up in two words:

Reduce variation

At one level statistical process control can be thought of as a technique to reduce variability in a process; for example, variability in delivery time, variability in faults that occur during operational use, etc. It involves measuring the repeated performance of a process and providing feedback to enable action to be carried out to improve the process.

Every process has natural limits and when these limits are exceeded the process is out of control.

Software developers should strive to develop stable processes where it is possible to predict, within limits, how the process will behave in the future.

WHAT IS A PROCESS?

Every task can be modelled as:

- The resources needed to perform the task
- The process used to carry out the task
- The products produced by the task.

This applies to any task such as writing a report, conducting a review or transforming a software specification into a software design. Figure 12.1 provides a high-level model of a cost estimation process.

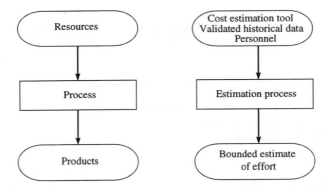

Figure 12.1   High-level model of a cost estimation process.

The high-level qualitative goals of any organization are to make better use of their resources, improve the efficiency of their processes and improve the quality of their products.

It should be noted that a process may consist of a number of subprocesses. For example, the overall software development process can be considered as a collection of subprocesses, such as requirements capture, planning and estimating, design, reviews, etc.

WHAT IS CONTROLLED AND UNCONTROLLED VARIATION?

We now discuss what is meant by a process being in or out of statistical control. There is always variation in anything that is being measured. If you are recording, regularly over time, a measurement associated with a process it will experience variation. For example, consider a process for predicting the effort needed to develop a software system. Here an important measure is the difference between the estimated effort and the actual effort needed to develop software projects. In general, this measure will vary from project to project.

Wheeler and Chambers (1986), state:

> While every process displays variation, some processes display controlled variation, while others display uncontrolled variation.

Controlled variation

Controlled variation is due to unassignable, chance or random causes (referred to by Deming as common causes). If a process exhibits controlled variation we can make predictions about its future behaviour with a good chance of success. We say that it is in statistical control, in other words stable and predictable (Fig. 12.2).

To quote Shewart (1980):

> A phenomenon will be said to be controlled when, through the use of past experience, we can predict, at least within limits, how this phenomenon may be expected to vary in the future.

Improving the process by reducing the common causes of variation requires action on the process. This is usually the responsibility of management because it requires changes to the process. For example, random variation may be due to the way the process has been designed and changes need to be made to the process. Another example is where software design reviews occasionally fail to detect a certain type of defect. Better training for the reviewers may be needed.

In the case of controlled variation, the group of values associated to a measure tend to form a pattern that can be described as a distribution, characterized by a certain location, spread and shape (Fig. 12.3).

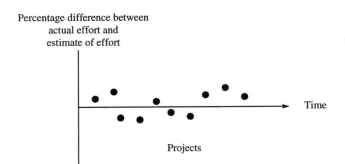

Figure 12.2 Stable cost estimation process.

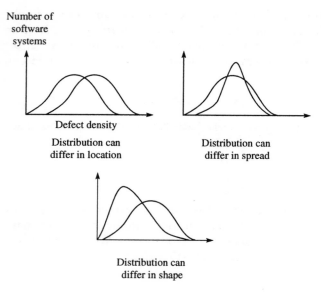

Figure 12.3 Distributions.

Uncontrolled variation

Uncontrolled variation is due to assignable causes (referred to by Edwards Deming as special causes). In general, resolving special causes does not require changes to the process. Instead, it usually requires local action by somebody who is directly connected with the process. For example, using inexperienced testers on a software project, due to staff shortages, may have a detrimental effect on the number of operational failures of the software system during operational use.

If a process exhibits uncontrolled variation over a period of time, then the output from the process is not stable over time and it is not possible to make accurate predictions about its future behaviour. In such cases we say that the process is out of statistical control, in other words unstable (Fig. 12.4).

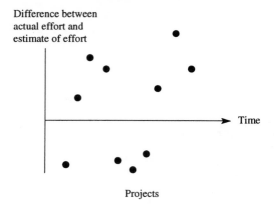

Figure 12.4 Unstable cost estimation process.

In the case of uncontrolled variation, when special causes are present, the group of values associated to a measure cannot be represented by a single distribution.

WHY IS IT IMPORTANT TO KNOW WHICH TYPE OF VARIATION IS PRESENT?

We now discuss why it is important to distinguish between controlled variation and uncontrolled variation. There are two main reasons.

First, the capability of a process is unknown while the process is out of statistical control. When a process is experiencing uncontrolled variation it is not possible to evaluate the effects of changes such as changing the work environment, introducing new tools, providing staff with training, etc. When special causes of variation have been eliminated, improvement to the process can be achieved by managers changing the process. More often than not it is the case that the staff working on the process can identify the special causes that impact on the ability of the process to achieve its full capability. That is why it is important to canvas the opinions of the staff who work on the process.

Secondly, misinterpreting either type of cause of variation as the other, and implementing changes based on this misunderstanding, may not only fail to have the desired effect but actually make things worse. For example, tampering with stable systems. The following story illustrates such a situation. It is related by Steve Smith and appeared in *Management Today* (October, 1987).

> One country's railroad decided to use the percentage of trains late on arrival at stations as a trigger for action. If trains were more than 3% late, immediate corrective action was taken. Only recently has a statistical analysis of the complex working of the railway shown that train times will vary normally by ± 5%. The management corrective action was disrupting a stable process and making things worse. In other words they were tampering with a stable process.

Another example concerned a major financial organization which was developing software systems which were unusable because of the high number of operational failures. To tackle the problem, management decided to increase the time spent on system testing. Unfortunately, this had little effect on the number of operational failures. What was required was a change to the process itself, through the introduction of inspections for each deliverable. Only then did the number of operational failures decrease.

HOW MUCH TIME SHOULD BE SPENT LOOKING FOR SPECIAL CAUSES?

It is estimated by pioneers such as Joseph Juran and Edwards Deming that between 2 and 15 per cent of the problems in a process are caused by special effects.

This raises the question of when should we take action to remove a special cause and should we remove all special causes before trying to optimize. In other words when to look and when not to look for a special cause.

Therefore, guidance is needed on when special causes need to be tackled. This topic is covered in Chapter 13 when we discuss Shewart's control charts, a valuable and powerful management tool for detecting uncontrolled variation.

IS SPC ONLY CONCERNED WITH PROCESS MONITORING?

There is a misconception by some people that SPC is only concerned with highlighting situations when the output of a process goes outside acceptable limits. This assumes the process is in a stable state. SPC is not just about monitoring a stable process: it is about determining whether a process is stable and improving the efficiency and quality of a stable process.

Essentially SPC can be viewed as a technique to determine if a process is stable and reduce variability in a process. In particular it can provide:

- An objective means of controlling quality by providing feedback on processes to minimize variability
- A better understanding of the processes used in software development.

WHAT IS PROCESS CAPABILITY?

Having achieved statistical control, the next step is to strive towards having a capable process, one that develops products that satisfy the customer's requirements. Just because a process is in statistical control, it does not automatically follow that it will produce products that conform to the requirements. For example, consider the case where there is excessive variation from common causes. In such cases management need to reduce variation from common causes to meet the specification. Motorola, for example, require all processes to be twice as good as the specification in terms of variability.

Achieving process capability cannot be viewed in isolation when that process is an integral part of a larger process. If a target for a process is set beyond its normal capability, the only way to achieve it is to distort the process in such a way as to cause trouble in other related processes. For example, suppose management has set the following unrealistic target for the accuracy of the effort to develop software systems:

- For at least 95 per cent of the projects, produce estimates of effort from the requirements that are correct to within 5 per cent of the actual effort expended.

Management pressure to meet this unrealistic target may be so great that project managers are forced to reduce the effort spent on reviews and testing. The consequences are almost certain to have an adverse effect on the number of operational failures.

Therefore it is important that any quantifiable goals for a process should be challenging, yet achievable. This can only come about from validated data from the process itself, not from the unrealistic wishes of management.

WHAT STATES CAN A PROCESS BE IN?

A process can be in one of four states (Fig. 12.5).

Stable but not capable	Stable and capable
Unstable and not capable	Capable but unstable

Figure 12.5   States of a process.

State 1 — Threshold: stable but not capable

The process is stable but not fully capable. The process requires management action to change the process to reduce common causes of variation.

State 2 — Ideal: stable and capable

The process is stable and capable. In other words the process is in control and the output conforms to the requirements. Furthermore, the control charts give timely warnings of any possible problems.

State 3 — Brink of chaos: capable but not stable

The process is capable but not stable. In other words the process is out of control although it has been producing outputs that conform to the requirements.

In a capable but unstable process, quality and productivity can deteriorate rapidly.

State 4 — Chaos: unstable and not capable

The process is unstable and not capable. In other words it is not possible to predict future behaviour and it is producing outputs that do not conform to the requirements. The process is susceptible to random fluctuations. In this state it is not possible to predict the future behaviour of the process. The first step out of this chaotic state is to eliminate those special causes that are having a detrimental effect on the process.

IS ENTROPY AN IMPORTANT CONSIDERATION IN SPC?

The sad fact of life is that processes left to their own devices do not remain in a constant state. They revert to an unstable and unpredictable state. Entropy continually acts upon all processes in a detrimental way. That is why it is so important to treat process improvement as a continuous activity.

WHAT ARE THE KEY POINTS CONCERNING SPC?

The key points associated with SPC are that:

- SPC can help to improve quality and efficiency.
- SPC can be applied to repetitive processes which are subject to performance variation.
- The results of SPC can be verified.

WHAT ARE THE PRINCIPLES OF SPC?

The main principles of SPC are:

- There is always variation in anything that is being measured.
- Every process has natural limits and when these limits are exceeded the process is out of control.
- A process needs to be stable before analysis and changes can be undertaken to improve it.
- Changes cause disturbances to a process, and require a stable state to be re-established.
- Processes are never entirely free of special causes.
- A state of statistical control is not a natural state for a process. It is achieved by removing special causes that have an excessive effect on variation.
- You never know anything to the second decimal point.
- SPC is a company-wide technique which involves all employees and should be driven from the top.

13

CONTROL CHARTS

This chapter provides an introduction to control charts, the basic tool for managers and engineers to detect variance.

Suppose we have a process and a measure associated with the process that generates a stream of numerical values. Then we need to know how to use this data to increase our knowledge about the process. One way that has been shown to work in practice is the use of control charts.

Control charts display information about a process in a visual form that is easy to understand. The power of the control chart comes from the way the information is acted upon.

Control charts were created by Walter Shewart in order to detect the presence of uncontrolled variation in a process. Control charts can be thought of as tools to identify the two types of variation, namely controlled and uncontrolled variation.

WHAT IS A CONTROL CHART?

A control chart for a process with an associated measure consists of:

- A central line
- An upper control limit (above the central line)
- A lower control limit (below the central line)
- Numerical values plotted on the chart generated by the measure.

The central line, upper control line and lower control line are calculated from the numerical data generated by the measure.

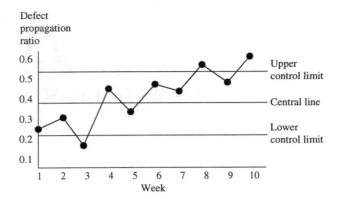

Figure 13.1 A control chart for trend in defect propagation ratio.

The purpose of drawing a control chart is to detect any changes in the process, signalled by abnormal points on the chart.

Figure 13.1 provides an example of a control chart plotting the defect propagation ratio over time for a software project where:

$$\text{Defect propagation ratio} = \frac{\text{number of defects created by correcting defects}}{\text{number of defects corrected}}$$

Essentially, historical data relating to a process is used to construct control limits. If the historical data falls within these limits, and if subsequent data collected also stays within these limits, then the process is said to be in statistical control and you can confidently predict what may happen in the future. In other words, it is likely that future data will remain within the control limits.

If the historical data does not fall within the limits then the process is said to be out of statistical control. In such a situation there is no reason to expect future data to remain within the control limits.

WHAT CAN CONTROL CHARTS DO?

Control charts can be used to:

- Help managers make predictions within limits about the future behaviour of a process
- Give an early warning of possible trouble
- Help managers avoid the situation of taking unnecessary action
- Determine if a sequence of data may be used for predicting what may happen in the future
- Help managers to know when they can make predictions from historical data, and when it is unsafe to do so.

HOW MANY TYPES OF CONTROL CHARTS ARE THERE?

There are six main types of control charts depending on the nature of the data, namely:

- *x–R* chart
- *x* chart
- *p* chart
- *np* chart
- *u* chart
- *c* chart.

However, we will only consider a simplified form of control chart, denoted as a basic control chart or B-chart. Further details on the six types of control charts can be found in Wheeler and Chambers (1986) and Ishikawa (1987).

HOW DO YOU MAKE B-CHARTS?

Consider a process and a measure of the process that has generated a set **V** of numerical values. Then the control lines for its associated B-chart are constructed as follows:

$$\text{Central line} = \text{mean } (\mathbf{V})$$
$$\text{Upper control limit} = \text{mean } (\mathbf{v}) + 3 \times \text{standard deviation } (\mathbf{V})$$
$$\text{Lower control limit} = \text{mean } (\mathbf{V}) - 3 \times \text{standard deviation } (\mathbf{V})$$

where for a set of *n* values $\mathbf{V} = (v_1, v_2, \ldots, v_n)$ the mean and standard deviation are calculated as follows:

$$\text{Mean } (\mathbf{V}) = \frac{v_1 + v_2 + \ldots + v_n}{n}$$

$$\text{Standard deviation } (\mathbf{V}) = \sqrt{\left(\frac{\Sigma v^2 - (\Sigma v)^2 / n}{n - 1} \right)}$$

where

$$\Sigma v = v_1 + v_2 + \ldots + v_n$$

and

$$\Sigma v^2 = v_1^2 + v_2^2 + \ldots + v_n^2$$

This type of chart is known as a 3-sigma control chart.

For example, consider the process of formally reviewing the requirements for a software system. Furthermore, suppose we have defined the following measure for the process:

$$\frac{\text{number of defects found during the review}}{\text{number of defects introduced during the requirements stage}} \times 100$$

Project	Defects found	Defects introduced	%
1	7	15	46.7
2	5	12	41.6
3	11	20	55
4	10	16	62.5
5	16	30	53.3
6	5	12	41.6
7	5	10	50
8	8	16	50
9	4	9	44.4
10	8	15	53.3

Figure 13.2   Data set from ten software projects.

where the number of defects introduced during the requirements stage refers to the number of such defects that were detected during development up to handover to the customer.

Now consider the data set from ten software projects shown in Fig. 13.2. Then for the data set $V = (46.7, 41.6, 55, \ldots, 53.3)$ we have:

$$\text{Mean (V)} = 49.8$$

$$\text{Standard deviation (V)} = 6.5$$

Using these values we can now construct a control chart for V as depicted in Fig. 13.3. Whether the detection rate was good, bad or indifferent, it was at least consistent.

The detection of defects in the requirements found during the formal review of the requirements can be considered to have been stable with an average ratio of approximately 50 per cent for the ten projects. The data for the next ten projects is shown in Fig. 13.4.

The continuation of the B-chart for this data is depicted in Fig. 13.5.

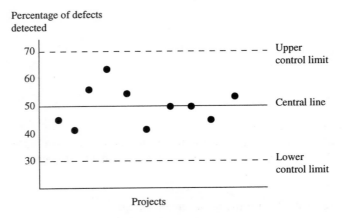

Figure 13.3   B-chart for defects detected during formal review of requirements.

Project	Defects found	Defects introduced	%
11	7	15	46.7
12	5	12	41.6
13	9	26	34.6
14	3	11	27.2
15	5	22	22.7
16	2	10	20
17	11	44	25
18	8	25	32
19	9	26	34.6
20	8	25	32

Figure 13.4   Data for the next ten projects.

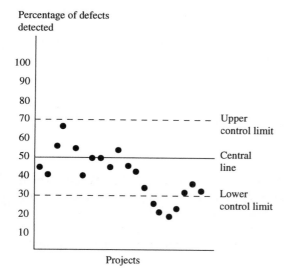

Figure 13.5   B-chart for defects detected during formal review of requirements for 20 projects.

The percentage of defects detected during the formal review of the requirements has decreased for the second set of ten projects. There is some assignable cause for this change and it is necessary to determine the cause.

COMMON QUESTIONS ABOUT CONTROL CHARTS

If the data used to construct the control chart is out of statistical control, will the limits obtained be still good enough to detect that lack of control?
Yes. The choice of 3-sigma was carefully chosen because it is not possible to know in advance if the data displays a lack of control or not. The data does not need to be

homogeneous (data collected in the same way, from a process which is known to display statistical control).

Why use 3 × standard deviation (3-sigma) for the limits?
We need to use limits that do not waste too much time looking unnecessarily for trouble. 3-sigma limits are action limits. They signal when action should be taken. 3-sigma limits strike a balance between raising too many false alarms and missing too many signals. Shewart found that empirical evidence showed the 3-sigma limit worked well in practice. 3-sigma limits have been thoroughly proven in over 60 years of practice to be the best action limits for processes.

In fact a homogeneous set of data can be characterized by its location and spread in the following way:

- Approximately 60 to 75 per cent of the data will be located within a distance of one standard deviation on either side of the central line.
- Usually 90 to 98 per cent of the data will be located within a distance of two standard deviations on either side of the central line.
- Approximately 99 per cent of the data will be located within a distance of three standard deviations on either side of the central line.

Does the data need to be normally distributed?
No. Control charts work well even if the data is not normally distributed. The normality of a data set is not a prerequisite for statistical control nor is it a consequence of statistical control.

How many data points are needed to construct a control chart?
It is possible to calculate control charts with whatever data is available. When a small amount of data is used (less than 10 data points) any out-of-control points on the chart are definitely out-of-control. The only risk of constructing a control chart with a small amount of data points is the risk of missing a signal. However, calculating control charts with more than 20 data points reduces the risk of an extreme value having an undue influence on the control limits.

Is it possible that a control chart will fail to indicate the existence of a special cause when one exists?
Yes. However, the risk is very small. It has been shown over and over again in practice that Shewart's control charts give very few false alarms.

Is it possible that a control chart will indicate the existence of a special cause when one does not exist?
Yes. However, the risk is very small.

What are the main characteristics of a control chart that exhibits statistical control?
The chart characteristics of a process operating with only common causes of variation are:

- All the data points are within the control limits.
- There are approximately an equal number of points above and below the central line.

- There is no specific pattern apparent; for example, there is not a continuous sequence of seven or more data points on one side of the central line.
- Approximately 60 to 75 per cent of the data points are within one standard deviation of the central line.

Any chart not satisfying these characteristics is likely to have special causes present.

When a special cause has been eliminated should the control limits be recalculated?
Yes except in the case where the reason for a special cause is not found. In such a case, the data point relating to the special cause remains part of the data set that generated the control limits.

What is a reasonable degree of statistical control?
Shewart provided a minimum criterion for a process to exhibit a reasonable degree of statistical control. When at least 25 consecutive values do not indicate any lack of control, then the process may be said to display a reasonable degree of statistical control.

In the field of software development, what is the relationship between SPC and testing?
Testing should be regarded as a subset of SPC.

14

HOW TO USE STATISTICAL PROCESS CONTROL

This chapter provides a step-by-step approach to using SPC to improve a process.

STEP 1 — GRAPHICALLY REPRESENT THE PROCESS

The first step should be to graphically represent your process. Flowcharts can be used as a tool for visualizing the overall complexity of a process. The main power of flowcharts come from the visual representations of the interrelationships between the various steps in the process.

The standard components of a flowchart (Fig. 14.1) are as follows:

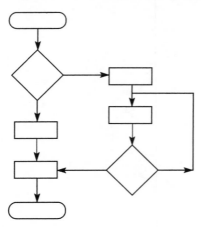

Figure 14.1 An example of a flowchart.

- Oval boxes which are used to signify the start and end points
- Rectangular boxes which are used to represent steps in the process
- Diamonds which are used for decision points
- Lines with arrows which are used to depict the flow of control.

STEP 2 — DEFINE MEASURES FOR THE PROCESS

This step is concerned with choosing measures for the process which:

- Can be used to control the process in terms of efficiency or quality
- Provide a warning when something is about to go wrong
- Capture an objective of the process.

In order that values from a measure can be compared against each other they may need to be normalized. For example, consider measuring the difference between the estimated effort to develop a software system and the actual effort. Then in order to make meaningful comparisons between projects, the values need to be turned into ratios. In this case we can use the ratio:

$$\text{Variance in estimate of effort} = \frac{\text{actual effort} - \text{estimate of effort}}{\text{estimate of effort}} \times 100$$

As an example of a measure that captures the objective of a process consider the process of formally reviewing the requirements specification for a software system. Then one objective of this process is to detect defects in the requirements. A measure relating to this objective is:

$$\frac{\text{Number of defects found during the review}}{\text{number of defects introduced during the requirements stage}} \times 100$$

Here the number of defects introduced during the requirements stage needs to be qualified. It could refer to the number of such defects that were detected:

- During development up to handover to the customer
- During development and during the first six months of operational use.

A measure which is used to control a process is called a control characteristic of the process. Such measures should have the following properties:

- Values generated by the measure should reflect the state of the process.
- Effects from outside influences should be minimized.
- Results should be readily available.
- The process of collecting the data from the process should be economical and should not disrupt the process itself.

The main message is to choose measures that are going to 'talk' to you!

STEP 3 — CONSTRUCT A CONTROL CHART AND ANALYSE IT

This step is concerned with collecting values for the measure and using these values to produce a B-chart. In order to collect values, the following questions need to be addressed:

- How will the values be obtained and who will collect the values?
- How often should the values be collected?
- How will the data be validated?
- What support tools will be needed (spreadsheets, databases, etc.)?

Before calculating the central line and control lines, abnormal values should be excluded from the calculations, otherwise the initial control lines may be excessively inflated. One way to detect abnormal values is to use the technique of constructing box plots for the data set. This technique is explained in Appendix B. Although abnormal values (outliers) are excluded from the calculations they are still plotted on the control chart.

The central line, upper control line and lower control line for a data set **V** should be calculated as explained in Chapter 13. Having constructed the control chart, it then needs to be analysed to determine:

- Whether action needs to be taken to remove special causes
- Whether a stable process needs to be made more capable.

STEP 4 — INVESTIGATE SPECIAL CAUSES

This step is concerned with investigating the values that fall outside the control limits. These values are signals that a special cause (assignable cause) is present. They need to be investigated, and if the cause results in a problem and is likely to recur, then corrective action needs to be taken to eliminate the special cause. Note that if a special cause is improving the process, then action should be taken to use this information to enhance the process.

Special causes are normally identified and removed by staff working within the process.

When a special cause has been eliminated, this data point should be removed from the data set and new control limits calculated unless the reason for the special cause has not been determined.

STEP 5 — REMOVE COMMON CAUSES

This step is concerned with removing common causes from a stable process. When all the special causes that have a significant impact on variation have been eliminated (the process is stable), management can concentrate on removing common causes and increasing the capability of the process. Management should introduce changes to the process to try and reduce common variation. Whenever a change is made to the process, data needs to be collected to determine the impact of the changes and new control limits need to be calculated. While this new data is being collected, and before the new control limits are calculated, the new data can be plotted against the old control limits to determine the impact of the changes.

The question then arises on how to determine where changes are needed. The cause and effect diagram, sometimes known as the fishbone diagram, is a versatile tool that can be used in helping to understand the factors that can influence a process. This analysis tool is described in Appendix B.

STEP 6 — CONTINUOUS PROCESS IMPROVEMENT

Continue to strive towards removing common causes of variation because process improvement is a continuous activity. Process improvement is best achieved through a series of small steps rather than giant leaps. The motto is to use an evolutionary approach not a revolutionary approach. Figure 14.2 illustrates the cycle of continual process improvement.

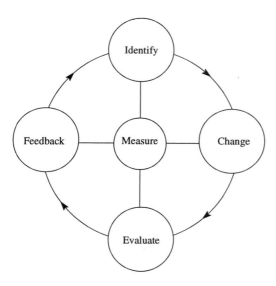

Figure 14.2   Process improvement cycle.

Identify where improvements are needed

First, use measurement to identify where the main problems are and which processes need improving. Then determine the causes of the problems before introducing changes to try to improve the situation. For example, management may be worried about productivity because they think too much effort is being spent on rework.

Make changes

Do not try to do everything at once. Use an evolutionary approach to implement the highest priority changes first.

Evaluate changes

Next, assess the impact of the changes.

Feedback

Use the results of the evaluation to inform managers and project teams.

Start again

Now start all over again because process improvement is a continuous activity.

15

HOW TO READ CONTROL CHARTS

In this chapter we discuss how to read control charts to determine when action should be taken; for example, when non-random patterns are present in a control chart. It should be noted that action does not necessarily mean corrective action. A data point outside a control line may indicate a marked improvement in the performance of the process; for example, a sudden increase in the percentage of defects found during the formal review of the requirements for a software project. Such a situation should prompt an investigation into the causes so that changes can be made so that it can be repeated continuously.

Action should be taken in the following situations.

Action Rule 1

When at least one of the data points lies outside the control limits.

Action Rule 2

When at least two out of three successive points are on the same side of the central line and these two points are also more than two standard deviations away from the central line. (Note that the third value may fall on either side of the central line.)

Action Rule 3

When at least four out of five successive points are on the same side of the central line and these four points are also more than one standard deviation away from the central line. (Note that the fifth value may fall on either side of the central line.) Figure 15.1 illustrates this situation.

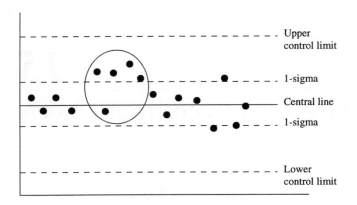

Figure 15.1   Control chart exhibiting abnormal behaviour — Action Rule 3.

Action Rule 4

When one of the following situations arises:

- Eight or more consecutive points are on one side of the central line.
- Eight or more consecutive points are all increasing or decreasing.
- At least 10 out of 11 consecutive points are on the same side of the central line.
- At least 12 out of 14 consecutive points are on the same side of the central line.
- At least 14 out of 17 consecutive points are on the same side of the central line.
- At least 16 out of 20 consecutive points are on the same side of the central line.

Since the probability of any of these situations occurring by chance is very unlikely, a special cause that needs investigating may be present. Figure 15.2 illustrates some of these situations.

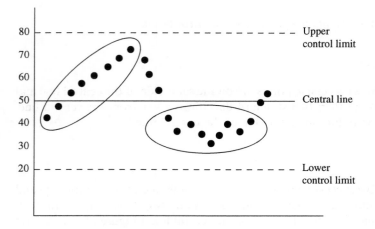

Figure 15.2   Control chart exhibiting abnormal behaviour — Action Rule 4.

Action Rule 5

When the number of data points lying within one standard deviation from the central line is less than 40 per cent of the total set of data points. Care should be taken in situations when the distribution of the data points is skewed.

GUIDELINES ON USING THE ACTION RULES

- The action rules should always be used with discretion and in the context of the particular process under consideration.
- Always start with Action Rule 1 and work through them consecutively.
- If the result of applying an action rule results in the removal of a data point, then apply subsequent rules to the reduced data set.

16

APPLYING SPC TO SOFTWARE DEVELOPMENT

This chapter shows how to apply statistical process control to software development by the use of two case studies. The case studies are concerned with addressing the following questions:

- How can we improve the accuracy of our estimates of effort to develop a software system?
- How can we improve the effectiveness of our formal review processes in identifying defects?

Before tackling these two questions, it is important to recognize the following. For most organizations, their overall software development process is not sufficiently well defined and stable to enable them to define a set of global measures to monitor its effectiveness and quality. For such organizations, the starting point is to treat their software development process as a set of subprocesses and to concentrate on improving these subprocesses.

CASE STUDY 1 — VARIATION BETWEEN ESTIMATES AND ACTUALS

This case study concerns an organization that wanted to improve the accuracy of its estimates of effort to develop a software system. We now describe the six steps involved in applying SPC to this situation.

Step 1 — Graphically represent the process

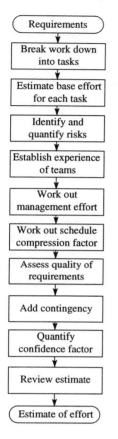

Figure 16.1   Cost estimation process.

The process used to generate an estimate of effort from a requirements specification is depicted in Fig. 16.1, namely:

Task 1   Use the work breakdown structure to decompose the work into tasks.

Task 2   Calculate the base estimates for each task using the following idealized assumptions:

- Staff are experienced (100 per cent productive)
- No constraints on timescales
- No risks
- No management overheads.

Task 3   Identify and quantify the risks and produce bounded estimates of effort for each task.

Task 4   Calculate the adjustment to take account of the experience of project teams (i.e. their potential productivity).

Task 5   Calculate the adjustment to take account of management effort which is calculated from the estimated size of the teams.

Task 6   Calculate the adjustment to take account of the constraint on the timescale using:

$$\text{Schedule compression} = \frac{\text{Available time}}{\text{Estimated elapsed time}}$$

Task 7   Calculate the adjustment to take account of the quality of the requirements.

Task 8   Calculate contingency, which is a management judgement. The estimated effort should be calculated as the midpoint of the bounded range and have the property that there is a 50 per cent chance that the actual effort will be greater than the estimated effort. Management may decide that they want to reduce this chance so they need to add in a contingency to the estimate to help ensure that there is a high probability (for example 90 per cent chance) that the actual effort will be in the interval:

[estimate − contingency, estimate + contingency]

Task 9   Quantify the confidence factor that the estimate will be in the interval [estimate − contingency, estimate + contingency].

Task 10   Review the estimate using the ratio method and at least two independent reviewers.

Step 2 — Define measures for the process

Management wanted to improve the accuracy of the estimates of effort needed to develop a software system. Therefore, the measure chosen was the variance between the estimate of effort and the actual effort for a project, where:

$$\text{Variance in estimate of effort} = \frac{\text{actual effort} - \text{estimate of effort}}{\text{estimate of effort}} \times 100$$

Step 3 — Construct a control chart and analyse it

Values were collected from projects that were completed during a 24-month period (Fig. 16.2) and used to construct the control chart depicted in Fig. 16.3.

     The values of estimated effort and actual effort in Fig. 16.2 refer to person months.

Project	Estimate	Actual	% difference
1	17	22	+29.4
2	24	32	+33.3
3	9	13	+44.4
4	100	240	+140
5	8	11	+37.5
6	30	42	+40
7	40	93	+132.5
8	19	29	+52.6
9	16	23	+43.7
10	18	26	+44.4

Figure 16.2   Values collected from projects completed during a 24-month period.

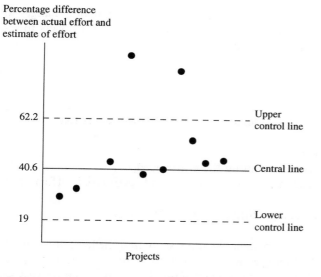

Percentage difference
between actual effort and
estimate of effort

Figure 16.3   Control chart for data in Fig. 16.2.

Then constructing a box plot (see Appendix B) for the percentage differences in Fig. 16.2 we have:

- Lower tail of the box plot = −29
- Upper tail of the box plot = 114.

Thus the data set has two outliers, namely the values 140 and 132.5. Excluding these values from the data set we then have:

- Mean of the percentage differences = 40.6 (excluding the two outliers)
- Standard deviation = 7.2 (excluding the two outliers)

Hence, it follows that:

- Upper control line = $40.6 + 3 \times (7.2) = 62.2$
- Lower control line = $40.6 - 3 \times (7.2) = 19$.

Next an analysis of this control chart was performed using the guidelines listed in Chapter 15. The only action rule that applied was Action Rule 1, namely:

When at least one of the data points lies outside the control limits.

Two data points met this criteria and required investigating.

Step 4 — Investigate special causes

Upon investigation, it was revealed that these two values were caused by major changes to the requirements. This situation was resolved by making it mandatory for projects to re-estimate whenever changes were made to the requirements.

Step 5 — Remove common causes

After removing the special causes, it was concluded from the control chart that:

- The estimation process was stable.
- In general, projects are always underestimating the effort needed.
- The average difference between the actual effort and estimated effort was approximately 40 per cent.
- The variation on the average percentage difference was ±20 per cent.

Although the process was stable it was not capable in the sense that the level of accuracy was unacceptable to management. Changes were needed to reduce variation and in particular reduce the mean (central line). Management needed to change the process so that:

- An estimate was as likely to be above as below the actual estimate.
- The average difference between the actual effort and estimated effort should be no more than 20 per cent.

It was decided that a formal approach to risk analysis needed to be incorporated into the process.

A cause and effect diagram was used to identify a list of risks. These risks were then used to produce a bounded estimate of effort where:

- The lower bound was calculated making the unrealistic assumption that nothing would go wrong.
- The upper bound was calculated assuming the risks would occur.

This change was introduced and a new set of data was collected (Fig. 16.4). This new data was then used to construct a new control chart (Fig. 16.5) where:

- Mean of the percentage differences = 5.6
- Standard deviation = 13.

Hence, it follows that:

- Upper control line $= 5.6 + 3 \times (13) = 44.6$
- Lower control line $= 5.6 - 3 \times (13) = -33.4$.

Project	Estimate	Actual	% difference
11	10	11	+10
12	24	21	−12.5
13	9	11	+22.2
14	30	36	+20
15	8	7	−12.5
16	17	17	0
17	27	31	+11.1
18	14	16	+14.2
19	12	11	−8.3
20	8	9	+12.5

Figure 16.4 New set of data after incorporating a formal approach to risk analysis.

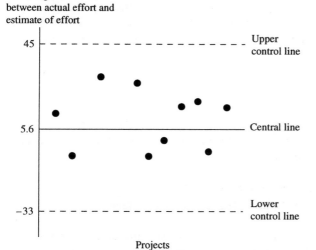

Figure 16.5 Control chart for data in Fig. 16.4.

The control chart depicted in Fig. 16.5 revealed that the change to the process had not made the process unstable and had dramatically reduced the average difference between the actual effort and estimated effort to approximately 5.6 per cent.

Step 6 — Continuous process improvement

Management were encouraged by the results of the changes and were committed to continuing to strive towards removing common causes of variation.

CASE STUDY 2 — IDENTIFYING DEFECTS DURING FORMAL REVIEWS

This case study concerns an organization which wanted to improve the effectiveness of its formal reviews in identifying defects. Formal reviews were conducted for each project deliverable. This case study concentrates on improving the formal review of the requirements specification. We now describe the six steps involved in applying SPC to this situation.

Step 1 — Graphically represent the process

The process used to formally review the requirements specification is depicted in Fig. 16.6.
The primary objectives of the formal review of the requirements specification were to:

- Ensure that the document meets its stated objectives
- Establish a level of confidence in the technical integrity and quality standard of the document
- Suggest enhancements to the document
- Detect defects in the document and assign responsibilities for removing them
- Provide an opportunity for the principal authors of the document to answer queries raised by the reviewers and where necessary provide clarification on issues and questions raised by the reviewers.

Step 2 — Define measures for the process

Management wanted to increase the number of defects detected during the formal review of the requirements specification. To assess the efficiency of the formal review process in detecting defects, the following measure was used:

$$\frac{\text{number of defects found during the review}}{\text{number of defects introduced during the requirements stage}} \times 100$$

where the number of defects introduced during the requirements stage refers to the number of such defects that were detected during development up to handover to the customer.

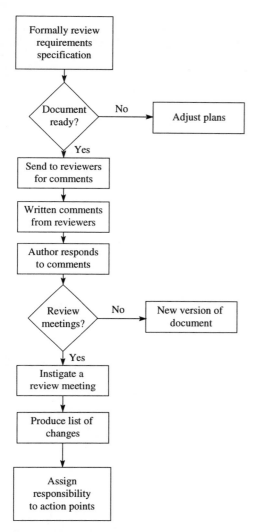

Figure 16.6 Formal review process.

Step 3 — Construct a control chart and analyse it

Values were collected from projects that were completed during a 12-month period (Fig. 16.7) and used to construct the control chart depicted in Fig. 16.8.

Then constructing a box plot for the data set $V = (26.9, 18.7, \ldots, 32)$ revealed there were two outliers (90.9 and 93.5).

Using the data set $V' = (26.9, 18.7, 28.2, 29.4, 30.7, 25, 25, 32)$ we see that:

$$\text{Mean } V' = 26.9$$
$$\text{Standard deviation } V' = 4.1$$

Project	Defects found	Defects introduced	%
1	7	26	26.9
2	6	32	18.7
3	11	39	28.2
4	10	34	29.4
5	16	52	30.7
6	5	20	25
7	10	11	90.9
8	29	31	93.5
9	4	16	25
10	8	25	32

Figure 16.7 Values collected from projects.

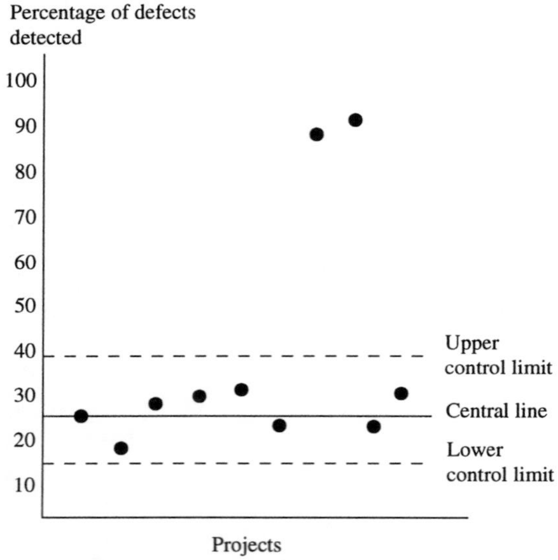

Percentage of defects
detected

Figure 16.8 Control chart for data in Fig. 16.7.

Hence, it follows that:

- Upper control line $= 26.9 + 3 \times (4.1) = 39.2$
- Lower control line $= 26.9 - 3 \times (4.1) = 14.6$

Next an analysis of this control chart was performed to detect any special causes using the guidelines listed in Chapter 14. Using the action rules described in Chapter 15, the control chart revealed that there were two special causes for the data set **V**.

Step 4 — Investigate special causes

Upon investigation, it was revealed that the two values corresponding to the special causes were the result of a number of factors, the most significant being:

- The reviews had predefined goals.
- Procedures were adhered to.
- The reviews were limited to one hour.

These findings were to some extent backed up when the cause of the data point 18.7 was investigated. At this review there was no formal structure or goals set for the review, procedures were not adhered to and the review dragged on all day.

It was decided to make the following changes to the process:

- Goals should be set for the review meeting by the review chairperson and the principal authors of the requirements specification. The goals of the review should define:
  - the expected results of the review
  - what actions will take place during the review
  - details of how the review will be conducted
  - criteria used to measure acceptability
  - decision processes that will be initiated at the end of the review
  - scope and areas of future actions.
- The chairperson and reviewers should not be part of the team that produced the document. Besides the chairperson, there should be at least two reviewers who should have knowledge of the subject matter. However, it is also useful to have one reviewer with no particular knowledge of the field, who can bring a fresh viewpoint. Where possible the reviewers should not all hold like-minded views with those of the authors.
- The length of a review meeting should be between 30 minutes and two hours. Authors should be encouraged to be concise and relegate background material to annexes, which need not be reviewed in detail.

These changes were introduced and a new set of data was collected from ten projects which had implemented these changes (Fig. 16.9).

Then for the data set $V = (46.7, 41.6, 55, \ldots, 53.3)$ we have:

$$\text{Mean } (V) = 49.8$$
$$\text{Standard deviation } (V) = 6.5$$

Project	Defects found	Defects introduced	%
1	7	15	46.7
2	5	12	41.6
3	11	20	55
4	10	16	62.5
5	16	30	53.3
6	5	12	41.6
7	5	10	50
8	8	16	50
9	4	9	44.4
10	8	15	53.3

Figure 16.9 New set of data after changes made.

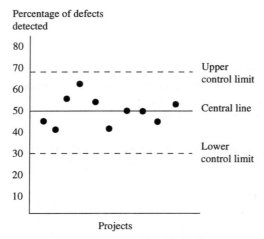

Figure 16.10   Control chart for data in Fig. 16.9.

Using these values a control chart was constructed as depicted in Fig. 16.10.

After removing the special causes, it was concluded from the control chart (Fig. 16.10) that the review process was stable but not capable in the sense that the level of accuracy was unacceptable to management.

Step 5 — Remove common causes

Changes were needed to be introduced to reduce variation and in particular increase the mean (central line). Management needed to change the process so that:

- The average detection rate per project was at least 85 per cent.
- 95 per cent of projects achieved a defect detection rate of at least 75 per cent.

To find out why the average detection rate was only approximately 50 per cent a cause and effect diagram was used. This revealed that projects spent little time preparing for review meetings. It was decided that adequate preparation for a review meeting should be given. Therefore, the following change was introduced: at least five days' notice should be allowed for reviewers to study the document before a review meeting. After implementing this change a new set of data was collected (Fig. 16.11).

This new data was then used to construct a new control chart (Fig. 16.12), where:

$$\text{Mean} = 91.4$$
$$\text{Standard deviation} = 3.5$$

Hence, it follows that:

- Upper control line $= 91.4 + 3 \times (3.5) = 100$ (truncated)
- Lower control line $= 91.4 - 3 \times (3.5) = 80.9$.

Project	Defects found	Defects introduced	%
11	12	14	85.7
12	29	33	87.8
13	21	24	87.5
14	24	25	96
15	16	17	94.1
16	10	11	90.9
17	17	19	89.4
18	22	23	95.6
19	40	43	93
20	16	17	94.1

Figure 16.11 New set of data after five days' notice allowed to reviewers.

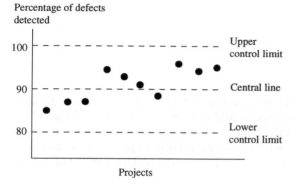

Figure 16.12 Control chart for data in Fig. 16.11.

The control chart depicted in Fig. 16.12 revealed that the change to the process had:

- Not made the process unstable
- Dramatically increased the detection rate.

Step 6 — Continuous process improvement

Management were encouraged by the results of the changes and were committed to continuing to strive towards removing common causes of variation.

17

SUMMARY

Improving a process cannot be achieved by mere guesswork of where changes are needed. It requires statistical understanding of the process and changes based on knowledge of the process gained through quantifiable information. Furthermore, there is no point introducing changes unless you have a way of assessing their impact and a means of determining when and when not to change a process based on data generated by the process.

SPC provides a set of systematic techniques for improving a process based on quantifiable information rather than subjective gut feelings. The power behind SPC is its:

- Simplicity
- Visual representation
- Proven worth based on empirical evidence gathered over 30 years.

The first step to continuous improvement involves achieving stability in the process. The next step is to shrink variation. Unless you have a stable process, it is pointless introducing changes because you will not be able to assess the impact of your changes.

SPC is about continual process improvement which is driven by top management and involves the whole organization. It can be summed up in two words:

Reduce variation

At the heart of SPC is the control chart, a powerful tool for managers and engineers that balances the economics of looking for special causes when none exist, and not looking when they do exist.

128

The main principles of SPC are:

- There is always variation in anything that is being measured.
- Every process has natural limits and when these limits are exceeded the process is out of control.
- A process needs to be stable before analysis and changes can be undertaken to improve it.
- Processes are never entirely free of special causes.
- A state of statistical control is not a natural state for a process. It is achieved by removing special causes that have an excessive effect on variation.
- SPC can be applied to repetitive processes which are subject to performance variation.
- The results of SPC can be verified.
- SPC needs to be driven from the top.
- SPC is a company-wide technique which involves all employees.
- You never know anything to the second decimal point.
-

Finally, to quote Edwards Deming (1986):

A process under statistical control has an identity; its performance is predictable; it has a measurable, communicable capability. Costs are predictable. Productivity, under the present system, is at a maximum.

Section 3

Specifying and Measuring Software Quality

*There is no such thing as perfection, but it doesn't
mean we shouldn't strive for perfection.*

Karl Popper

This section discusses the concept of software quality. It defines a generic set of qualitative requirements that are common to all systems. It then defines a set of measures that can be used to:

- Specify in quantifiable terms how well each requirement does what it is supposed to do
- Measure the 'quality' of a software system.

18

INTRODUCTION

The philosophy of one of the largest computer manufacturers in the world is that quality must come first. To show their commitment to quality every employee has to wear a quality badge. Each year all the top executives and senior managers attend a meeting which is addressed by the chairperson. As each delegate enters the hall the chairperson checks to make sure they are wearing their quality badge. At one such meeting one unlucky manager had arrived without his badge. In front of everyone else the chairperson asked him to stand up and explain why he was not wearing his badge. Looking down at his lapel and seeing his badge was not there he apologized and said he must have forgotten to take it off his pyjamas. What can we glean from this story apart from admiring the quick thinking of the unlucky manager? It is that one of the main ingredients for sustaining a quality culture in an organization is the commitment from senior management which is communicated to all the employees.

USER COMPLAINTS

When users are asked what is wrong with their software systems their main complaints are that:

- It does not do what was wanted.
- It breaks down too many times.
- It takes too long to recover from breakdowns.
- It is slow to respond to users' commands.
- The interface is not intuitive.
- The error messages are uninformative.
- The training facilities are inadequate.

- The user manuals are difficult to read.
- It is difficult to make changes.

And yet these software systems supposedly met their requirements. In general, the problem is that the requirements are not stated in quantifiable terms. Thus the end result is an unhappy customer who invariably makes statements of the form:

This is not what I wanted.

KEY QUESTIONS

At system handover, the customer wants answers to two key questions, namely:

- Does it do what I want?
- How well does it do what I want?

If these questions were not considered in detail when the requirements were produced, then it is unlikely that the system will satisfy the customer's needs. To help in avoiding this situation, these two key questions need to be refined into a set of quantifiable statements. For example:

- *What is the system required to do?*
  The system shall be able to stop unauthorized users from gaining access to the system.
- *How well does it do it?*
  At most only one in two thousand attempts by unauthorized users to access the system will be successful.

Figure 18.1 What the system is required to do and how well does it do it.

MAIN GOAL

A venture capitalist was asked what were the most important criteria he used to decide on which start-up companies to invest in. His reply was:

- First criterion, the quality of management
- Second criterion, the quality of management
- Third criterion, the quality of the process
- Fourth criterion, the quality of the product.

Software quality can be viewed (Fig. 18.2) as consisting of:

- The quality of the management.
- The quality of the project teams.
- The quality of the requirements of a software project in terms of how well each requirement is supposed to be met.
- The quality of the software development process.
- The quality of the product in terms of whether it meets the users' needs.
- The quality of the culture of the IS department.

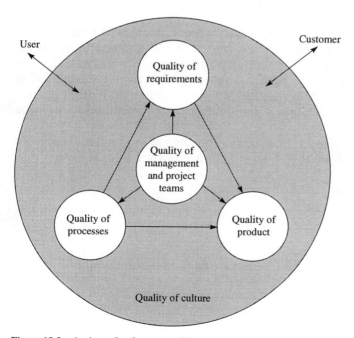

Figure 18.2   A view of software quality.

In this section we will concentrate on:

- The quality of the requirements for a software system
- The quality of the development process
- The quality of the product.

Our goal is to devise:

- A generic set of qualitative requirements that are common to all software systems
- A set of measures together with example benchmarks that can be used to express each generic qualitative requirement in quantifiable terms. In other words, a set of measures to support the task of specifying in quantifiable terms how well a software system should do what it is supposed to do; for example, specifying how well a software system should avoid a system failure during operational use. It is no good specifying that the system shall be reliable: that goes without saying. All systems should be reliable. You would hardly specify that the system should be unreliable. The point is that you need to specify in quantifiable terms the degree of reliability.

Before we go any further we should make it clear that:

There does not exist a single quality benchmark against which a software system can be compared to determine its quality.

DEFINITIONS OF SOFTWARE QUALITY

We do not provide a definition of software quality. This is because the quality of a software system has many contributing factors, and it is not meaningful to try to encapsulate them into a single subjective definition. Furthermore, if we assume that the quality of a software system should be viewed from the perspective of the user, then quality will mean different things to different users in different situations. We now provide a discussion on the shortcomings of some of the more common definitions of software quality.

If you asked ten users and developers what software quality means you would probably get back ten different answers. Typical high-level notions of software quality are:

- Conformance to requirements
- Degree of user satisfaction
- Degree of excellence
- Number of defects
- Exceeding the customer's expectations
- Fitness for purpose
- Value for money
- Cost of rework
- ISO definition.

We now provide an overview of these notions of software quality.

Conformance to requirements

This notion of software quality suffers from the problem that, in general, the requirements are not stated in quantifiable terms that can be tested against; for example, specifying that the system shall be highly reliable instead of stating in quantifiable terms the level of reliability. Also it is not possible to conform to requirements which are inconsistent, incomplete and incompatible. This may sound obvious but these problems may only surface during the latter stages of development.

Degree of user satisfaction

This notion of software quality is used in Japanese quality management. To quote Katsuyuki Yasuda of Hitachi (Yasuda, 1989):

> Meeting the needs of the user is the ultimate determinant of quality.

It is based on two fundamental principles:

- Does the system meet the requirements?
- Do the requirements meet the user needs?

Degree of excellence

This definition is used by the *Oxford English Dictionary*. It is meaningless unless we define what excellence is. However, a dictionary usually defines excellence in terms of quality. It is a bit like the old joke professors tell their students. How does a dictionary define the word recursive? The entry for recursive is: for recursive see recursive.

Number of defects

Many software managers and software engineers define software quality as the absence of defects that would cause a program to stop or to produce incorrect results.

The number of defects is often used to define quality while neglecting such attributes as usability because it is assumed usability is difficult to measure. A system that has no defects does not mean the user is going to view it as a useful and valuable system. It is easy to demonstrate that the number of defects is not an adequate definition of quality. If quality is tied up with how happy a user is with the system, there are many cases where a system has defects but is still regarded by the users as a quality product. All operating systems and word processors have defects but they do not detract from the overall worth of the product. A necessary condition for quality is that a system does not have too many failures during operational use. However, a low defect rate is not a sufficient condition for declaring that a system is a quality system. Software developers need to minimize defects and maximize value to the customer.

A common measure of defects for a software system is:

- The number of defects per thousand lines of code detected during the first six months of operational use.

However, in general, it is not the number of defects that users are worried about but the severity of the defects in terms of their effect.

A typical slogan relating to using defects as a definition of quality is:

Zero defects

This is not a realistic goal because it has been shown that the effort to detect the few remaining defects is prohibitively expensive. It took Bell Laboratories eight years to increase the availability of one of their systems from 99.9 per cent to 99.98 per cent.

Exceeding the customer's expectations

This definition may be fine for products with a mass market (word processors, spreadsheets, etc.) but is a recipe for disaster on fixed-price contracts.

Fitness for purpose

Joseph Juran, an American quality guru who along with Edwards Deming helped the Japanese industry after the Second World War, is credited with equating quality to 'fitness for purpose'. (Juran, 1979). Fitness for purpose views quality from the user's perspective and is concerned with helping to ensure that the software system addresses the user's needs. This definition suffers from the problem that users may perceive the software as being of poor quality, because they have a misconception of what the software system is supposed to do. This misconception is usually compounded by requirements that are not stated in quantitative terms.

Value for money

The kindest thing that can be said about this definition is that it cannot be tested against unless you define what value for money means. To some customers it simply means being able to use the product.

Cost of rework

Philip Crosby, author of *Quality Is Free* and *Quality Without Tears* (Crosby, 1984, 1986), argues that quality should be measured in financial terms by calculating the costs of doing things wrong.

Typical slogans concerning rework are:

- It is always cheaper to do the job right first time.
- There is never enough time to do it properly but there is always time to correct it.
- The best way to deal with defects is to prevent them.

ISO definition

The ISO definition of quality is:

- The totality of features and characteristics of a product, process or service that bear on its ability to satisfy stated or implied needs.

The ISO definition is of little use as it does not tell anyone how to evaluate the quality of a software system.

Let us now briefly examine each of these definitions using the following criteria:

C1 Is it objective?
C2 Is it stated in testable terms that enables quality to be designed into a system and tested against?
C3 Does it view quality from the user's viewpoint?
C4 Does it encompass the concept of the quality of the requirements in terms of how well each requirement is to be met?
C5 Does it encompass the notion that software quality is not absolute; in other words that it means different things in different situations?
C6 Does it encompass the notion that software quality has many contributing factors?

Figure 18.3 compares each definition using these criteria.

Definition of quality	C1	C2	C3	C4	C5	C6
Conformance to requirements	✓	✓			✓	✓
Degree of user satisfaction			✓			
Degree of excellence						
Number of defects	✓	✓				
Exceeding the customer's expectations			✓			
Fitness for purpose			✓			
Value for money						
Cost of rework	✓					
ISO definition					✓	✓

Figure 18.3 Comparison of quality definitions.

19

WHAT IS QUALITY?

In this chapter we discuss what is meant by software quality. Unfortunately, there is no simple explanation, even though the word quality has become commonplace, and some would say devalued, through advertising hype and slogans expounded by quality gurus, such as:

- Quality is free
- Zero defects
- Right first time
- Fitness for purpose.

Many people claim that quality, like beauty, is in the eye of the beholder. In other words quality means different things to different people in different situations. But you can be sure that although customers may not know how to define quality, they know when they have not got it.

A readable and thought-provoking philosophical discussion of quality can be found in Pirsig (1974):

And what is good, Phaedrus, And what is not good — Need we ask anyone to tell us these things?

Another thought-provoking philosophical discussion of quality can be found in Sartre (1943). However, we will not concern ourselves with a philosophical discussion on quality. Instead we will take a practical approach to software quality.

DOES QUALITY = ABSENCE OF ERRORS?

The answer is no. A necessary condition for a software system to be regarded as a quality product by the user is that it is available to be used when it is needed. However, absence of errors is not a sufficient condition for guaranteeing quality (whatever that may be). To quote Weinberg (1992):

> Though copious errors guarantees worthlessness, having zero errors guarantees nothing at all about the value of software.

DOES QUALITY = CONFORMANCE TO REQUIREMENTS?

The answer is no. Conformance to requirements is not a definition of quality since, among other things, it takes no account of the quality of the requirements. Conformance to requirements means precisely what it says. So why use another word? There is more to quality than conformance to requirements. We illustrate this point with two examples.

Our first example concerns a software system that conforms to the following requirement:

- The system shall have no more than ten breakdowns per day and it shall take no more than two hours to repair each one.

By most people's standards a system that had up to ten breakdowns per day and where each breakdown took up to two hours to repair would be practically unusable and hence of extremely poor quality. This example highlights that quality is often qualified by terms such as good, bad, poor, etc.

Our second example concerns two cars, the Trabant which was produced in East Germany, and a Rolls-Royce whose name is revered throughout the automobile industry. Both cars conform to their requirements. But whereas a Rolls-Royce has a reputation for quality recognized by millions of people throughout the world, you would be hard pushed to find anyone who would describe the Trabant as a quality car. So where does the difference lie? At one level, both cars are very similar in the sense that they both have four wheels, an engine, a place to sit, etc. But differences start to emerge when we examine how well they satisfy each of their requirements. For example, a Rolls-Royce can reach 0 to 40 mph in 6 seconds, whereas in a Trabant you would struggle to engage first gear within 6 seconds. A Rolls-Royce has eighteen coats of paint to both protect it from chipping and to provide a deep shine, whereas a Trabant only has three coats of paint. But is it fair to compare a Trabant to a Rolls-Royce when you can buy 20 Trabants for the price of a single Rolls-Royce? Just because one car goes faster than another, breaks down less often than another, does not automatically make it a quality car. Certainly these are important considerations, but they alone do not automatically imply quality. Furthermore, quality does not usually change with time. It is most unlikely that if the Trabant had been developed in the 1920s it would have been described as a quality car.

Is there something more to a Rolls-Royce than simply having high standards for each of its constituent parts? We argue that part of what people perceive as quality in a Rolls-Royce is intimately related to the way its development process has evolved and improved through experience. A Rolls-Royce is still hand-built by a highly skilled work force who take a pride in their work.

A product or a process is made up of many parts. But a product or a process is more than the sum of its parts. Similarly, in an informal way the quality of an object is more than the sum of the quality of its constituent parts.

In short, quality is more than a set of measures but it is beyond the scope of this book to explore this philosophical argument in any depth. To illustrate this viewpoint consider the highly skilled job of painting a car. Nowadays mass-produced cars are painted by industrial robots. These robots have been programmed to duplicate the movements of the best professional car sprayers. However, humans can still produce a better finish than a robot. But it is very difficult to measure this difference. The professional is bringing years of judgement to the job and many subtle things that science at this point in time would find difficult if not impossible to measure.

To some this would suggest that quality is that special something extra that we cannot measure. As soon as it can be measured, it no longer becomes part of quality because we can then use the measures to design our products to more exacting standards. Then we are no longer talking about quality but conformance to requirements. On the other hand a set of requirements can generally be realized in more than one way. To some people quality is a relative measure of the differences between two such realizations. To other people quality is a measure of the gap between the formal requirements and what the customer perceives is going to be delivered, which are often two different things.

WHAT IS A SOFTWARE QUALITY MODEL?

Most software quality models are hierarchical in nature and based on the idea that there are a number of high-level quality attributes of software products, like reliability, usability, etc., which need to be specified in the requirements. These attributes are refined into sub-attributes such as error tolerance, operability, modularity, etc. Sub-attributes are supposed to be defined more objectively than high-level attributes and in some sense are the definition of the high-level attributes. Finally measures are associated with the lowest level attributes.

Essentially a software quality model (Fig. 19.1) consists of:

- A set of attributes based on the user view of the system
- A refinement of these attributes into sub-attributes (the sub-attributes may themselves be refined further)
- Relationships between the attributes of the form:

If reusability is increased then, in general, this will have an adverse effect on integrity.

There are many software quality models in existence, for example:

- Boehm's model (Boehm, 1981)
- McCall's model (McCall et al., 1977)
- MQ model (Watts, 1987)
- LOQUM (Gillies, 1992).

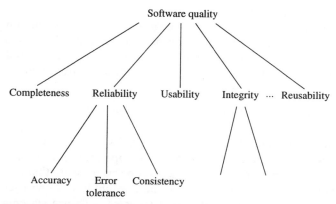

Figure 19.1 Example of a software quality model.

The main weaknesses with most software quality models are that they:

- Do not provide sufficient measures
- Do not provide benchmarks for measures
- Provide a narrow focus of software quality
- Mix quality of the process and quality of the product
- Lack guidance on how to use models.

COMMON QUESTIONS AND ANSWERS

Does there exist a standard definition of software quality that is stated in quantifiable terms?
No.

Is software quality absolute?
No. What is adequate quality to one person may be inadequate quality to another person. Consider a requirement of the form:

- During the first six months of operational use the system shall have no more than x defects per thousand lines of code.

If we view the variable x as a tolerance level, then by adjusting the tolerance level we can start to see why quality, in the restrictive sense of number of defects, means different things to different users. To one user 1.3 defects per thousand lines of code may be acceptable, whereas to another user 2 defects per thousand lines of code may be acceptable.

Is software quality specific to a particular system?
In general, yes. If you consider the various notions of what developers and users mean by quality it becomes apparent that software quality is specific to an application or operational environment.

Can software quality be encapsulated in a single number?
No. This point is best illustrated by the following analogy. The health of a person relies on a variety of attributes. For simplicity, suppose the health of a person was defined in terms of their blood pressure, heart rate and temperature. Then it does not make sense to try and combine these three measures into a single number. It is the same for software quality.

Does there exist a standard set of measures that can be used to determine the quality of a software system?
No. Furthermore, even if we restrict our definition of software quality to the number of system failures per thousand lines of code during the first year of operational use, then even in this restricted sense, there are no standard tolerance levels on this measure that can be used to determine the quality of a software system. In fact, there would have to be a set of standard tolerance levels to take account of the different types of software systems (safety critical systems, etc.).

Suppose we have defined software quality in an objective way. Does it make sense to say that one software system has a higher quality than another system?
The answer will depend on how software quality has been defined. Suppose we take a very narrow view of software quality for systems written in the same programming language and define it to be the number of system failures per thousand lines of code during the first year of operational use. Then in this very restricted sense we can compare the quality of two software systems.

Now consider the situation where we extend our definition of software quality to be:

- Number of system failures per thousand lines of code during the first year of operational use
- Effort needed to learn the system.

Then, in general, it does not make sense to say that one system has a higher quality than another system because you can have the situation where:

- System A has ten system failures per thousand lines of code during the first year of operational use and requires two hours to train a user in how to operate the system.
- System B has two system failures per thousand lines of code during the first year of operational use and requires 15 hours to train a user in how to operate the system.

However, we can say that:

- System B has higher quality (tighter constraints) than system A with respect to the number of system failures per thousand lines of code during the first year of operational use.
- System A has higher quality (tighter constraints) than system B with respect to the effort needed to learn to use the system.

PRINCIPLES OF SOFTWARE QUALITY

It may be argued that it is not possible to discuss the principles of software quality until it has been defined in an objective way. However, we take the view that although it is not meaningful to provide a definition of software quality, it is still meaningful to discuss certain principles that will lead us to a better understanding of this seemingly all-encompassing concept.

We now list the general principles surrounding software quality:

- Software quality is not absolute, it is relative. It means different things to different people.
- Quality is easy to recognize but difficult to define and measure.
- Software quality is more than conformance to requirements. You cannot fully capture the concept of quality simply by examining the constituent parts of something.
- The quality of a software system is intimately related to the process that developed it. Quality depends on the skills, motivation and creativity of the development staff.
- Software quality must be designed into a system, not tested in.
- Achieving software quality is a continuous process.
- Software quality must be related to what the user wants, not what the developers think the user wants.
- Software quality starts with the requirements which must state in quantifiable terms how well each requirement is to be met.
- Part of specifying the quality of a software system involves assigning values to a set of attributes (characteristics, factors, criteria, call them what you want) such as reliability, usability, etc., whose values will vary according to the type of system and type of user. In other words you need to specify the quality of the requirements in terms of the severity of the constraints placed on the quantitative measures associated with how well each requirement is to be satisfied. In general, these attributes are not independent. For example:
  - storage capacity is generally adversely affected by defensive programming techniques
  - increase in efficiency generally has an adverse affect on ability to correct defects and the ability to run the system on other hardware.
- Trade-offs may need to be made between the values assigned to the various measures used to define how well each requirement is to be satisfied.

20

SPECIFYING THE REQUIREMENTS

In this chapter we provide an overview of the important aspects of defining the requirements for a software system.

The requirements for a software system can be divided into:

- What it does
- How well it does what it is supposed to do.

For example, most requirements relating to what it does will be stated in qualitative terms. All requirements relating to how well it does what it is supposed to do need to be stated in quantifiable terms so that they can be designed into a system and evaluated during acceptance testing.

An example of what it does could be:

- The test strategy shall ensure that all paths in the code are tested.

An example of how well it meets this requirement could be:

- Each path in the code will be tested at least twice.

Specifying the requirements of the customer is one of the most difficult tasks in software development. In general, there is not one but many customers each with different needs which may be conflicting. When producing the requirements it is necessary to consider what would be the effect of not being able to meet certain requirements due to excessive costs. One possibility could be to increase the budget. Another possibility is that other requirements could be relaxed. These types of problems generally lead to a juggling act between costs and requirements. A common way to help alleviate these potential problems is to grade the requirements as:

146

- *Mandatory* (essential and non-negotiable)
- *Negotiable*
- *Useful* but can be procured at a later date (this is especially applicable if an evolutionary development process was adopted).

Adopting this strategy is important, as it provides a way of focusing on the relative importance of each requirement from the customer's viewpoint, and in particular the mandatory requirements. Having categorized the requirements, this information needs to be communicated to the developers so that they know where to direct their best efforts. Questions that need to be considered are as follows:

- Are all the requirements needed?
- Can some of the requirements be met by tailoring existing systems?
- Do all the requirements need to be operational at the same time?
- Are the requirements stated in quantifiable terms?
- Are the requirements mutually compatible?
- Does the customer understand what they will get?

CATEGORIZING THE REQUIREMENTS

The requirements for a software system can be divided into six categories, namely those that:

- Refer to the timescales and cost
- Refer to the contract
- Are specific to the development process
- Are generic to the development process
- Are specific to the application
- Are generic to all applications.

A GENERIC SET OF QUALITATIVE REQUIREMENTS

We now define a generic set of qualitative requirements that are common to all systems. In defining this generic set we consider four categories of requirements, namely requirements relating to:

- The development process
- Using the system
- Changing the system to meet new requirements
- Repairing the system.

Our generic set of qualitative requirements is:

- The development process shall be mature.
- The software system shall be tested.
- The software system shall be complete.

- The software system shall be reliable.
- The software system shall be usable.
- The software system shall be robust.
- The design of the software system shall be structured.
- The software system shall be repairable.

There are other generic requirements that need to be considered but are outside the scope of this book. For example:

- How accurate should the outputs be (level of tolerance)?
- How secure should the system be?
- How efficiently should the system run on the hardware?
- How easy should it be to interface with another system?
- Which parts of the system should be designed for reuse?
- How much storage should be available?
- How easy should it be to move the system onto another machine?

We now refine our generic set of qualitative requirements into questions that require quantifiable answers.

THE DEVELOPMENT PROCESS SHALL BE MATURE

We need to produce quantifiable statements on the maturity of the software development process that will be used to develop the software system. One way to do this is to use the SEI CMM (Capability Maturity Model) developed by the Software Engineering Institute of Carnegie Mellon University (Appendix D). The SEI CMM can be thought of as a tool to help:

- Identify weaknesses and strengths in a software development process
- Support process improvement initiatives
- Procurers to evaluate the capability of software vendors.

Questions that require quantifiable answers

The requirements relating to the maturity of the development process should answer:

- What level of maturity is the development process when it is assessed using the SEI CMM?
- How many defects should be detected during formal reviews at the end of each phase of development?
- How well does the development process inhibit the propagation of defects caused by correcting defects?
- What percentage of defects detected are corrected during each phase of development?
- What percentage of modules are found to be defective during testing?
- How much effort is spent on correcting defects found during development?

THE SOFTWARE SYSTEM SHALL BE TESTED

Testing is the execution of a program on selected sets of input data with the intention of finding defects. Testing is not a process of confirming that a program is correct, nor is it a demonstration that errors are not present. The weakness in testing is its inability to guarantee that a program has no defects. It must be recognized that generally it is impossible or impractical to construct sets of test data which will fully exercise a program. Furthermore, even if it was possible to construct such test data most software development budgets and timescales would not enable such testing to be performed. Thus the requirements need to state in quantifiable terms the amount of testing that is required and the quality of the tests in terms of coverage (number of paths to be tested, etc.).

At this point the reader may question why it is necessary that the requirements should be concerned with testing because it is the developer's responsibility and not the concern of the requirements. The main reason why a minimum level of testing needs to be specified is that most software is not rigorously tested. For example, Hennell (1989) has used the dynamic test tool TESTBED to analyse actual test data supplied for industrial systems. The analysis revealed that, in general, the percentage of statements tested did not surpass 40 per cent.

The main problems associated with testing are that:

- It is a non-trivial task to choose test data that reflects the salient properties of a function that the program is supposed to implement.
- In general, testing cannot assure that a program will always terminate.
- Defects are sensitive to the specifics of the data being processed.
- Correcting defects may introduce new defects.
- Unless measurement is used it is rarely clear when to stop testing and assert that most of the defects have been detected.

Questions that require quantifiable answers

The requirements relating to the effectiveness of the testing should answer the following questions concerning how much of the code should be tested:

- What percentage of the paths in the code should be tested?
- How many times should each path be tested?
- How many times should each statement in the code be tested?
- How many times should each branch in the code be tested?
- How well should each loop exit condition be tested?
- How many times should each boundary condition be tested, such as loop variables, array subscripts, input parameters, etc.?

THE SOFTWARE SYSTEM SHALL BE COMPLETE

We need to produce quantifiable statements on how complete the system needs to be in terms of meeting its requirements. In particular, in terms of:

- Mandatory requirements

- Negotiable requirements
- Useful requirements.

We also need to determine which requirements bring 'real' value to the customer. For example, which requirements are going to help the customer do their job more efficiently and more effectively.

Questions that require quantifiable answers

The requirements relating to the completeness of the software system should answer:

- Which requirements are mandatory (essential and not negotiable)?
- Which mandatory requirements bring 'real' value to the customer?
- Which requirements are negotiable?
- Which requirements are useful but can be procured at a later date?

THE SOFTWARE SYSTEM SHALL BE RELIABLE

The present state of software technology cannot guarantee to produce error-free-software. Therefore, users are interested in how long a system will operate before it fails and what will be the impact of the failures. To quote from Currit *et al.* (1986):

> Increasing inter-fail times represents progress towards a reliable product, whereas increasing defect discovery may be a symptom of an unreliable product.

Thus the requirements need to state in quantifiable terms the level of reliability that is required. In order for a user to assess the reliability of a software system they want answers to two questions:

- How many breakdowns will occur?
- How long will it take to recover from a breakdown?

Questions that require quantifiable answers

The requirements relating to the reliability of the system should answer the following questions:

- During a given period of operational use, how many system failures of a given severity should be tolerated?
- During a given period of operational use, what should be the maximum number of defects per thousand lines of code?
- What should be the availability of the system over a given period of time?

By a system failure is meant a departure from expected behaviour as specified in the requirements. It should be noted that certain parts of a system may need to be more reliable than other parts.

THE SOFTWARE SYSTEM SHALL BE USABLE

We need to produce quantifiable statements on how usable the system needs to be; in particular, in terms of:

- The context in which the system will be used
- Level of experience, knowledge and skill needed by the user
- Effort needed to learn to understand the system
- Effort needed to operate the system.

Questions that require quantifiable answers

The requirements relating to the usability of the system should answer the following questions:

- How much effort is needed to learn to use the system?
- What skills do users need to operate the system?
- How much effort is needed to install the system?
- How much effort is needed to prepare inputs?
- How much time will be spent doing 'productive' work?
- How much effort is needed to interpret outputs?
- How much effort is needed to learn to maintain the system?
- What should be the average response times to users' commands?
- What parts of the system should be provided with on-line help facilities?
- How informative should the error messages be?
- How should the system reduce the possibility of the user doing something that they did not mean to do but cannot reverse the situation? For example, accidentally deleting the wrong file and being unable to retrieve the file.

A detailed coverage of software usability can be found in the deliverables from the ESPRIT project MUSiC (Measuring Usability of Systems in Context; see Kirakowski *et al.*, 1992).

THE SOFTWARE SYSTEM SHALL BE ROBUST

The robustness of a software system covers the ability of the system to cope with:

- Erroneous inputs made by the user
- Loss of data
- Corrupted data
- Invalid data.

Questions that require quantifiable answers

The requirements relating to the robustness of the system should answer the following questions:

- How accurate do the inputs need to be (level of tolerance to error)?
- Should the system be required to recover automatically from certain failure scenarios?
- How often should the system crash when the user presses a wrong key?
- What percentage of failures should result in no loss of information on recovery?
- Which input data should be checked before it is processed?
- What should be the probability that the system is able to detect erroneous input data?
- Which variables need to be assigned range values so that actual values assigned to the variables can be checked?
- Should all assignments to variables be checked to detect illegal assignments?
- Which modules should check incoming data for correctness?
- Which parts of the system should use defensive programming techniques?
- What should be the tolerance level for incorrect input data?
- How well should the system limit the impact of a failure?

THE SOFTWARE SYSTEM SHALL BE STRUCTURED

It has long been appreciated that the writing of well-structured programs which are modular has helped to produce more comprehensible programs which are easier to change. Structured programming employs the use of hierarchies to reduce complexity, pushing details into ever lower and simpler structures. This raises the question of what we mean by complexity. Like quality, complexity means different things to different people in different situations.

The goal of software designers is to keep it simple. Wirth (1974) summed up the quest for elegant simplicity in software design as follows:

> You vow to make it simple at all cost. You accept complexity as your enemy. Then you build it, doing your best to control complexity ... and it comes out complex anyway.

It is beyond the scope of this book to discuss what constitutes a well-structured program other than to provide the following guidelines:

- All loops in the control structure of a program should have a single entry point.
- Minimize the linkage between pairs of modules (known as module coupling).
- Maximize the degree to which the components within a module are related (known as cohesion).

Coupling is an attribute of a pair of modules and cohesion is an attribute of an individual module. For a more detailed account of the important topic of structured programming the interested reader should consult Parnas (1972), Wirth (1974) and Fenton (1991).

The use of modularity in the design of software systems is recognized as the key factor in understanding a software system in order to change it. A large monolithic program consisting of one module is very difficult to understand and change. On the other hand a program consisting of very small modules of less than eight lines of code would also be very difficult to understand and change. If we accept the principle of divide and conquer where it is easier to solve a problem when you divide it into a set of subproblems, it raises the question of what bounds if any should be placed on:

- The size of a module in terms of lines of code

- The number of paths through a module
- The nesting of loops
- The number of decision points in a module
- The coupling between pairs of modules.

Unfortunately there are no standard bounds because among other things the size of a module will be influenced by its application. Instead the following guidelines should be adhered to by software designers:

- Each module should implement at most one function.
- Each module should maximize its cohesion.
- Each module should minimize its interaction with other modules.
- Minimize the depth of nested loops.

It should be noted that for poorly structured programs we cannot even define the concept of loop nesting.

Questions that require quantifiable answers

The requirements relating to the control structure of the code should answer the following questions:

- What should be the control structure of the code?
- What should be the average size of a module?
- What should be the average number of paths through a module?
- What should be the maximum nesting of loops?
- What should be the average coupling between pairs of modules?

THE SOFTWARE SYSTEM SHALL BE REPAIRABLE

We need to define quantifiable statements for how easy it will be to correct defects found during operational use.

Questions that require quantifiable answers

The requirements relating to the repairability of the system should answer the following questions:

- How long should it take to repair a system failure?
- How long should it take to locate the cause of a system failure?
- What percentage of modules should be defect-free during a given period of time?

21

SOFTWARE QUALITY INDICATORS

In this chapter we provide a set of indicators that can be used to:

- Answer the questions generated in Chapter 20
- Help gauge the quality of a:
  - software development process
  - software system.

In general, the indicators are like the temperature, blood pressure and heart rate of a hospital patient. They do not tell the doctor what is wrong but they give an indication that something might not be quite right and requires further investigation.

BENCHMARKS FOR INDICATORS

For each indicator we also provide a benchmark. It should be noted that these benchmarks should be used as guides. They are not taken from any standard benchmarks but rather from what can reasonably be expected to be achieved by an organization which is embarking on a process improvement programme to reach level 2 on the SEI capability maturity model. They are derived from the following sources:

- Actual figures from IS departments
- Practical experience of software developers.

Initially, IS departments should use historical data from their software systems or rely on the experience of staff to set benchmarks as there are no industry standards at present. However, this situation is being addressed by a number of initiatives. For example,

SOFTWARE QUALITY INDICATORS

Brameur Ltd are in the process of setting up a European benchmarking club which is partially sponsored by the European Commission under its ESSI (European System and Software Initiative) programme. The purpose of the benchmarking club will be to collect data from IS departments from various industrial sectors on a set of key performance indicators covering productivity, quality and accuracy of estimates.

Note that care needs to be taken when quoting benchmarks using lines of code (LOC) as a size measure because different programming languages will give different results and LOC can be counted using different rules. Here LOC means source lines of code and does not include comment statements. Where benchmarks are defined in terms of LOC they refer to high-level programming languages such as Ada, Pascal, etc.

More and more organizations are now using Function Point Analysis (FPA) (see Appendix C) as a size measure. One of the advantages of Function Point Analysis over LOC is that it is language independent.

PROCESS QUALITY INDICATORS

We now provide templates for the following process indicators:

Defect density	Maturity
Defect detection efficiency	Maturity
Defect propagation ratio	Maturity
Defect removal efficiency	Maturity
Defect-prone module ratio	Maturity
Spoilage	Maturity
Test case density	Testability
Test time density	Testability
Test effectiveness ratio	Testability

Defect density		*Maturity*
Definition		
	$$\frac{\text{number of defects detected during development}}{\text{size of software system}}$$	
Comment		
Size can be measured using LOC, FPA, etc. Defect density can be calculated for each phase of development. The benchmark refers to the cumulative defects found during the development process (summed over all phases of development). The benchmark should be viewed in conjunction with the quality of the reviews and tests.		
Benchmark		
Good		*Average*
less than 15 defects per KLOC		[20–40] defects per KLOC

Defect detection efficiency		Maturity
Definition		
	$$\frac{\text{number of defects detected during development}}{\text{number of defects present}} \times 100$$	
Comment		
The number of defects present refers to those defects that were detected during development and during the first year of operational use. The benchmark for defect detection efficiency refers to the percentage of defects present that were detected at the end of testing.		
Benchmark		
Good		*Average*
more than 85%		[65–80%]

Defect propagation ratio		Maturity
Definition		
	$$\frac{\text{number of defects created by correcting defects}}{\text{number of defects corrected}}$$	
Comment		
The defect propagation ratio can be calculated for each phase of development. Some software projects found that correcting a defect during the latter stages of development created between 0.1 and 0.3 new defects.		
Benchmark		
Good		*Average*
less than 5%		[10–20%]

Defect removal efficiency		Maturity
Definition		
	$$\frac{\text{number of defects corrected during a phase of development}}{\text{number of defects detected during a phase of development}} \times 100$$	
Comment		
Defects corrected in a particular phase of development can include defects introduced at an earlier stage. Therefore defect removal efficiency can be more than 100%. As a general rule, clear all defects detected before embarking on the next phase of development.		
Benchmark		
Good		*Average*
100%		[80–95%]

Defect-prone module ratio		*Maturity*
Definition		
$$\frac{\text{number of defective modules}}{\text{total number of modules}}$$		
Comment		
This should be calculated either during system testing or during a period of operational use. A rule of thumb is that 80% of the problems can be traced to 20% of the modules.		
Benchmark		
Good		*Average*
less than 10%		[15–30%]

Spoilage		*Maturity*
Definition		
$$\frac{\text{effort to correct defects}}{\text{total project effort}} \times 100$$		
Comment		
Defects refers to defects found during development. Spoilage should be compared with the effort spent on preventing defects occurring, such as conducting formal inspections. Spoilage can be calculated for a particular type of defect.		
Benchmark		
Good		*Average*
less than 10%		[20–30%]

Test case density		*Testability*
Definition		
$$\frac{\text{number of tests}}{\text{size of software system}}$$		
Comment		
Size can be measured using: FPA, LOC, number of branches, number of paths.		
Benchmark		
Good		*Average*
[0.07–0.05] per LOC		[0.05–0.03] per LOC

Test time density		*Testability*
Definition		
	$$\frac{\text{CPU time spent during testing}}{\text{size of software system}}$$	
Comment		
The size of the system can be measured using: FPA, LOC, number of branches or number of paths.		
Benchmark		
Good		*Average*
greater than 0.5 seconds per LOC		[0.2–0.3] seconds per LOC

Test effectiveness ratio		*Testability*
Definition		
	$$\frac{\text{number of objects tested at least once}}{\text{total number of objects}} \times 100$$	
Comment		
An object can be: • A statement in the code • A branch in the code • A path in the code.		
Benchmark		
Good		*Average*
100%		[40–60%]

PRODUCT QUALITY INDICATORS

We now provide templates for the following product indicators:

Conformance ratio	Completeness
Mean time to failure	Reliability
Availability ratio	Reliability
Breakdown ratio	Reliability
Failure density	Reliability
Flesch–Kincaid Index	Usability
Automatic recovery ratio	Robustness
Information loss ratio	Robustness
Volume information loss ratio	Robustness
Module robustness ratio	Robustness
Erroneous data detection	Robustness
Average module size	Structuredness
Module input/output ratio	Structuredness
Cohesion ratio	Structuredness
Coupling ratio	Structuredness
Mean downtime	Repairability
Mean recovery effort	Repairability
Mean effort to repair a failure	Repairability
Mean restart time	Repairability
Defect-free module ratio	Repairability

Conformance ratio		*Completeness*
Definition		
	$$\dfrac{\text{number of requirements correctly implemented}}{\text{total number of requirements}} \times 100$$	
Comment		
This ratio can be calculated for the following grades of requirements: • Mandatory (essential and non-negotiable) • Negotiable • Useful (can be procured at a later date).		
Benchmark		
Good		*Average*
100% w.r.t. mandatory		[80–95%] w.r.t. mandatory

Mean time to failure		Reliability
Definition		
	$$\frac{\text{total operation time over a given period}}{\text{number of failures observed}}$$	
Comment		
The mean time to failure (MTTF) will be dependent on the type of application. The benchmark refers to large one-off systems.		
Benchmark		
Good		*Average*
greater than 100 hours		[30–50 hours]

Availability ratio		Reliability
Definition		
	$$\frac{\text{total operating time over given period}}{\text{time system is supposed to be operational}} \times 100$$	
Comment		
The benchmark is taken from a major telecommunications circuit switch network. A total downtime of one hour over a one-year period equates to an availability of 99.98%.		
Benchmark		
Good		*Average*
greater than 99.8%		[95–98%]

Breakdown ratio		Reliability
Definition		
	$$\frac{\text{number of breakdowns over a given period}}{\text{total number of failures during period}} \times 100$$	
Comment		
A breakdown refers to a failure that results in the system being unable to be used. A low breakdown ratio does not necessarily imply a low number of breakdowns.		
Benchmark		
Good		*Average*
less than 5%		[10–20%]

Failure density		Reliability
Definition		
	number of failures detected during operational use / size of software system	
Comment		
The six on-board flight software systems in the Space Shuttle achieved a defect rate of 0.1 defects per thousand lines of code during the first three years of operational use. Achieving this figure cost $1000 per line of code.		
Benchmark		
Good		*Average*
[0.9–1.5] failures per KLOC		[3–8] failures per KLOC

Flesch–Kincaid Index		Usability
Definition		
	$0.39 \times A + 11.8 \times B - 15.9$ where A = number of words in a sentence B = average number of syllables per 100 words	
Comment		
Used to measure the difficulty in reading and understanding text. It is a measure on a sentence. It is used by the US DoD for the production of user and training manuals and is defined in standard MIL-M-38784A. A similar measure is the fog index $= 0.4 \times (A + C)$ where C is the percentage of words of three or more syllables.		
Benchmark		
Good		*Average*
less than 5		[7–10]

Automatic recovery ratio		Robustness
Definition		
	$\dfrac{\text{number of automatic recoveries from failures over a period}}{\text{total number of failures during period}} \times 100$	
Comment		
May be difficult to determine when a system has failed if it has recovered automatically. An adaptable routing mechanism for a packet switch network is an example where it may be difficult to determine when a failure has occurred. The benchmark is taken from a telecommunications packet switch network.		
Benchmark		
Good		*Average*
greater than 60%		[10–20%]

Information loss ratio		Robustness
Definition		
$$\frac{\text{number of failures that result in loss of information}}{\text{total number of failures}} \times 100$$		
Comment		
Refers to information that is lost upon recovery.		
Benchmark		
Good		*Average*
less than 10%		[15–25%]

Volume information loss ratio		Robustness
Definition		
$$\frac{\text{volume of information before failure } - \text{ volume of information on recovery}}{\text{volume of information before failure}} \times 100$$		
Comment		
This indicator refers to information that is lost upon recovery from a failure. The volume can be measured in a variety of ways, such as bytes of information.		
Benchmark		
Good		*Average*
less than 10%		[15–25%]

Module robustness ratio		Robustness
Definition		
$$\frac{\text{number of modules that use defensive programming techniques}}{\text{total number of modules}} \times 100$$		
Comment		
Defensive programming techniques refers to modules that check the validity of incoming and outgoing data, etc. Safety-critical software should require 100% module robustness. Defensive programming techniques have an adverse effect on other attributes, such as efficiency. The benchmark refers to non-safety-critical software.		
Benchmark		
Good		*Average*
40–60%		[5–30%]

Erroneous data detection		*Robustness*
Definition		

$$\frac{\text{number of erroneous inputs detected}}{\text{number of erroneous inputs}} \times 100$$

Comment	

In certain situations some erroneous inputs may never be detected.
    Can be calculated at a system level or a module level. Can also be calculated for erroneous outputs.

Benchmark	
Good	*Average*
100%	[95–98%]

Average module size		*Structuredness*
Definition		

$$\frac{\text{total lines of code for the system}}{\text{total number of modules}}$$

Comment	

This indicator should not be strictly adhered to in the sense that all modules should not be constrained to be less than a certain number of LOC.
    Module size can also be measured in terms of paths through the module.

Benchmark	
Good	*Average*
[20–50] LOC	[30–150] LOC

Module input/output ratio		*Structuredness*
Definition		

$$\frac{\text{number of modules with only one entry and one exit point}}{\text{total number of modules}} \times 100$$

Comment	

All loops should have a single entry point to help assist in understanding and changing the module.

Benchmark	
Good	*Average*
100%	[50–75%]

Cohesion ratio	*Structuredness*
Definition	

$$\frac{\text{number of modules performing a single function}}{\text{total number of modules}} \times 100$$

Comment	

Can be calculated for varying degrees of cohesion, such as:

- Unrelated activities (bad)
- Logically related activities
- Time-related activities
- Ordered activities
- Activities on same data
- Sequence of data transformations.

Benchmark	
Good	*Average*
100%	[50–75%]

Coupling ratio	*Structuredness*
Definition	

$$\frac{\text{number of pairs of modules that communicate via data parameters}}{\text{total number of pairs of modules that communicate}} \times 100$$

Comment	

Can be calculated for varying degrees of coupling, such as:

- Modules that share code
- Access to global data shared
- Passing of control parameters
- Passing entire data structure
- Passing of data parameters.

Benchmark	
Good	*Average*
100%	[50–75%]

Mean downtime		Repairability
Definition		

$$\frac{\text{downtime over a given period}}{\text{number of breakdowns in given period}}$$

Comment	

Downtime is the time between the occurrence of a breakdown of the system and the completion of the recovery (correcting the defect(s) and restart from the breakdown).

Benchmark	
Good	*Average*
less than 1 hour	[2–4 hours]

Mean recovery effort		Repairability
Definition		

$$\frac{\text{effort spent on correcting breakdowns}}{\text{number of breakdowns}}$$

Comment	

A breakdown refers to a failure in operational use that results in the system being unable to be used.

Benchmark	
Good	*Average*
[1–3 hours]	[5–10 hours]

Mean effort to repair a failure		Repairability
Definition		

$$\frac{\text{effort spent on correcting failures}}{\text{number of system failures}}$$

Comment	

Failures refer to defects found during operational use. The effort spent correcting a particular failure is dependent on where the defect was introduced. In general, many failures are not corrected individually over a period of time, but all at once.

Benchmark	
Good	*Average*
[1–3 hours]	[5–10 hours]

Mean restart time		Repairability
Definition		

$$\frac{\text{effort spent on restarting system after recovery from a breakdown}}{\text{number of breakdowns}}$$

Comment	
The benchmark will depend on the application and the amount of information that has been lost.	

Benchmark	
Good	*Average*
less than 30 minutes	[1–1.5 hours]

Defect-free module ratio		Repairability
Definition		

$$\frac{\text{number of modules that have no defects detected during a period of operational use}}{\text{total number of modules}} \times 100$$

Comment	
The Pareto principle states that 80% of the problems can be traced to 20% of the modules (see Section 4).	

Benchmark	
Good	*Average*
greater than 80%	[40–60%]

22

QUANTIFIABLE STATEMENTS

In this chapter we provide templates to support the task of producing quantifiable statements relating to the generic set of qualitative requirements defined in Chapter 20, the questions devised in Chapter 20 and the indicators defined in Chapter 21.

TEMPLATES FOR MATURITY REQUIREMENTS

- The defect density with respect to lines of code shall be less than (x).
- The defect detection efficiency shall be greater than (x).
- The defect propagation ratio shall be less than (x).
- The defect removal efficiency shall be greater than (x).
- The defect-prone module ratio shall be less than (x).
- The effort spent on correcting defects found during development shall be less than (x) per cent of the overall development effort.

TEMPLATES FOR TEST REQUIREMENTS

- The test case density with respect to lines of code shall be greater than (x).
- The test case density with respect to branches in the code shall be greater than (x).
- The test case density with respect to paths in the code shall be greater than (x).
- The test time density with respect to LOC shall be greater than (x).
- The test time density with respect to branches in the code shall be greater than (x).
- The test time density with respect to paths in the code shall be greater than (x).
- The test effectiveness with respect to statements in the code shall be greater than (x).
- The test effectiveness with respect to branches in the code shall be greater than (x).

- The test effectiveness with respect to paths in the code shall be greater than (x).
- Each boundary condition shall be tested at least (x) times.

TEMPLATES FOR COMPLETENESS REQUIREMENTS

- The conformance ratio with respect to mandatory requirements shall be 100 per cent.
- The conformance ratio with respect to negotiable requirements shall be greater than (x).
- The conformance ratio with respect to useful requirements shall be greater than (x).

TEMPLATES FOR RELIABILITY REQUIREMENTS

- During the first (x) months of operational use the mean time to failure shall be greater than (y).
- During the first (x) months of operational use the availability ratio shall be greater than (y).
- During the first (x) months of operational use the breakdown ratio shall be less than (y).
- During the first (x) months of operational use the defect density per thousand lines of code shall be less than (y).

TEMPLATES FOR USABILITY REQUIREMENTS

- The average time for a category (x) user to achieve level (y) of competence with the system shall be less than (z) hours.
- A category (x) person shall be able to install the system within (y) minutes.
- The average time needed to prepare system inputs of class (x) by a category (y) user shall be less than (z) minutes.
- The average time needed to interpret outputs of class (x) by a category (y) user shall be less than (z) minutes.
- The average response time to class (x) of user commands shall be less than (y) seconds.
- The average time for a class (x) of user to learn to maintain the system to a level (y) of competence shall be less than (z) hours.
- On-line help facilities shall be available for (x) per cent of screens.
- On-line help facilities shall be available for (x) per cent of system prompts.
- The ratio of the number of on-line help screens to the number of menu options shall be greater than (x).
- In (x) per cent of the cases where a user tries to enter illegal input data there shall be an error message.
- (x) per cent of error messages shall have an on-line help facility that suggests the response the user should adopt.
- A category (x) user shall not have to refer to a manual for at least (y) per cent of the error messages.
- In (x) per cent of the cases where a user tries to execute an illegal command, there shall be an error message.

- In the user guide to the system, associated with every user command there shall be at least (x) examples showing how that command can be used.

TEMPLATES FOR ROBUSTNESS REQUIREMENTS

- The system shall be able to recover automatically from at least (x) per cent of failures.
- At least (x) per cent of failures shall result in no loss of information on recovery.
- At least (x) per cent of wrong keys pressed by a user will not result in a system breakdown.
- At least (x) per cent of input data shall be checked before it is processed.
- The probability that the system is able to detect erroneous input data shall be greater than (x).
- At least (x) per cent of assignments to variables shall be checked to detect illegal assignments.
- At least (x) per cent of modules shall check incoming data for correctness.
- At least (x) per cent of modules shall check outgoing data for correctness.
- The knock-on effect of a module producing an incorrect output should be limited to those modules that are directly called by the module.

TEMPLATES FOR STRUCTURE REQUIREMENTS

- The module ratio shall be greater than (x) per cent.
- The average module size shall be less than (x) LOC.
- The cohesion ratio shall be greater than (x) per cent.
- The coupling ratio shall be greater than (x) per cent.
- The impact on other modules of changing a module should be limited to those modules that are directly called by the module or directly call the module.
- Each loop shall have a single entry and less than (x) exit points.
- The average number of times a module is referenced by other modules shall be less than (x) per cent of the total number of modules.

TEMPLATES FOR REPAIRABILITY REQUIREMENTS

- The mean downtime during the first (x) months of operational use shall be less than (y) hours.
- The mean recovery time during the first (x) months of operational use shall be less than (y) hours.
- The mean time to repair a failure during the first (x) months of operational use shall be less than (y) hours.
- The mean restart time during the first (x) months of operational use shall be less than (y) hours.
- The average time to locate the cause of a failure shall be less than (x) hours.
- The percentage of modules that are defect-free during the first (x) months of operational use shall be more than (y) per cent.

23

SUMMARY

There is no objective definition of software quality that satisfies everyone's concept of quality. Software quality is not absolute, it is relative. It means different things to different people in different situations.

What is required is a set of measures that can be used to specify how well a requirement is to be met. Ideally, benchmarks should be provided for these measures. Historical data and industry best practices can help in determining realistic benchmarks.

The main points to remember are that:

- Quality is usually easy to recognize but difficult to define and measure.
- Quality is more than conformance to requirements.
- You cannot fully capture the concept of quality simply by examining the constituent parts of something.
- There does not exist a quality benchmark against which a software system can be compared to determine its quality.
- Quality must be related to what the user wants, not what the developers think the user wants.
- The requirements must state in quantifiable terms how well each requirement is to be met.
- Reliability and usability must be designed into a system, not tested in.

Section 4

Defect Analysis As An Improvement Tool

Truth emerges more readily from error than from confusion.

Sir Francis Bacon

This section provides a step-by-step guide on how to use defect analysis as a tool to improve your software development process. In particular, it shows how to use defect analysis to reduce rework by helping to prevent defects occurring.

This section does not put forward any sophisticated statistical techniques. Rather, it concentrates on using an evolutionary approach, starting off with techniques that can be easily implemented by a project or department.

The main message of this section is that defects should be treated as a valuable source of information that can be used to improve your software development process.

24

INTRODUCTION

When should we stop testing? Which modules give us the most trouble and need to be rewritten? How effective are our testing techniques? What are the most common causes of defects? How much effort is spent on rework? How can we reduce the effort spent on rework? What are the most defect-prone development activities?

Too often when managers ask these questions they fail to get satisfactory answers.

THE CHALLENGE

Two of the main challenges a software project manager faces are to:

- Remove as many defects from the software system within the limits of the budget and timescales before the system is delivered to the customer
- Remove defects as early as possible.

Software developers faced with such a challenge need to know how to go about the job in a systematic way. The key is to learn from our mistakes and the mistakes of others. For example, analysis of the data related to defects can be used to:

- Help remove the gamble from determining when to stop testing the system and release it for operational use
- Help estimate the defect density at handover to the customer
- Help to determine how much effort will be required to correct defects found during reviews and testing
- Assess the effectiveness of design reviews and testing techniques
- Identify defect-prone development activities
- Identify defect-prone modules that need to be rewritten.

SCOPE

Defect analysis is not only a very important subject but is also very extensive. Therefore, it is impractical to cover such a vast topic all at once. The main objective of this section is show an IS department how to get started. In particular, it will answer the following four questions:

- What is a defect?
- What is defect analysis?
- How can defect analysis be used to help gauge the health of a software project or software department?
- How can defect analysis be used as a tool to improve software development?

Before embarking on a detailed discussion of defect analysis it is important to understand that defect analysis should not be used to assess the performance of individual software developers. It should be used to help identify and improve those processes that cause defects. However, it is important to recognize the distinction between using defect analysis to assess the performance of staff and using defect analysis to improve the performance of staff. An important part of defect analysis is providing feedback to developers to enable them to learn from their mistakes and the mistakes of others.

25

WHAT IS A DEFECT?

In this chapter we provide some general information about software defects. In particular, we answer the following questions:

- What constitutes a defect?
- When is a defect a defect?
- Are all defects equal?
- What needs to be recorded?
- What are the main types of defect?
- What are the main causes of a defect?
- What activities can detect defects?

WHAT CONSTITUTES A DEFECT?

The basic concepts surrounding software defects can be expressed informally as:

- People make *errors*
- Errors lead to *defects* in software products
- Defects manifest themselves by causing *failures*
- A failure is an observed departure from the expected behaviour of the software system during operational use
- Failures vary in *severity*
- Not all failures result from a defect (they may be caused by a hardware failure, incorrect installation, etc.).

In general, failures should be viewed as two failures. First, an error was made that led to a defect and, secondly, the defect was not identified during development.

Software products

The term software product denotes the outputs from a software development process, such as:

- Project plan
- Requirements specification
- Design specification
- Test specification
- Code
- User manual
- Etc.

Notation

Sometimes the term fault is used to denote defects which have been discovered during operational use. Where no confusion arises, we will use the term defect to mean both defect and fault.

It is not always easy determining what constitutes a defect. For example:

- Does a defect have to be something written down?
- Should we record defects that we make while thinking about a problem but we correct before we have written anything down?

Furthermore, should the concept of a defect encapsulate the possibility that rectifying a perceived defect may in fact result in an enhancement? At this point you might wonder what all the fuss is about. Are we making it unduly complicated? One of our aims is to provide a coherent description of defect analysis which is simple to understand and yet still provides a powerful tool for developers to use. Let us carry on and see how these issues can be resolved.

Definition of a software defect

A software defect is a perceived departure in a software product from its intended properties, which if not rectified would under certain conditions contribute to a software system failure (departure from required system behaviour during operational use).

Main characteristics of a software defect

- A defect can occur (be created) during any phase of the development process.
- The cause of a defect can be due to a variety of factors, such as the combination of one or more of the following:
  - misunderstanding of the requirement, design, etc.
  - incorrect logical reasoning
  - inappropriate or faulty tools such as an incorrect compiler
  - inexperienced personnel.

In fact, there can be a chain of causes; for example, poor management of the process which led to inappropriate training which led to inappropriate staff skills which led to an ineffective test strategy.

- In general, defects that are inherent in an operational system are not evenly or randomly distributed throughout the system. Empirical evidence suggests that, in general, they tend to be confined to less than 20 per cent of the modules.
- The effect of a defect may lead to more than one software system failure.
- Not all defects that go undetected during testing cause failures during operational use because some are latent and are never activated during the lifetime of the system.
- The process of correcting defects can create more defects.
- The impact of a defect can be minimized by the use of defensive programming techniques; for example, checking the value of an array variable for incorrect bounds.

WHEN IS A DEFECT A DEFECT?

This question needs to be considered if we are going to record information about defects. In particular, we need to consider whether we record:

- Defects detected by a compiler
- Repeated failures in testing
- Repeated failures in operational use
- Defects that are not corrected
- Defects produced by an author of a document but corrected by the author (during proofreading, etc.) before the document is formally reviewed
- Defects produced by a programmer but discovered by the programmer during unit testing
- Typographical or grammatical mistakes in documents (excluding the code itself).

The type of defects to record will depend on the goals for defect analysis. However, whatever the goals are, careful consideration needs to be given to determining how much data to collect. There needs to be a balance between recording information on every defect, which would inevitably result in recording difficulties, and the problems of collecting too little information which would result in inconclusive evidence to support your goals.

To avoid confusion and to minimize the amount of data collected, a defect should only be recorded if it is identified during:

- A formal review or inspection of a software product
- The testing phase of development
- A phase of development but was introduced at an earlier phase
- Any phase of development and it is not known where it was introduced
- Operational use.

Thus defects introduced during the requirements phase, design phase or coding phase but identified during that phase outside a formal review or inspection should not be recorded. This avoids having to record defects that were introduced in a document but found during proofreading, or an informal discussion with a colleague, etc.

In general, issues of when to record and when not to record should be fairly easy if you have a well-defined set of rules for what to record and what not to record. A consistent and pragmatic approach should be used. The motto should be:

> If in doubt, record it.

Typographical and grammatical mistakes

Typographical and grammatical mistakes can be tricky. Clearly, in most cases it would be impractical and pointless to record such defects. However, care needs to be taken. For example, consider the case where a typographical mistake in the instructions for entering input data has the potential to cause a software system failure. This situation can be further complicated by the fact that one person can recognize the typographical mistake whereas another person may not and consequently perform an incorrect action.

Typographical and grammatical mistakes should not be recorded if they do not have a direct effect on the software system; that is, if they are not code-related or related to instructions that directly affect the operational use of the software system. Although this is a rather subjective judgement, in practice there should not be a problem of deciding what typographical mistakes should be recorded.

ARE ALL DEFECTS EQUAL?

Not all defects are equal in terms of their impact on the behaviour of the software system. Some defects may cause the total failure of a software system, whereas other defects may have a trivial effect such as a misaligned printout. However, it is important to remember that, in general, the impact of a defect will be application dependent. For example, a misaligned printout could be a disaster for a book or newspaper. Furthermore, there is no relationship between the effort needed to correct a defect and the severity of its symptoms. For example, a typographical mistake which is trivial to rectify may have the potential to cause a software system failure.

MARINER 1, the first attempt by NASA to send a spacecraft to Venus, failed minutes after launch in 1962. The guidance instructions from the ground stopped reaching the rocket due to a problem with its antenna, so the on-board computer took control. Unfortunately, there was a defect in the guidance software, and the rocket promptly went off course, so the Range Safety Officer destroyed it. Although the defect is sometimes claimed to have been an incorrect FORTRAN DO statement, it was actually a transcription error in which the bar (indicating smoothing) was omitted from the expression 'R-dot-bar sub n' (nth smoothed value of derivative of radius). This error led the software to treat normal minor variations of velocity as if they were serious, leading to incorrect compensation.

Thus the severity of a defect should not be measured in terms of the effort required to correct the defect. In general, the severity of a defect will be application dependent.

WHAT NEEDS TO BE RECORDED?

The type of information to record about a defect will be dependent on your goal. For example, if it is to identify defect-prone modules then you need to record the effort spent in correcting defects. However, in general, the following information should be recorded, where possible:

- Where the defect was identified (design phase, operational use, etc.)
- The activity that identified the defect (design review, system test, etc.)
- Cause of the defect
- Origin of the defect (where it was created)
- Type of defect
- Effect/potential effect of defect on the system, if known
- Effort to correct defect
- Elapsed time taken to correct a defect.

Data relating to the cause of a defect is the most difficult to collect since it may not be possible to determine the cause of a defect. For example, there may be incomplete documentary evidence regarding the circumstances that led to the cause of a defect.

WHAT ARE THE MAIN TYPES OF DEFECT?

The following is a list of the types of software defect that can occur during software development:

- Missing or incorrect function
- Data flow defects:
  - variable used before it is initialized
  - variable initialized but never used
  - etc.
- Control flow defects:
  - unreachable code
  - statement from which a program exit cannot be reached
  - statements without successors
  - unreferenced labels
  - control flow given to incorrect statement
  - etc.
- Computational defects:
  - incorrect operand in logical expression
  - incorrect use of parenthesis
  - sign convention error
  - incorrect variable type
  - computation produces an overflow or underflow
  - incorrect equation used
  - missing computation

– precision loss in arithmetic calculations
– etc.
- Logical defects:
  – incorrect subroutine called
  – mismatch of parameters
  – data referenced at incorrect location
  – logic activities out of sequence
  – wrong variable being checked
  – missing logic on a condition test
  – non-termination of a loop
  – a loop iterated incorrect number of times
  – etc.
- Interface defects
- Input/output defects
- Timing defects
- Documentation defects.

It is recognized that this is not an exhaustive list. However, we have tried to make the list as general as possible and tried to provide a balance between being too vague or too specific. In general, the choice of defect types should be derived from the goals of defect analysis.

WHAT ARE THE MAIN CAUSES OF A DEFECT?

In general, a defect can be attributed to one or more of the following causes:

- Requirements technically infeasible
- Requirements economically infeasible
- Requirements incompatible
- Inaccurate or incomplete documentation
- Correction of another defect
- Typographical
- Misinterpretation
- Changing requirements
- Inaccurate translation
- Undocumented assumptions
- Inappropriate development method/tools
- Incorrect logical expressions
- Unstructured control flow
- Erroneous numerical analysis techniques
- Misinterpretation of language constructs
- Boundary value problems
- Violation of language rules
- Working with incorrect version of code
- Inexperienced personnel

- Insufficient validity checks for input data
- Non-standard interfaces
- Failure to fully take account of all interactions between modules
- Inadequate test strategy
- Inadequate level of user involvement
- Non-adherence to standards
- Inadequate configuration control procedures.

WHAT ACTIVITIES CAN DETECT DEFECTS?

The following is a list of the main activities that can detect a defect:

- Requirements analysis
- Formal reviews (inspections, walkthroughs, etc.)
- Informal reviews
- Static analysis
- Dynamic analysis
- Symbolic testing
- Exception testing
- Random testing
- Unit testing
- Path testing
- Functional testing
- Integration testing
- System testing
- Regression testing
- Interoperability testing
- Acceptance testing
- Operational use
- Corrective maintenance
- Enhancements to operational system
- Compiling the code
- Audit
- Risk analysis
- Simulation and modelling.

26

A STEP-BY-STEP APPROACH TO DEFECT ANALYSIS

In this chapter we provide an overview of defect analysis, discuss what it can be used for and provide a step-by-step guide on how to use it. Quite simply, defect analysis is the process of recording and analysing the data associated with software defects in order to:

- Help answer specific questions about a software project or software system the defects relate to, such as:
  - When should we stop testing?
  - Do we need to devote more time to testing a particular part of the system?
- Help identify where improvements are needed to the software development process in order to prevent defects being introduced, by answering such questions as:
  - What activities uncover most defects?
  - How effective are reviews at finding defects?
  - How effective are inspections at finding defects?
  - How effective is our test strategy?
  - Which are the most error-prone development activities?
  - What are the most common causes of defects?
  - How effective are our quality assurance techniques?
- Help evaluate changes to the development process
- Help in providing a comparative evaluation of testing techniques, by answering such questions as:
  - Which test techniques are most effective?
  - Which test techniques are best at finding a particular type of defect?
- Help predict the reliability of a software system before it goes into operational use, by answering such questions as:
  - Are critical failures (the system cannot be used at all) more likely to be uncovered early in testing?
  - Is there a correlation between the number of defects found during operational use and the number of defects detected during system testing?
- Help evaluate software engineering tools
- Help validate and calibrate reliability models.

Defect analysis may not be able to fully answer these questions but it gives an indication of where further investigation is necessary. For example, defect analysis may reveal that on a certain project more defects are being found during system testing than would normally be expected. Further investigation is then required to determine the reason, such as:

- Changes made to the test strategy (use of an independent test team)
- More experienced testers
- Ineffective reviews
- Unreliable software.

Defect analysis provides a systematic way to identify problem areas. By analysing the origin and cause of defects we can use this information to help prevent defects in future systems.

It is always possible to do more inspections and reviews, and conduct more static analysis and dynamic testing. Defect analysis provides the information that is necessary to understand the costs and benefits of performing inspections, reviews, static and dynamic analysis and tests.

PRINCIPLES OF DEFECT ANALYSIS

The main principles of defect analysis are:

- Learn from mistakes
- Understand why problems occur
- Determine priorities and focus on problems that really matter
- Use an evolutionary approach; tackle one problem at a time
- Use feedback to improve the prevention and detection of defects
- Don't use defect analysis to assess the performance of individuals
- Defect prevention takes time and commitment
- 80 per cent of the problems can be fixed with 20 per cent of the effort
- 80 per cent of software defects can be traced to 20 per cent of the modules
- 80 per cent of the problems can be traced to 20 per cent of all possible causes.

The last three principles are derivations of the Pareto principle, named after the Italian economist Vilfredo Pareto.

STEP-BY-STEP APPROACH

We now discuss the steps that need to be carried out to be able to use defect analysis as an improvement tool (Fig. 26.1).

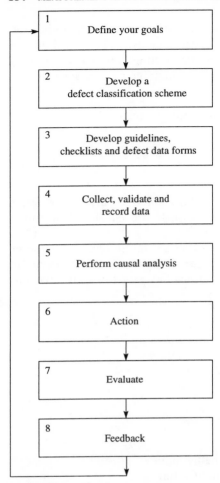

Figure 26.1 Defect analysis process.

STEP 1 — DEFINE YOUR GOALS

The first step is to define your goals for defect analysis in order to make sure everyone knows what is to be done, why it is to be done and what defect data needs to be collected. For example, a company developing software systems may be losing their market share because their customers are fed up having their business disrupted by defective software systems. In response to this situation, the company's high-level qualitative business goal may be to deliver software products to the customer with substantially fewer critical defects. Here critical can be defined as defects that result in a very irate user, total loss of all functionality, etc. Defect analysis may reveal that the average number of defects for a particular class of software systems is:

- 1.5 defects per thousand lines of code found during the first two years of operational use

- 0.4 critical defects per thousand lines of code found during the first two years of operational use.

Having established your current position, you should determine what you think you can achieve and state your goal accordingly. What you think you can achieve will be dependent on the type of process changes that you are introducing. For example, for your type of systems, the industry average may be 0.6 defects per thousand lines of code, if such data exists for an IS department at your level in the SEI CMM model. Therefore, your goal (remembering one of the principles of goal setting is to make them achievable) might be that within six months, the number of defects inherent in your software systems at handover to the customer will be no more than:

- 1.1 defects per thousand lines of code during the first year of operational use in 90 per cent of the cases
- 0.2 critical defects per thousand lines of code during the first year of operational use in 90 per cent of the cases.

That is, for a system of 100 000 lines of code the system is to be delivered to the customer with no more than 110 defects of which 20 will have a critical effect on the software system. In other words, for 90 per cent of the systems no more than 110 unique defects will be discovered during the first two years of operational use and only 20 of these will have a critical impact on the working of the software system.

Remember we are advocating using an evolutionary approach to the long-term goal of eradicating defects being introduced during the development process. In other words, approach the goal of zero defects in incremental steps.

Returning to setting goals for using defect analysis, examples of typical qualitative goals are:

- Improve the testing strategy by identifying and improving ineffective test techniques.
- Reduce the effort spent on corrective maintenance by identifying and rewriting defect-prone modules.

Inputs and outputs

The inputs to this step are:

- Business objectives of department/company
- Main problem areas associated with defects.

The output from this step is:

- A set of quantifiable goals that relate to defect prevention.

STEP 2 — DEVELOP A DEFECT CLASSIFICATION SCHEME

The second step is to develop a software defect classification scheme. The first thing that needs to be understood is that there is no universally correct way to classify defects because the classification will depend on your goals, your type of development process, etc. Trying to develop a classification scheme to cater for every conceivable goal would be impractical. However, the main characteristics of any defects classification scheme are that it:

- Can be applied to all phases of software development
- Records the activity that identified the defect in order to help in assessing the efficiency of defect-detection techniques
- Records the cause of the defect in order to help make improvements to prevent defects recurring
- Records the origin of the defect in order to allow defects to be directed to the appropriate groups for analysis and to help identify error-prone phases of development
- Records the effort to correct a defect in order to help estimate the effort needed during system testing and corrective maintenance
- Supports the prediction of residual defects in operational software by recording the number of defects introduced and detected during each phase of development
- Takes account of the severity of defects in order to help in system hazards analysis
- Requires only minimal training in its use.

During the 1970s and 1980s many different schemes were defined (Collofello and Balcom, 1985; Ostrand and Weyuker, 1984; Bowen, 1980; Amory and Clapp, 1973). The following scheme was developed for the European Space Agency (Ashley, 1989) and is general enough to be applied to all types of development methodologies. Essentially, the classification scheme consists of recording the following information relating to a defect:

- *Where* defect detected
- *Activity* that detected defect
- *Cause* of defect
- *Origin* of defect
- *Type* of defect
- *Effect* of defect on system
- *Effort* to correct defect
- *Elapsed time* to correct defect.

It should be noted that the effort to correct a defect does not include the effort to fix the process to help stop the defect recurring.

Problems and solutions with recording defects

If you have repeated identical failures, do you record the defect more than once?
An identical failure is said to occur when the circumstances that lead to a particular failure are repeated and the same deviation from the expected behaviour of the system occurs. Identical failures occur because the defect that causes the failure has not been corrected. In

general, as test plans try to avoid repeating the same input states, identical failures in testing are unlikely. In general the following guidelines should be used:

- In testing do not count repeated identical failures
- In operational use count repeated failures because they help to provide an indication of the efficiency of defect removal.

If a decision is made not to correct a defect, should it still be recorded?
The reasons for not correcting a defect may be that the cost is too high or the defect does not affect the functionality of the system. In some cases the requirements are changed to eradicate the defect. Even if a decision is made not to correct the defect, then the defect should still be recorded.

Do you count defects that are caused by a faulty compiler?
In general no, since it is likely that the compiler will be reliable by the time the system is finally recompiled for delivery.

A defect is defined to be a departure in a software product from its intended properties. As the properties are defined in the requirements specification, does this rule out the possibility of defects in the requirements document?
No. You can view the requirements specification as resulting from the user's needs. So a difference in the requirements specification and the user's needs can be regarded as a requirements defect.

Inputs and outputs

The inputs to this step are:

- Your goals for using defect analysis as an improvement tool
- Other classification schemes.

The output from this step is:

- A defect classification scheme that supports your goals for defect analysis.

STEP 3 — DEVELOP GUIDELINES AND CHECKLISTS

The third step consists of developing the following set of guidelines and checklists to support and record the detection and correction of defects:

- Guidelines on activities that need to be performed to detect defects
- Guidelines on how to determine the type of defect to record
- Guidelines on how to determine the cause of a defect
- Guidelines on how to determine the origin of a defect
- Guidelines on how to determine the severity of the defect
- Checklist to determine actions to be performed to correct a defect

- Checklist of processes associated with defect prevention
- Checklist of the most common defects for each phase of development.

Note that it may be necessary to develop guidelines and checklists for each phase of development. The guidelines and checklists need to be updated on a regular basis to take account of the information gained from defect analysis.

Inputs and outputs

The inputs to this step are:

- Existing guidelines (Jones, 1985; Humphrey, 1989; Hollocker, 1990)
- QA procedures, etc.

The output from this step is:

- A set of guidelines and checklists to support defect analysis.

STEP 4 — COLLECT, VALIDATE AND RECORD DEFECT DATA

The fourth step is concerned with collecting, validating and recording the data relating to defects.
A plan for data collection should be produced covering:

- What data is to be collected
- Bounds for each data item
- When the data is to be collected
- Frequency of data collection
- Where the data is to be collected from
- Who will collect, validate and store the data
- How the data is to be collected, validated, recorded and stored
- Where the data is to be stored.

Data collection forms should be used to record data and should have the following properties:

- Be self-explanatory, except for common technical terms which should be defined elsewhere
- Be based on quantifiable answers to questions
- Where variable information is required choices should be given
- Be contained on one side of A4 paper which should state:
  - title of form
  - reference for form
  - instructions for completing the form
  - who recorded the data

- date when form was completed
- date when data was collected.

Once data has been collected it must be validated. We can ask a number of questions about the data:

- *Is it accurate?* That is, does it fall within previously laid down criteria on accuracy and have the correct methods and terms of reference been used as agreed in the data collection plan?
- *Is it complete?* That is, has all relevant data been collected over the correct period or correct stage of the lifecycle?
- *Is it what was wanted?* That is, does it specifically relate to a goal?

The techniques described in Chapter 5 can be used to validate the data collected.

Inputs and outputs

The inputs to this step are guidelines and checklists to support recording the information relating to defects.

The outputs from this step are the completed defect data forms.

STEP 5 — PERFORM CAUSAL ANALYSIS

The fifth step is concerned with analysing the cause of a defect. This should be performed as early as possible after the defect is detected. Experience has shown that data should be analysed as part of the process, not in isolation. Causal analysis should be more concerned with the prevention of defects rather than their detection.

The primary objectives of causal analysis are to determine:

- What caused the defect?
- How can the defect be detected more quickly?
- What needs to be done to prevent a particular type of defect recurring, such as:
  - How can reviews and inspections be improved?
  - What is the optimum time for a review?
  - What tools would be useful?
- What corrective actions are needed?
- What is the cost effectiveness of the proposed solutions?

Which defects should be analysed?

If you try to analyse all defects you will use up too much of your resources. Therefore, you need to concentrate on those defects that are rich in information. Initially, the choice of which defects to analyse should be based on the experience of the development teams.

Who should perform causal analysis?

The team which performs causal analysis should be made up of people that have a knowledge of the processes and staff who have experience of carrying out the processes.

How do you perform causal analysis?

The cause and effect diagram, sometimes known as the fishbone diagram, is a versatile tool that can be used in helping to identify the causes of a defect. This analysis tool is described in Appendix B. Figure 26.2 provides an example.

A detailed description of what needs to be done to determine the cause of a defect and how to do it can also be found in Jones (1985), Humphrey (1989) and Ishikawa (1987).

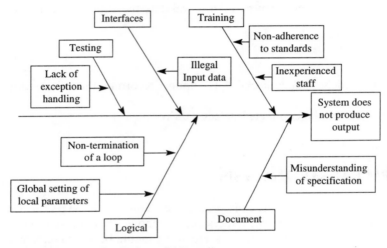

Figure 26.2   Example of using a fishbone diagram.

Inputs and outputs

The input to this step is the information relating to the defects as recorded via the defect classification scheme.

The outputs from this step are:

- A prioritized list of development processes that need to be changed in order to reduce the likelihood of introducing defects
- A set of recommended changes.

STEP 6 — ACTION

The sixth step is concerned with acting on the information from analysing the cause of the defects. Otherwise, what is the point of collecting and analysing the data? This action may take the form of implementing changes to help meet the defect analysis goals. Any changes should be accomplished using an evolutionary approach starting with the high priority problems.

Inputs and outputs

The input to this step is a list of recommended changes that were produced in Step 5.

The output from this step is the implementation of an incremental improvement programme for the software development process which will lead to a refined set of development processes.

STEP 7 — EVALUATE

The seventh step is concerned with using defect analysis to determine the impact of the changes. In other words, evaluate results against your goals; for example, to determine whether certain types of defects have been eradicated or at least drastically reduced.

Inputs and outputs

The input to this step is defect data from the refined development processes and products.

The output from this step is an evaluation report that states in quantifiable terms the impact of the changes.

STEP 8 — FEEDBACK

The eighth step is concerned with using the information generated from defect analysis to:

- Help developers learn from their own mistakes and to learn from other people's mistakes
- To make managers and developers aware of the effort spent on rework in contrast to the benefits gained from conducting formal reviews and inspections, etc.
- To improve guidelines and checklists
- To improve the data classification scheme.

Inputs and outputs

The input to this step is the results of defect analysis.

The output from this step is feedback to the developers and management.

STEP 9 — WHAT NEXT?

The final step is to start all over again because defect prevention is a continuous activity.

GENERAL GUIDELINES

We now provide a general set of guidelines to help in using defect analysis as a tool to improve a software development process:

- In general, the results of analysing defects in small systems (typically under 10 000 lines of code) cannot be extrapolated to large systems (typically greater than 500 000 lines of code).
- It may be the case that the effect of a defect may be eradicated, not by correcting the defect, but by changing the requirements or the design, since this may be easier to accomplish.
- Some software reliability models are incapable of taking into account the severity of defects.
- It may be the case that data is corrupted in an area far removed from the defect.
- The use of fault-tolerant techniques such as software diversity may mask the occurrence of defects.
- Since some defects that go undetected during system testing do not cause failures during operational use, it is useful to develop a model relating defects to operational failures; for example, the percentage of defects that result or would have expected to result in an operational failure.
- In general, it may not be possible to determine whether a particular defect discovered during development will have a catastrophic effect on the system.
- The recognition that a defect has occurred may consist of more than one piece of information. For example, it may be the result of a number of views from different personnel. Also, a number of observations may correspond to different manifestations of a single defect.
- The recording of compilation defects may introduce bias. For example, some programmers may use the compiler to detect defects without checking the code manually. Other programmers may thoroughly check the code manually before submitting the code for compilation. The number and/or severity of compilation defects therefore depends on the programmer's attitude and does not necessarily reflect the reliability of the product.
- There can be a wide variation in the defect density between projects, departments and companies depending on how defects are defined and recorded and how the size of a system is measured. This needs to be taken into account when you derive models of defect density, etc. from 'similar' projects. This emphasizes the need for standards.
- Failure reports do not always imply that a failure of the system has occurred. For example, the user may be unhappy with the response time of the system to a command and report it as a failure. Another example is where the user may think a user manual is unclear. Also, users can make mistakes!
- Some failures cannot be replicated.
- Grady and Caswell (1987) point out that there can be a significant difference in the type of defects occurring on projects using different development environments.

A CASE STUDY

This case study concerns an IS department which used defect analysis to improve the effectiveness of its inspections of project deliverables. We now describe the eight steps involved in applying defect analysis to this situation.

Step 1 — Define your goals

The goal was to:

- Help improve the effectiveness of design inspections by producing a checklist of the defects that are likely to be present in a design specification.

This checklist could then be used by the reviewers to assist them in the inspection process.

Step 2 — Develop a defect classification scheme

The following classification scheme was devised to classify the type of a defect detected:

- Missing function
- Incorrect function
- Computational
- Logical
- External interface
- Internal interface
- Input/output
- Timing defects.

Step 3 — Develop guidelines and checklists

A guideline on how to determine the type of defect to record was produced. This included a set of checklists for helping to determine the type of a particular defect.

Step 4 — Collect, validate and record defect data

Defect data from projects was collected, validated and recorded on a database.

Step 5 — Perform causal analysis

Each defect detected during testing was analysed using the fishbone diagram technique to determine whether its cause was due to the design process.

Step 6 — Action

The information generated from Step 5 was used to produce a checklist of the defects that are likely to be present in a design specification. This checklist was then used by the reviewers to assist them in the inspection process.

Step 7 — Evaluate

The impact of this enhancement to the design inspections was an improvement in the effectiveness of the design inspections and a reduction in the time needed to perform the inspections.

Step 8 — Feedback

The information generated from this exercise was fed back to development teams to encourage them to think about ways of improving the design process in order to minimize the type of design defects that were being produced.

27

INDICATORS DERIVED FROM DEFECT DATA

This chapter defines the following eight indicators that are derived from defect-related data, namely:

- Defect density
- Defect-detection efficiency
- Defect propagation ratio
- Defect removal efficiency
- System stability ratio
- Defect-prone module ratio
- Breakdown ratio
- Spoilage.

The indicators were derived to help answer the following questions posed by an IS department, namely:

- Which testing techniques are most effective at detecting a particular type of defect?
- When should we stop testing and declare a system reliable?
- What is the estimated defect density of the system at handover to the customer?
- Which processes are in most urgent need of improvement?
- Which are the most defect-prone modules?

The indicators are like the temperature, blood pressure and heart rate of a hospital patient. They don't tell the doctor what is wrong but they give an indication that something might not be quite right and requires further investigation. The indicators can be used to help identify the health of a project or department with respect to how well it is preventing and correcting defects.

DEFECT DENSITY

$$\text{Defect density} = \frac{\text{number of defects detected during a period of time}}{\text{size of system}}$$

The defect density can be calculated at various times such as during development, during system testing and during a period of operational use.

The defect density can also be calculated for individual modules, critical defects and testing techniques.

Using historical data from completed projects a model of defect density can be constructed, such as the one depicted in Fig. 27.1.

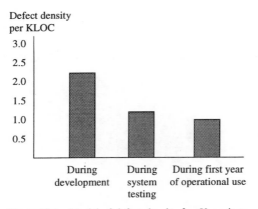

Figure 27.1 Model of defect density for 50 projects.

This model shows the average defect density, that is defects per KLOC (thousand lines of code), for 50 projects. The way to interpret this graph is as follows. For 50 software systems, the average number of defects found per system during the first year of operational use was 1.1 defects per thousand lines of code. Therefore, it would be reasonable to assume, that unless the development process had dramatically changed, the estimated defect density for a new software system on handover to the customer would be somewhere in the range [0.6, 1.6] defects per thousand lines of code with the most likely defect density being 1.1 defects per thousand lines of code. Note that the range [0.6, 1.6] could be derived using a variety of techniques such as using the standard deviation on the data set of 50 projects assuming a normal distribution.

This model can be enhanced by calculating the maximum and minimum defect densities for each category.

Problem with using LOC as a size measure

Comparing the defect densities of two projects may be misleading if the systems are written in different programming languages. For example, consider a system developed in both Assembler and PL/1 by the same development team in the same development environment having the following statistics:

	Assembler	PL/1
Number of LOC	500 000	150 000
Total defects	300	220
Defect per KLOC	0.6	1.4

Intuitively, you would expect that the defect density of the system written in PL/1 would be less than the defect density of the system written in Assembler. Using Function Point Analysis (Appendix C) as a size measure would overcome this problem.

DEFECT-DETECTION EFFICIENCY

$$\text{Defect-detection efficiency} = \frac{\text{number of defects detected}}{\text{number of defects present}} \times 100$$

The defect-detection efficiency should be related to a pair of development phases. For example, we can define the defect-detection efficiency for the pair (requirements phase, testing phase) as the percentage of defects introduced during the requirements phase that were detected at the end of testing.

For example, using historical data from completed projects, a defect-detection efficiency model can be constructed, such as the one depicted in Fig. 27.2.

Phase of development	Defect-detection efficiency
Requirements	60%
Design	70%
Code	80%
Test	85%

Figure 27.2 Model of defect-detection efficiency.

This model shows that on average, at the completion of testing the following applies:

- 60 per cent of the defects introduced during the requirements phase will have been detected.
- 70 per cent of the defects introduced during the design phase will have been detected.
- 80 per cent of the defects introduced during the coding phase will have been detected.
- 85 per cent of the defects introduced during testing will have been detected. Note that defects caused by correcting defects detected during testing are classified as being introduced during testing.

When calculating the defect-detection efficiency, the number of defects present means the number of defects detected during the lifetime of the system. The number of defects present can be approximated using the following approach. The number of defects detected during development and the number of defects detected during a period of operational use (typically six to twelve months) can be used to approximate the total number of defects introduced. These defects should then be allocated to the phases of development in which they were introduced. It should be noted that it is reasonable to expect that most operational failures will occur during the first six to twelve months of operational use. Of course, this will be dependent on how many times the system is run during this period. A model should be developed for your systems to see if this hypothesis is reasonable.

DEFECT PROPAGATION RATIO

$$\text{Defect propagation ratio} = \frac{\text{number of defects created by correcting defects}}{\text{number of defects corrected}}$$

The defect propagation ratio is an important indicator of the quality and stability of a software development process. Some software projects found that, on average, for every ten defects corrected during development, one new defect was created which was directly attributable to the corrections.

The graph depicted in Fig. 27.3 shows the defect propagation ratio for a project over a period of weeks. It indicates that the project is in trouble. Management need to introduce reviews of corrections to try and resolve the situation, even corrections that only involve changing one line of code!

The purpose of this graph is to help:

- Indicate the 'quality' of the work associated with correcting defects
- Indicate the 'complexity' of the software products being changed.

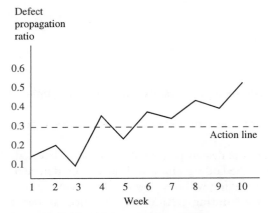

Figure 27.3 Trend in propagation of defects.

A word of warning. Defects created by correcting defects may not be detected until much later in the development process or in operational use and may account for a sudden surge in the upward trend.

DEFECT REMOVAL EFFICIENCY

$$\text{Defect removal efficiency} = \frac{\text{number of defects corrected}}{\text{number of defects detected}} \times 100$$

The defect removal efficiency should be calculated for a particular point in time t and should be calculated as the number of defects corrected from the start of the project up to time t divided by the number of defects detected from the start of the project up to time t.

The graph in Fig. 27.4 depicts the trend in the defect removal efficiency over a period of months during the development of a project.

One purpose of this graph is to warn managers when the defect removal efficiency falls below a threshold level (action line). The calculation of this action line should be based on historical data or failing that the experience of the project team and quality group.

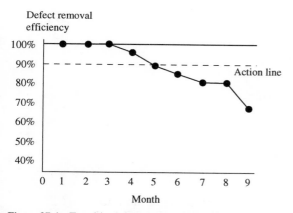

Figure 27.4   Trend in defect removal efficiency for a project.

SYSTEM STABILITY RATIO

$$\text{System stability ratio} = \frac{\text{number of defects corrected}}{\text{estimated number of total defects}}$$

The system stability ratio is the ratio of the number of defects corrected up to a certain point in time during development per the estimated number of defects initially in the system. The number of defects introduced during the development of the system can be estimated from historical defect data from similar projects (Chapter 28). For example, suppose 120 defects were detected and corrected up to and including unit testing of the code and suppose the total estimated number of defects is 160. Then at that point in time we have system stability ratio = 120/160 = 0.75.

The graph depicted in Fig. 27.5 can be used as a warning for management when the graph starts to climb above the action line.

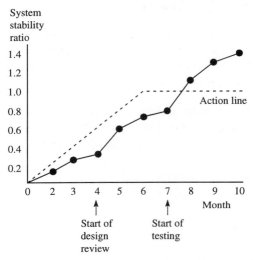

Figure 27.5   Trend in system stability ratio of a project.

DEFECT-PRONE MODULE RATIO

$$\text{Defect-prone module ratio} = \frac{\text{number of defective modules}}{\text{total number of modules}}$$

The number of defective modules refers to the number of modules that have been identified as containing defects during operational use. When analysing the cause of defective modules, it should be determined whether there is a relationship between:

- The control structure of the modules and the defective modules
- Effort spent on testing the modules and the defective modules.

The defect-prone module ratio can be refined by defining defective modules as those modules whose defect density rises above a threshold value.

BREAKDOWN RATIO

$$\text{Breakdown ratio} = \frac{\text{number of critical defects detected during operational use}}{\text{total number of defects detected during operational use}}$$

A critical defect occurs where the software system cannot be used at all.

Care needs to be used when interpreting this ratio. A very low breakdown ratio does not necessarily indicate a very low number of critical defects.

SPOILAGE

$$\text{Spoilage} = \frac{\text{effort to correct defects}}{\text{total project effort}}$$

Spoilage can be calculated as:

- The effort to correct defects found during the development of a project
- The effort to correct defects found during operational use of a system
- The aggregate spoilage over all projects on a month by month basis.

USE OF INDICATORS TO SUPPORT GOALS

Figure 27.6 shows where indicators can be used to help answer a variety of questions.

Question	Indicator							
	Defect density	Defect-detection efficiency	Defect propagation ratio	Defect removal efficiency	System stability ratio	Defect-prone module ratio	Breakdown ratio	Spoilage
Which testing techniques are most effective at detecting a particular defect?	✓	✓						
When should we stop testing and declare the system reliable?	✓	✓	✓		✓			
What is the estimated defect density of the system at handover to the customer?		✓					✓	
Which processes are in most urgent need of improvement?	✓		✓	✓				✓
Which are the most defect-prone modules?						✓		

Figure 27.6 Use of indicators to answer questions.

28

WAYS TO USE DEFECT ANALYSIS

This chapter shows how defect analysis can be used to answer the following questions:

- Which testing techniques are most effective at detecting a particular defect?
- When should we stop testing and declare a system reliable?
- What is the estimated defect density of the system at handover to the customer?
- Which processes are in most urgent need of improvement?
- Which are the most defect-prone modules?

DEFECT ANALYSIS AND COMPARING TEST STRATEGIES

We now discuss how defect analysis can help in the goal:

- Improve testing techniques

by providing a comparative evaluation of testing techniques.

Step 1

Use historical data from at least five projects to construct a model showing which test strategies found which type of defect. Figure 28.1 provides an example of such a model. Here the model shows that path testing found 53 per cent of the logical defects detected during the testing phase.

Step 2

Analyse the data using a checklist having questions such as:

- Which testing techniques are good at identifying a particular type of defect?

Technique	Type of defect			
	Computational	Logical	Interface	Others
Unit testing	7%	1%	0%	1%
Path testing	27%	53%	37%	17%
Symbolic testing	5%	7%	4%	5%
Exception testing	6%	9%	5%	9%
Static analysis	18%	8%	3%	6%
Stress testing	15%	10%	11%	25%
Random testing	15%	9%	33%	34%
Other techniques	7%	3%	7%	3%

Figure 28.1   Model of defects found during system testing.

- Which testing techniques are poor at identifying a particular type of defect?

Caution needs to be used when comparing testing techniques. It may be the case that a particular testing technique, such as path testing, failed to detect many defects simply because this form of testing was very limited. It is a sobering experience to hear the answers from project managers when you ask them to quantify the path coverage performed by their test strategy. The chances are that you will not get an answer that can be backed up by quantifiable evidence.

Statistical analysis techniques should be used to determine whether the differences are significant or simply the result of random variation.

Step 3

Having got an indication of which testing techniques are effective and ineffective at identifying particular types of defects, further investigation is required. In particular, determine if there are any reasons (special circumstances) for the differences in the results. For example:

- The technical features of the testing techniques
- The experience of the personnel applying the techniques
- Extraordinary features of the design or code under test.

Remember, in most cases defect analysis can only provide an indication of what is wrong or needs improving. The next step is to investigate further.

Note

This approach can be enhanced by comparing how well the testing techniques identify defects when they are classified by the phase in which they were introduced.

The same approach can be used to compare the effectiveness of the various defect-detection processes such as design reviews, etc.

Case history

The following story concerns a US telecommunications company which used defect analysis to uncover the reasons why experimental evidence did not agree with its intuitive beliefs. It assumed that if you increased the throughput rate on a software system controlling a telecommunications circuit switch then the defect rate would be proportional to the increased workload. In practice this turned out not to be the case. When the workload on the software system for the circuit switch experienced a tenfold increase from its normal workload the defect rate increased by between 100 and 500 times the normal rate. Defect analysis revealed that the heavy workload induced exception handling such as busy lines, lack of available memory space, boundary value problems, inserting an item in a full array, etc., which manifested themselves in a vastly increased defect rate. This information was then used to improve the test strategy by concentrating more effort on exception testing.

DEFECT ANALYSIS AND DEFECT DETECTION

We now discuss how defect analysis can help in the goal:

- Improve the reliability of the software system

by helping to determine when to stop testing and declare the system reliable.

The present state of software development cannot guarantee to produce defect-free software. Therefore, a balance needs to be found between the cost of producing software with very few defects and customer satisfaction in terms of how many defects will be tolerated by a user. For example, if a company like Microsoft waited until they were confident that their word processing package contained no defects, then they would not only miss their window of opportunity but probably go bankrupt in the process.

Unless measurement is used it is rarely clear when to stop testing and declare a system reliable. The weakness in testing is its inability to guarantee that a program has no defects. As Dijkstra, a well-known computer scientist who was instrumental in spreading the word about structured programming, said:

> Testing shows the presence of errors not the absence of errors.

You could say that Dijkstra was expressing the philosophy of Albert Einstein who looked for experiments whose agreements with his predictions would by no means establish his theory, while a disagreement, as he was the first to stress, would show his theory to be untenable.

Reliability cannot be tested into a system and no amount of measurement will directly improve its reliability. The reliability of a software system is established by the correctness of the specification, design and implementation stages. Testing alone is insufficient as a means of uncovering defects. To be most effective it needs to be done in conjunction with inspections and reviews. Studies have shown that carrying out inspections, reviews and testing to uncover defects results in lower development costs and shorter schedules compared with only performing testing to uncover defects. Data relating to the cost of finding and fixing defects can be found in Basili and Selby (1987).

Specifying the defect density during a period of operational use is often used as part of the reliability requirement for a software system. For example, IBM Houston won a NASA quality award for the on-board Space Shuttle software. They developed over 2 million lines of code which had 0.11 defects per KLOC while in operational use over a three-year period.

It should be noted that such reliability requirements do not take into account the severity of the effect of a defect. A system with ten inconsequential defects is better than a system with one defect that causes a total software system failure.

Suppose the requirement is for a defect density of 0.5 defects per KLOC during the first five years of operational use. Then defect analysis can help in removing defects during the development of a software system in the following way.

Step 1

Using defect data from similar projects, develop a defect removal model for your project. Figure 28.2 depicts an example of such a model.

This model should be interpreted as follows. Suppose the model was compiled from 50 software projects. Then the average number of defects detected during the design phase of development was 5.6 defects per KLOC. The maximum and minimum number of defects detected on a single project during the design phase was 7.6 defects per KLOC and 2.5 defects per KLOC respectively. In other words, for a new project it would be reasonable to assume that the number of defects that will be detected during the design phase will be around 5.6 defects per KLOC, unless there were major changes to the development process or differences in the characteristics of the new project compared with the 50 projects used to produce the model.

Step 2

If significantly fewer defects were found during a certain phase of development when compared with the model in Fig. 28.2, then a careful analysis should be made to determine the reasons. For example, it may be because:

- The document under review was of 'high quality'
- The defect removal process (design review, etc.) was inefficient

Activity	Estimated number of defects per KLOC that should be detected		
	Minimum	Average	Maximum
Requirements	0.1	2.0	3.5
Design	2.5	5.6	7.6
Code	3.2	5.8	8
Test	1.5	4.0	7
Operational use	0.8	1.6	3.3

Figure 28.2 Defect removal model.

- The staff were inexperienced or lacked the necessary skills
- There were fewer to find!

Similarly if significantly more defects are found during a particular phase of development, further investigation is required to determine the reason why. Remember, in most cases defect analysis can only provide an indication about something; further investigation may be required.

A potential problem with this approach is that during the requirements or even design phase of development, the size of the system in terms of lines of code is not available. However, using function point analysis (Appendix C) as a size measure can help to overcome this problem as it can be derived early on in the development process. Furthermore, the function point count for a system can be converted into lines of code if necessary. For further information on this topic, see Ashley (1992).

Step 3

During the testing phase, plot a graph of defects found against time (Fig. 28.3) to help in determining when to stop testing. The purpose of this graph is to:

- Show the rate at which defects are being detected during testing
- Help in determining when it is cost-effective (in terms of finding defects) to stop testing.

Ideally as the project progresses we should expect the graph to level off, that is, reach its saturation point. The saturation point is the estimated number of defects present which can be calculated from historical defect data from similar projects.

During the initial testing phase, we would expect most of the defects to be found. If we plot the cumulative number of defects found against time we should notice that the graph takes the general shape of that shown in Fig. 28.3. Here we are interested in the gradient of the graph. Once the gradient begins to level off, we have a reasonably stable system,

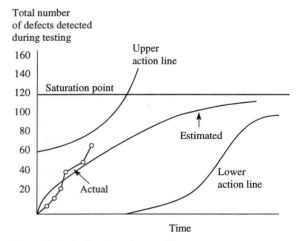

Figure 28.3 Defect detection profile.

assuming the quality of the test cases has not fallen. Here stable should be interpreted as stable in terms of the defects that can be found by this particular testing technique. Note that in a realistic project the graph would fluctuate to varying degrees depending on both the project and the procedures applied during that project, from simple perturbations to a situation so chaotic that the graph would no longer be applicable. However, it should be noted that one of the principles of defect analysis for predicting defects is:

> If the number of detected defects plotted against time remains linear (steadily increases), the probability of there being more undetected defects increases.

The purpose of the two action lines is as follows. The upper action line can be used to determine when to abort a test run. If the number of defects crosses the upper action line then the likely inference is that the software is riddled with defects and it would be time-wasting to carry on testing. It suggests corrective action is required immediately.

The lower action line can be used to indicate a number of things such as:

- The ability of the test cases to detect defects
- The level of defects in the software.

If the line representing the actual number of defects crosses the lower action line then it may indicate that the test cases are not effective at detecting defects or that more test cases are required. On the other hand it may be that the software has very few defects. There are a variety of techniques for assessing the ability of the test cases to detect defects; for example, the technique of seeding the software with known defects. Further information on the topic of test coverage can be found in Fenton (1991). The action lines should be calculated from historical data. If historical data is not available, then the action lines should be generated using the experience of the project teams and quality group.

It should be noted that another way to help to determine when to stop testing is based on testing for a predefined number of hours without discovering any defects. Further information on this technique, which is used by some of Hewlett Packard's software development departments, can be found in Grady and Caswell (1987).

DEFECT ANALYSIS AND ESTIMATING DEFECT DENSITY

We now discuss how defect analysis can help in the goal:

- Improve the reliability of the software system

by helping to estimate the defect density of a software system at handover to the customer.

Let us suppose we have completed system testing and we now wish to estimate the defect density of our software system. Using defect data from previous projects and defect data collected during the development of our project it is possible to estimate the number of defects that will be found during the operational lifetime of the project, using the following approach.

Step 1

Use historical defect data from past projects to produce a defect-detection efficiency model as depicted in Fig. 28.2.

Step 2

Now consider a project where after system testing the following data is available:

- 12 defects were detected during development up to and including testing, which were introduced during the requirements phase.
- 7 defects were detected during development up to and including testing, which were introduced during the design phase.
- 20 defects were detected during development up to and including testing, which were introduced during the coding phase.
- No defects were introduced during testing.

Now using the model depicted in Fig. 28.2 we can estimate the number of defects that will be found during the operational lifetime of the system as follows:

Estimated number of defects that will be detected during operational use
$$= 12 \times (10/6) + 7 \times (10/7) + 20 \times (10/8) = 55$$

Step 3

This step involves validating the data, by comparing the defects detected during development against a model of defects detected during development. Such a model should be developed from historical data and take the following form:

- On average, 29 per cent of the defects detected during development were introduced during the requirements phase.
- On average, 20 per cent of the defects detected during development were introduced during the design phase.
- On average, 50 per cent of the defects detected during development were introduced during the code phase.
- On average, 1 per cent of the defects detected during development were introduced during testing.

Note that these figures are used as an illustration. Actual figures should be generated from at least ten projects.

If any data values (in our example the data values are [12, 7, 20, 0]) are not within 10 per cent of the values in the model, then investigations need to be conducted to establish the reasons.

Step 4

This method can be enhanced in a number of ways, such as:

- Use historical data to develop a model of latent defects; that is, those defects that go undetected during testing which never get activated during the lifetime of the system. For example, suppose we assume that 15 per cent of defects that go undetected during testing are latent. Then in our example we can estimate there will be approximately:

$$55 \times 85/100 = 47 \text{ operational failures.}$$

- Assume we have a model of the origin of defects, such as:
  - 40 per cent of defects introduced during requirements specification
  - 50 per cent of defects introduced during design
  - 10 per cent of defects introduced during coding and testing.

Then using the defect removal efficiency model implies that on average 67 per cent of defects will have been removed at system handover ($40 \times 6/10 + 50 \times 7/10 + 10 \times 8/10$). For our example, where we have 39 detected defects, the estimated number of defects detected during operational use will be $39 \times 100/67 = 58$. Our estimated number of defects is taken to be the larger of the two numbers.

- Use the maximum and minimum defect removal efficiency rates to produce an interval estimate.
- Consider failures due to defects in supporting documentation.
- Classify defects using the severity of the failure, as our evolutionary approach to using defect analysis becomes more sophisticated.

DEFECT ANALYSIS AND IMPROVING PROCESSES

We now discuss how defect analysis can help in the goal:

- Reduce rework

by helping to determine which processes are in most urgent need of improvement. This will be carried out by answering the question:

- What is the breakdown of defects found during operational use in terms of origin?

Step 1

Using historical data from at least ten 'similar' projects, develop a model of the origins of defects found during operational use. Figure 28.4 provides an example of such a model. It shows where defects detected during operational use were introduced. The way to interpret this graph is as follows:

- On average, 30 per cent of defects found during operational use were introduced during the requirements phase of development.

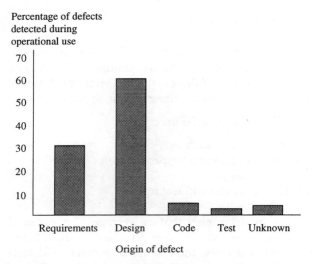

Figure 28.4   Model of origin of defects found during operational use.

- On average, 60 per cent of defects found during operational use were introduced during the design phase of development.
- On average, 5 per cent of defects found during operational use were introduced during the coding phase of development.
- On average, 2 per cent of defects found during operational use were introduced during testing.
- On average, 3 per cent of defects found during operational use were of unknown origin.

Step 2

The information from this model can then be used to help prioritize the phases of development that are in most urgent need of improvement. In this case it suggests that reviews of the design process should be investigated further. It should be pointed out that there may be a variety of reasons why the design phase contained more defects. For example:

- Inadequate design reviews and testing
- Poor design process
- Untrained staff
- Poor management of the design process.

Furthermore, it may be necessary to collect data relating to the cause of defects, see Chapter 25, in order to identify the most defect-prone activities within a phase of development.

DEFECT ANALYSIS AND IDENTIFYING DEFECT-PRONE MODULES

We now discuss how defect analysis can help in the goal:

- Reduce rework

by helping to answer the following questions:

- Is there a relationship between the defect density of a module before release and during operational use?
- Which modules are the most defect-prone?
- Do larger modules have relatively more defects than smaller modules?

Step 1

For each module determine its defect density before release and after release. The results can be represented graphically as in Fig. 28.5.

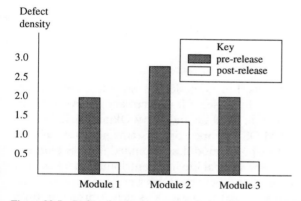

Figure 28.5 Defect density per module before release and after one year of operational use.

The main purposes of this graph are to:

- Depict the defect density for modules relating to a software system before release and after one year of operational use
- Help identify defect-prone modules.

Step 2

This step is concerned with determining whether there is a relationship between the size of a module and its defect density during operational use. The way to proceed is to construct a scattergraph, such as Fig. 28.6, of the size of a module plotted against its defect density. The purpose of this graph is to:

Defect density

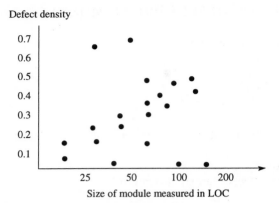

Size of module measured in LOC

Figure 28.6   Relationship between the size of a module and its defect density.

- Depict whether there is a potential relationship between the defect density for each module and the size of the module.

This approach can be expanded to see if relationships exist with other factors, such as programming language, control structure, development teams, etc.

Step 3

This step is concerned with analysing the results. For example, for those modules with the highest defect density, determine the reasons why to see if it is necessary to rewrite them.

Weinberg (1992) relates a story about how in 1970 he and Gary Okimoto studied the history of defects in many releases of the IBM OS/360 operating system and discovered the existence of defect-prone modules. The defect-prone modules accounted for less than two per cent of the code in OS/360 yet over their operational life had contributed more than 80 per cent of the defects. Initially it was thought that these modules were poorly structured. Recently Weinberg has come to the conclusion that in most cases defect-prone modules are modules that for one reason or another never received their planned test coverage.

A major problem when analysing data is the problem of interpretation. For example, even if you find a good correlation between two variables, all it tells you is that further investigation is required. Suppose analysis of the scattergraph in Fig. 28.6 revealed that smaller modules had a lower defect density than larger modules. You may be tempted to insist modules are split up into smaller ones (for example, less than 50 lines of code). This action may be incorrect, apart from the fact that modules should not be governed by size alone. It may be the case that the smaller modules were implemented first and handed over for testing before the large modules. Furthermore, it may have been the case that the test team spent more time functionally testing the modules delivered early but then ran out of time when the last modules arrived. Consequently the testers did not perform sufficient testing of these later modules which in this case were the 'larger' modules.

The way to avoid such problems of misinterpretation is to investigate all the assumptions. For example, determine whether all the modules were tested as planned, etc.

29

SUMMARY

The main points put forward in this chapter are as follows:

- Defect analysis should be used as a tool to help prevent defects occurring during software development.
- Defects should be treated as a source of valuable information. In other words we should learn from our mistakes.
- Use a goal-driven approach to using defect analysis. Do not collect defect data without a purpose, a goal.
- It is important to recognize the distinction between using defect analysis to assess the performance of individual staff and using defect analysis to improve the performance of staff. An important part of defect analysis is providing feedback to developers to enable them to learn from their mistakes and the mistakes of others.
- Concentrate on preventing defects occurring by analysing the causes of defects and implementing changes in the development process to try and eradicate the causes of defects.
- Use an evolutionary approach by prioritizing your problems and tackling the highest priority problems one at a time.

Finally, you can carry on as usual and ignore the valuable information that can be derived from analysing defects, but do not assume your competitors will do the same.

Section 5

Estimation Techniques

Work expands so as to fill the time available for its completion.

Cyril Northcote Parkinson

This section provides guidelines on the information that needs to be recorded for an estimate of effort for a software project in order to:

- Assess its plausibility
- Provide an audit trail
- Support an estimation process.

It also provides guidelines for helping to determine the feasibility of project timescales.

30

INTRODUCTION

One day I went to a garage to get a quote for repairing some dents to the bodywork of my car. The manager of the garage spent ten minutes estimating the cost by looking at the damage, taking measurements and making calculations. All very impressive I thought. After the manager had quoted me a price I asked how he had worked it out. That's easy he said. First of all, to repair the damage to your door we will need to fit a new skin, which is a standard job, and so has a fixed price. Then for all the little dents I measured the size of them and multiplied the size by a weighting factor to reflect how difficult it is to get at the dent. For instance, whether the front grille needs to come off, or if the headlights need to be removed. All very straightforward and systematic. Then he told me that if he asked the mechanics who would carry out the work to estimate the effort, they would probably underestimate by at least 30 per cent. So I asked him where he got his figures from, was it from his own experience of carrying out the work. At this suggestion he looked visibly shocked. He insisted he didn't know the first thing about repairing dents. He said he just looked at the mechanics' timesheets to see how long it actually took them to carry out the work. The morale of this story: is do not just rely on the person who is going to carry out the work to provide an estimate, use validated historical data.

For many IS departments, estimating is just a polite term for guessing. Dictionaries define a guess as an estimate based on inadequate knowledge. If the quality of the information used to derive the estimate is very subjective or, worse, non-existent, then who is going to have any confidence in the estimate?

You do not become a 'good' estimator simply by adding a 30 per cent contingency to your estimate to compensate for an inadequate estimation process. Experience has shown that this type of approach leads to lower productivity. The quality of an estimate of effort for a software project, in terms of the variation between the actual and the estimate, needs to be related to productivity.

There is no magic wand to wave to produce an accurate estimate. The best way to produce accurate estimates of effort for software projects is to base your method on using validated historical data.

When a manager is given an estimate they need to assess its plausibility. They need some way of determining whether it is a good estimate or whether it is an optimistic assumption that has little chance of coming true. To begin with they should ask the estimator the following two questions:

- What is the chance of finishing over budget?
- What is the chance of finishing under budget?

This leads us to the question of how to express an estimate. Suppose you were planning to drive to a business appointment and you asked a colleague how long it would take you. What confidence would you have if you were told one hour, three minutes and twelve seconds? On the other hand suppose your colleague asked you some questions and found out you were travelling on a Monday morning and needed to arrive at nine a.m. Using this information, your colleague told you that nine out of their last ten journeys had taken between forty minutes and sixty-five minutes depending on the traffic. Which answer would you have confidence in?

FORMAT OF AN ESTIMATE

The format for an estimate of the effort needed to carry out a software project should be stated along the following lines:

- There is a 95 per cent chance that the actual effort will be within the interval [5 months, 7 months] with the most likely effort being six months based on the following assumptions:
  - subcontractors will deliver on time
  - no premature loss of key personnel
  - supporting documentation will be up to date.

In other words, an estimate of effort for a software project should consist of four numbers, namely:

- The most likely effort
- A lower bound (sometimes referred to as the base estimate) that does not take risk into account
- An upper bound that incorporates risk
- A confidence value, expressed as a percentage, that quantifies the chance that the actual value will be within the bounds.

VARIANCE BETWEEN ESTIMATES AND ACTUALS

When calculating the variation between the actual effort and the estimated effort the following apply:

- The estimated effort is defined as the most likely effort and does not include contingency.
- The estimated effort includes estimates of planned changes agreed during development.

The estimated effort does not include re-estimates which do not relate to planned changes.

ACCURACY OF AN ESTIMATION PROCESS

The goal of producing accurate estimates should be stated in quantifiable terms along the following lines:

- Within six months produce estimates of effort from the high-level design that are within 20 per cent of the actual effort in 85 per cent of the cases.

PRINCIPLES OF ESTIMATING

The main principles associated with estimating are as follows:

- Estimates are dynamic and should be revised as more information becomes available or when the requirements change.
- The estimation process should use historical data from previous 'similar' projects for both calculating the estimate and for assessing its plausibility.
- The estimation process should use more than one method.
- The estimation process should be repeatable and traceable. Thus all the assumptions and calculations used in producing the estimate should be recorded.
- The estimation process should include a technique for measuring the effectiveness of the estimation process in terms of how well estimates converge to the actual value.
- The estimation process should employ a feedback mechanism to help improve the estimation process. Learn from bad estimates.
- Effort and timescales are not interchangeable. That is, reducing timescales generally means increasing effort. The productivity of a project team of twelve people working full time for one month will, in general, be less than the productivity of one person working for twelve months. In general, the productivity of project teams decreases as the size of the team increases.
- The accuracy of an estimate must not be viewed in isolation, but must be related to productivity.
- Work expands to fill the time available for its completion. This is one of the famous sayings of the twentieth century. The implications of the saying have a serious side: it implies it is no good trying to improve the chances of coming in under budget by adding in a huge contingency.
- The difference between the amount of time it takes individuals to complete a task can be up to a factor of ten. However, experiments have shown that in general, for projects of seven or more staff, individual differences cancel each other out.
- Most people underestimate the effort needed to carry out a task, because they often fail to take proper account of the risks involved. Experience shows us that what can go wrong will go wrong.
- The longest distance between two points is the shortcut.

PROPERTIES OF AN ESTIMATE OF EFFORT

The main properties of an estimate of effort for a software project are that it should:

- Be produced using a consistent and auditable method
- Be broken down for phases and tasks
- Take account of risk
- Take account of experience of staff who will perform the work (productivity of project teams)
- Take account of management effort
- Take account of constraints on timescales
- Take account of the quality of the documents used to produce the estimate
- Have an equal chance of being above or below the actual effort before contingency is added
- Include a contingency to help ensure there is a high probability (for example 90 per cent chance) that the actual effort will be in the interval:

    [most likely effort − contingency, most likely effort + contingency]

- Quantify the confidence in the estimate.

FACTORS THAT AFFECT THE ACCURACY OF AN ESTIMATE

The accuracy of an estimate of the effort needed to carry out a software project depends on a variety of factors, the main ones being:

- The quality of the documents used as input to the estimation process, such as the requirements specification
- The quality of the historical data available; for example, whether the historical data took into account the amount of unpaid or unrecorded overtime worked
- When the estimate was produced (from requirements specification, high-level design, etc.)
- The size of the project
- Technical complexity of the work to be performed
- Experience of staff available to perform the work
- The size of the project team
- Management effort
- Constraints on timescales
- Degree of novelty of project.

31

OVERVIEW OF AN ESTIMATION PROCESS

In this chapter we provide an overview of a process to estimate the effort needed to carry out a software project (Fig. 31.1).

The process consists of the following tasks that should be performed by the estimation group on receipt of a requirements specification for a new software system or change request to enhance an operational system:

Task 1   Identify tasks
Task 2   Estimate lower bound (base effort)
Task 3   Estimate upper bound (identify and quantify risks)
Task 4   Work out increase due to experience of teams
Task 5   Work out increase due to management effort
Task 6   Work out increase due to constraints on timescales
Task 7   Work out increase due to quality of documents
Task 8   Calculate most likely effort
Task 9   Work out contingency
Task 10   Quantify confidence factor
Task 11   Review estimate
Task 12   Record estimates and assumptions

TASK 1 — IDENTIFY TASKS

Determine which development activities (tasks) defined in the standard work breakdown structure (WBS) need to be carried out.

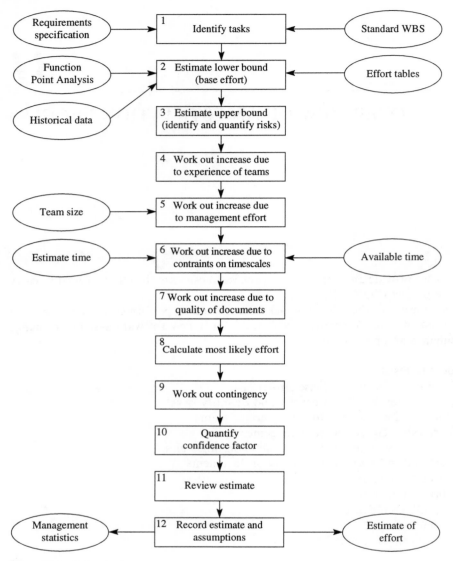

Figure 31.1 Estimation process.

TASK 2 — ESTIMATE LOWER BOUND (BASE EFFORT)

Having identified the tasks to be performed, the next step is to calculate the base estimate of effort (lower bound) for each task. The base estimate of effort for a task is calculated using the following idealized assumptions:

- No risks
- Staff are experienced (100 per cent productive)

- No management overheads
- Productivity of project teams does not vary with size
- No constraints on timescales.

In other words, base estimates are calculated by making the unrealistic assumption that nothing will go wrong during development and there are no overheads.

Base estimates can be produced using one or more of the following methods:

- Expert opinion using the wideband Delphi technique
- Analogy method
- Effort tables.

These methods are described in Chapter 32. It should be noted that there are other methods, but they are outside the scope of this book. Further information can be found in DeMarco (1982).

TASK 3 — ESTIMATE UPPER BOUND

The upper bound for a task is derived by identifying and quantifying the risks in terms of increased effort and adding this effort to the base estimate. We now describe the steps involved in producing the upper bound for the effort needed to carry out a task.

Step 1 Identify the main risk factors that will have an influence on the estimate of effort. This should be accomplished using the support of a checklist of known risk factors from previous projects. For example:

- Availability of staff to perform the work
- Premature loss of key personnel
- Subcontractors delivering late.

Step 2 Categorize each risk factor to reflect their importance using the following three categories:

- Critical
- Significant
- Minor.

A checklist should be produced for each risk factor in order to help in determining its importance.

Step 3 Weight each risk factor to reflect their chances of occurring using the following three categories:
- Very likely – more than 70 per cent chance of occurring
- Likely   – 30–70 per cent chance of occurring
- Unlikely   – less than 30 per cent chance of occurring.

A checklist should be produced for each risk factor in order to help in determining its likelihood of occurring.

Step 4   Record the information. Figure 31.2 provides an example of a form to record information about the risks for a task.

Step 5   Work out the increased effort due to each risk using a look-up risk table. Figure 31.3 provides an example of a look-up risk table produced from historical data.

For example, for risk x, let its importance be categorized as significant and the chance of it occurring be categorized as very likely. Then the estimated increased effort due to risk x is calculated as:

$$\text{lower bound} + 5 \text{ per cent of lower bound}$$

Note that the example form for recording risks in Fig. 31.2 provides the estimator with the option to define their own percentage increase for a risk.

Name of *project*	*Name of* *phase*	*Name of* *risk assessor*	*Date*
Risk		Optional user-defined weighting factor 0–100%	Chance of occurring *very likely* *likely* *unlikely*	Importance *Critical* *significant* *minor*

Premature loss of key personnel
Shortfall in specialist skills
Incorrect mix of skills in team
Inexperience of IS project manager
Size of project team greater than estimated
Productivity of staff lower than estimated
Lack of familiarity with method
Complexity of interface to other projects
Subcontractors delivering late
Dependence on other projects which deliver late
Interdependencies of tasks underestimated
Incompatibility of constraints
Detrimental impact of schedule constraints
Size and scope of the work greater than anticipated
Underestimated complexity of the project
Stability of system to be changed is overestimated
Impact due to novelty of work underestimated
Amount of rework greater than estimated
Support tools and facilities not available
Communication overhead due to split site working underestimated
Support documentation missing or out of date

Figure 31.2   Example form for recording risks.

It should be noted that the values in the table in Fig. 31.3 are only examples. The percentages should be based on historical data. If this is not available, the initial values should be supplied by staff familiar with risk analysis. Then, as validated historical data becomes available, it can be used to calibrate the initial values.

Risk assessment	Importance		
	Critical	Significant	Minor
Chance of occurring			
very likely	10%	5%	1%
likely	5%	2.5%	0%
unlikely	1%	0.5%	0%

Figure 31.3   Example look-up risk table for assessing the impact of a risk.

We then define the unadjusted bounded estimate of effort for a task to be: [lower bound, upper bound].

TASK 4 — WORK OUT INCREASE DUE TO EXPERIENCE OF TEAMS

Step 1   Identify the technical skills needed to perform each task.

Step 2   Where possible identify the staff available to perform each task. If this information is not available, assume project teams are 80 per cent productive.

Step 3   Classify the productivity of each member of the team assigned to a particular task using a staff productivity look-up table such as the one depicted in Fig. 31.4. Note that historical data should be used to quantify the productivity of team members. Checklists should be used to help determine the level of experience of a team member. For example, a designer may be regarded as experienced if:

- The designer has at least 12 months' experience of designing systems
- The designer is fully conversant with the design methodology.

Category of team member	Productivity
Experienced	100%
Semi-experienced	80%
Inexperienced	50%

Figure 31.4   Example of categorization of project teams.

Step 4   Classify the productivity of the project team for a task by taking the average productivity of the project team members.

Step 5   These productivity rates are applied to both the lower bound and upper bound for each task. For example, consider a task with an associated unadjusted bounded estimate [10 months, 20 months] and suppose a team has been assigned to carry out the work which has a productivity rate of 90 per cent. Then the adjustment to take account of the experience of the project team will be:

$$[10 + 10 \times (100 - 90) / 90), 20 + 20 \times (100 - 90) / 90)]$$
$$= [11.1 \text{ months}, 22.2 \text{ months}]$$

When determining the level of experience of a team, the following facts need to be taken into consideration:

- The difference between the amount of effort it takes individuals to complete a task can be up to a factor of ten. However, experiments have shown that the effect of these differences disappears as the size of the project team increases because individual differences cancel each other out. For example, DeMarco (1982) points out that, in general, for projects of seven or more staff, individual differences cancel each other out.
- Skills may not be readily interchangeable. For example, a person may be 100 per cent productive as a tester but may be only 50 per cent productive as a designer.

TASK 5 — WORK OUT INCREASE DUE TO MANAGEMENT EFFORT

The main part of management effort is made up of:

- Effort of project manager
- Effort of team leaders, etc. with respect to their management role
- Communications on a project
- Progress meeting.

In general, as project teams increase in size their productivity tends to decrease due to communication overheads. For example, when a new member joins the team, an existing member will have to spend time training the new member. The adjustment to take account of management effort is calculated from the information supplied concerning the estimated size of the teams. (Note that the available time to complete a task is used as input to estimate the size of a team.) The calculation consists of the following steps:

Step 1   Calculate the size of the project team for a task.

Step 2   Determine whether work on the task will be intermittent and spread over at least twice the 'normal' timescale. Here normal timescale refers to the timescale needed if progress on the project was continuous.

Team size	'Normal' timescale	Long timescale
1	2%	3%
2 to 4	10%	12%
5 to 10	15%	18%
11 to 15	20%	23%
Greater than 15	25%	28%

Figure 31.5 Example look-up table for determining management effort.

Step 3   Use a look-up table for determining management effort (percentage increase to unadjusted bounded estimate of effort) such as the one depicted in Fig. 31.5. Note that historical data should be used to quantify the percentage increase for each category of team size.

Step 4   The percentage increase to take account of management effort is applied to the unadjusted bounded estimate of effort for each task. For example, consider a task with an associated unadjusted bounded estimate of effort [4 months, 6 months] and suppose the size of the team has been estimated as 18 staff working full time. Then the adjustment to take account of management effort would be an increase of 25 per cent on the unadjusted bounded estimate of effort, namely:

$$[4 + 4 \times 25/100, 6 + 6 \times 25/100] = [5 \text{ months}, 7.5 \text{ months}]$$

TASK 6 — WORK OUT INCREASE DUE TO CONSTRAINTS ON TIMESCALES

To meet timescales more people may need to be added to a team in the situation where tasks, or subtasks within a task, can be produced in parallel. However, in general, one person working on a package of work that can be subdivided into work packages that can be carried out in parallel is more efficient than two or more people working in parallel. Thus, in general, adding more people to a task will increase the effort needed to complete the task.

The adjustment to take account of the constraint on the timescale is calculated from the schedule compression factor (SCF) which is defined as:

$$\text{SCF} = \frac{\text{available time in months}}{\text{estimated elapsed time in months}}$$

where estimated elapsed time in months for a task is defined using the assumption that work on a task that can be done in parallel is in fact done in sequence. The increase in effort should be calculated using a look-up table such as the one depicted in Fig. 31.6.

Historical data should be used to quantify the percentage increase for each category of team size.

SCF	Percentage increase				
	Team size 1	Team size 2 to 4	Team size 5 to 10	Team size 11 to 15	Team size greater than 15
$0.9 \leq SCF < 1.0$	2	4	5	7	10
$0.8 \leq SCF < 0.9$	4	8	10	12	15
$0.7 \leq SCF < 0.8$	10	15	20	25	30

Figure 31.6 Example look-up table for SCF.

Empirical evidence suggests that it is infeasible to meet a timescale with an SCF of less than seven. In such cases the following options should be considered:

- Reduce functionality
- Increase available time
- Opt for package solutions.

The increase in effort due to the constraints on timescales are applied to the unadjusted bounded estimate of effort for each task. For example, consider a task with:

- An unadjusted bounded estimate of effort of [22 months, 27 months]
- Team size $= 8$
- Available time $= 6$ months.

Then the SCF $= 0.8$ and the adjustment to take account of the SCF will be a percentage increase in effort of 10 per cent, namely:

$$[22 + 22 \times 10/100, 27 + 27 \times 10/100] = [22.2 \text{ months}, 29.7 \text{ months}]$$

TASK 7 — WORK OUT INCREASE DUE TO QUALITY OF DOCUMENTS

The adjustment to take account of the quality of the documents used to produce the estimate (such as the requirements specification) should be calculated using a look-up table similar to the one depicted in Fig. 31.7.

Quality of requirements	Percentage increase
Complete	0%
Nearly complete	15%
Incomplete/ambiguous	30%

Figure 31.7 Example look-up table for quality of requirements.

Checklists can be used to determine which category to assign a requirements specification. Furthermore, historical data should be used to quantify the percentage increase of each category.

These percentage increases are applied to the unadjusted bounded estimate of effort for each task. For example, consider a task with an associated unadjusted bounded estimate of effort of [10 months, 12 months] and suppose the quality of the requirements are nearly complete. Then the adjustment to take account of the quality of the requirements will be:

$$[10 + 10 \times 15/100, 12 + 12 \times 15/100] = [11.5 \text{ months}, 13.8 \text{ months}]$$

TASK 8 — CALCULATE MOST LIKELY EFFORT

We have now worked out the unadjusted bounded estimate of effort for each task, and the increases due to:

- Experience of teams
- Management effort
- Constraints on timescales
- Quality of requirements.

We now need to work out the adjusted bounded estimate of effort. Let us look at an example. Consider a task where the following information has been generated:

- Unadjusted bounded estimate of effort = [10 months, 20 months]
- Category of team = semi-experienced
- Estimated size of project team = 6 staff
- Available time = 6 months
- Quality of requirements = complete.

Then the SCF = 0.88 and we have:

Lower bound for the adjusted bounded estimate of effort =
$$(10 + [10 \times (100 - 80)/80] + [10 \times 15/100] + [10 \times 10/100] + [10 \times 0/100])$$
$$= 15 \text{ months}$$

Upper bound for the adjusted bounded estimate of effort =
$$(20 + [20 \times (100 - 80)/80] + [20 \times 15/100] + [20 \times 10/100] + [20 \times 0/100])$$
$$= 30 \text{ months}$$

Thus the adjusted bounded estimate of effort = [15 months, 30 months].

Having worked out the adjusted bounded estimate of effort for a task, it is now necessary to work out the most likely effort for a task. That is, a point between the adjusted lower bound and upper bound having the property that there is an equal chance that the actual effort will be above or below the most likely effort. Now in theory it is possible to work out this point using probability theory. However, due to the uncertainty involved in assessing all the risks (and their interrelationships) associated with estimating the effort, it is impractical. Furthermore, the proposed technique used to assess risk is somewhat subjective. Therefore, it is much simpler, and probably just as sensible and accurate, to approximate the most likely effort as the midpoint of the adjusted bounded estimate of effort. Thus for our example where the adjusted bounded estimate of effort was [15 months, 30 months], the most likely effort = 22.5 months.

Then the most likely effort for the project is calculated by summing the most likely efforts for each of its associated tasks.

TASK 9 — WORK OUT CONTINGENCY

Contingency is a management judgement. The most likely effort should have the property that there is a 50 per cent chance that the actual effort will be greater than the most likely effort. Management may decide that they want to reduce this chance so they need to add in a contingency to the most likely estimate to help ensure there is a high probability (for example 90 per cent chance) that the actual effort will be in the interval:

[most likely estimate − contingency, most likely estimate + contingency]

Thus contingency is a judgement taken by management that:

- Reduces the chance that the actual effort will be greater than the most likely effort plus contingency
- Takes account of any risks that may have been overlooked during risk analysis
- Takes account of the fact that, in general, most people underestimate. Therefore, the base estimates may have been underestimated
- Takes account of political decisions. For example, for fixed priced projects it may be unacceptable to go back to the customer to ask for more money to complete the project.

Contingency is expressed as a percentage of the most likely effort and has three constituent parts:

- Reduce the chance that the actual will be above the estimate
- Overlooked risks
- Underestimating base estimates.

The limitations on the quantification of these constituent parts should be based on a look-up table such as the one depicted in Fig. 31.8. Historical data from previous projects should be used to support management in determining the level of contingency.

Constituent part	Maximum contingency
Reduce the chance that the actual will be above the estimate	15%
Overlooked risks	5%
Underestimating base efforts	5%

Figure 31.8   Example look-up table for contingency.

TASK 10 — QUANTIFY CONFIDENCE FACTOR

This task is concerned with quantifying the confidence that the actual effort will be in the interval:

[most likely estimate − contingency, most likely estimate + contingency]

We now describe a simple method for doing this.

For each piece of information used in the production of the estimate of effort, grade it as either subjective or quantitative.

Judging whether a piece of information is subjective or quantitative can itself be a subjective process. Therefore, in order to help in deciding whether a piece of information is subjective or not, checklists should be produced to assist the process. Using this type of approach it should be possible to classify information as:

- Quantitative
- Nearly quantitative
- Subjective
- Missing.

Regard information as quantitative if it is quantitative or nearly quantitative and regard information as subjective if it is subjective or missing.

Then express the confidence factor as follows:

- If more than 80 per cent of the information is quantitative, express the confidence factor as:
  − there is a 95 per cent chance that the actual effort will be within the interval:

  [most likely estimate − contingency, most likely estimate + contingency]

- If between 50 and 80 per cent of the information is quantitative, express the confidence factor as:
  − there is an 80 per cent chance that the actual effort will be within the interval:

  [most likely estimate − contingency, most likely estimate + contingency]

- If between 25 and 49 per cent of the information is quantitative, express the confidence factor as:
  − there is a 75 per cent chance that the actual effort will be within the interval:

  [most likely estimate − contingency, most likely estimate + contingency]

- Otherwise, express the confidence factor as:
  − there is a 60 per cent chance that the actual effort will be within the interval:

  [most likely estimate − contingency, most likely estimate + contingency]

It should be noted that there is a correlation between the size of a bound and its associated confidence factor, where the size of a bound is defined as:

$$\frac{\text{upper bound} - \text{lower bound}}{\text{lower bound}}$$

The larger the bound the more confidence there is in the actual effort being within the bounds. Furthermore, as a project progresses and re-estimates are made, the size of the bounds should get progressively smaller, and eventually converge to the actual value (Fig. 31.9).

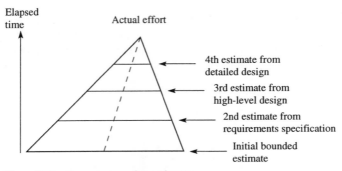

Figure 31.9 Convergence of re-estimates.

TASK 11 — REVIEW ESTIMATE

The bounded estimate of effort should be reviewed by at least two independent people, one of whom should be familiar with the system being developed. The review should use a variety of techniques, such as:

- A checklist of questions
- Using historical data to assess the plausibility of its confidence factor
- Comparing the estimate with historical data
- The ratio method
- Sensitivity analysis.

We now briefly describe these techniques.

Checklist

A checklist should be used for assessing the plausibility of an estimate and should include the following questions:

- Has the standard WBS been used to identify the tasks to be performed?
- Has the estimate been broken down into phases and tasks?
- Have the risks been identified, quantified and incorporated into the estimate?
- Has the productivity of the proposed team been taken into account?
- Has the management effort been taken into account?

- If the SCF is less than 1 for a phase of development, has this information been reflected in calculating the effort required?
- Has the quality of the information upon which the estimate has been produced been taken into account?
- If the (phase estimated effort/overall estimated effort) × 100 differs by more than 10 per cent from the standard ratio, have reasons been provided for the differences? Figure 31.10 provides an example of a table of standard phase ratios which should be produced from historical data.

Phase	% effort
Analysis	20
Design	20
Code and unit test	35
Test	20

Figure 31.10 Example table of standard phase ratios.

It may be necessary to produce a set of phase ratio tables corresponding to different types of systems. For example, phase ratios for enhancement projects to an old system that is monolithic and poorly documented will, in general, be different from phase ratios for an enhancement project to a system that was developed using structured design techniques.

- Has a contingency been incorporated?
- Has historical data been used to validate the estimate?
- Has the estimate been reviewed by at least two independent people?

Confidence factor

The estimate should be compared against historical data to assess the plausibility of its confidence factor. A look-up table should be produced from historical data that provides a standard set of confidence factors associated with the documents from which the estimate was produced (Fig. 31.11).

If this technique reveals a variation of more than 10 per cent, then the reasons for this should be investigated to determine if the estimate should be revised.

Document	Accuracy
High-level requirements	85% chance that the actual will be within ±40% of most likely effort
Requirements specification	90% chance that the actual will be within ±30% of most likely effort
High-level design specification	95% chance that the actual will be within ±20% of most likely effort
Specification of code modules	98% chance that the actual will be within ±5% of most likely effort

Figure 31.11 Example of expected accuracy of estimates.

Compare with historical data

The bounded estimate should be compared to actual effort for implementing similar projects, assuming this data is available.

If this technique reveals a variation of more than 10 per cent, then the reasons for this should be investigated to determine if the estimate should be revised.

Ratio method

We now provide an overview of the ratio method to check the plausibility of an estimate.

A rule of thumb in software development is that effort for the four phases of development, namely: analysis, design, code and unit test and test (system test, acceptance test, regression test) are usually in the ratio:

$$20 : 20 : 35 : 25$$

These ratios will then need to be adjusted to take account of the cost drivers associated with a particular implementation. As validated historical data becomes available the ratios can be calibrated to the development environment. In fact, it may be the case that there will need to be a set of ratios corresponding to the set of systems that are maintained.

Figure 31.12 provides an example of a look-up table of effort ratios that should be produced from historical data, corresponding to the following three cost drivers:

- *Size of team* which is categorized as:
  - one person
  - small (between 2 and 4 people)
  - medium (between 5 and 10 people)
  - large (between 11 and 15 people)
  - very large (greater than 15 people).
- *Staff experience* which is categorized as:
  - experienced
  - semi-experienced
  - inexperienced.
- *Technical difficulty* which is categorized as:
  - complex
  - average
  - simple.

Cost drivers			Effort ratios			
Size of team	Staff experience	Technical difficulty	Analysis	Design	Code	Test
2 to 4 people	Experienced	Average	20	15	45	20
2 to 4 people	Semi-experienced	Complex	25	15	35	25
5 to 10 people	Experienced	Complex	25	20	30	25
⋮	⋮	⋮	⋮	⋮	⋮	⋮

Figure 31.12   Look-up table of effort ratios.

If this technique reveals a variation of more than 10 per cent, then the reasons for this should be investigated to determine if the estimate should be revised.

Sensitivity analysis

The bounded estimate of effort should be analysed to explore its sensitivity to the input data used in its calculation. The aim is to determine if the estimate is overly sensitive to any cost drivers. The simplest approach is to identify what is felt are the five most important cost drivers and use these to perform a sensitivity analysis. For example, the estimate should be analysed for its sensitivity to the calibrated values used to work out the increase in effort due to risk.

If this exercise reveals that the estimate is overly sensitive to one or more cost drivers, then the reasons for this should be investigated and action taken if necessary.

TASK 12 — RECORD ESTIMATE AND ASSUMPTIONS

Record the following information associated to an estimate of effort for a software project:

- List of tasks
- Effort expended in producing the estimate
- Bounded estimate for each task or phase of development
- Bounded estimate of effort needed to perform corrective maintenance during the first year of operational use
- Adjusted bounded estimate for each task or phase of development
- Contingency and confidence factor
- Actual effort for each phase and task
- Actual effort to perform corrective maintenance during the first year of operational use
- Risks and their associated weightings
- List of assumptions associated to estimate, such as political decisions
- List of reasons for variation between actual effort and estimated effort (see Appendix E for an example of a form to record this information)
- Size and experience of project team
- For an enhancement, the estimated and actual size of a change in terms of:
  - the number of modules changed/created
  - the control structure of the modules changed/created
  - for each module the percentage of code changed/added
  - the interaction of the modules
  - number of test cases changed/created
  - the number of documents changed/created
  - for each document the number of pages changed/created.
- The characteristics of each project, such as:
  - programming language
  - impact on other systems

  — development method
  — team structure
  — etc.

This information should be used to:

- Assess the plausibility of an estimate
- Support the production of future estimates
- Generate management statistics.

Figure 31.13 provides an example of a form to record the information associated to an estimate. Note that on the form, bounded estimates for tasks have been combined to give bounded estimates for each phase of development.

Management statistics

The data generated from the estimation process should be used to produce statistics, such as:

- The accuracy of estimates for each phase of development
- Ratio of effort for phases of development
- Most time-consuming development activities
- Which systems/modules are the most difficult to change/test
- Main reasons for discrepancies between estimates and actuals
- Trend of accuracy of estimates of effort and timescales.

Form To Record A Software Project Estimate					
Name of project		*Name of estimator*		*Date*	
Development phase	**Assumptions** *staff 100% productive* *no management overheads* *no constraint on timescales*		Estimated size of team	Estimated productivity of team	Available time in months
	lower bound (base estimate) in months	**upper bound** (risk included) in months			
Analysis					
Design					
Code and unit test					
Test					
Installation					
Warranty					
Quality of the documents used to produce the estimate	*Complete and detailed*	*Nearly complete*		*Incomplete and ambiguous*	
Unadjusted bounded estimate of effort in months					
Adjusted bounded estimate of effort in months					
Most likely effort in months					
Contingency in months					
Confidence factor as a percentage					
Total (most likely effort + most likely effort × contingency)					

Figure 31.13 Example form for recording an estimate.

32

THREE METHODS FOR CALCULATING BASE ESTIMATES

In this chapter we describe three methods that can be used to estimate the base estimates for a task associated with developing a new software system or enhancing an operational software system, namely:

- Expert opinion
- Analogy method
- Effort tables.

EXPERT OPINION — WIDEBAND DELPHI TECHNIQUE

This method is based on harmonizing the expertise of a number of staff and is known as the wideband Delphi technique. It was developed by the Rand Corporation during the Second World War as a way of forecasting uncertain outcomes (Boehm, 1981). The title suggests some sophisticated technique. In fact it is a simple process based on common sense. We now provide an overview of the steps involved in this method.

Step 1   A group of estimators is each given information relating to the project or task to be estimated and an estimation form.

Step 2   They meet to discuss the project or task and any specific points regarding the estimation such as quality of documentation available, required accuracy, etc.

Step 3   They then each anonymously complete the estimation forms using different methods.

Step 4   The estimates are given to the estimate coordinator, who tabulates the results and returns them to the estimators together with the group estimate calculated as the average of the estimates. Only each estimator's personal estimate is identified, all others are anonymous.

Step 5   The estimators meet to discuss the results, revising their estimates as they feel appropriate. In particular the reasons for any wide variations are explored.

Step 6   The cycle continues until all the estimates converge to an acceptable range, usually within 15 per cent of the average. Typically, up to three iterations are needed.

In general, this procedure produces more accurate estimates than an individual estimator.

ANALOGY METHOD

This method uses direct comparisons with completed projects/tasks that are similar in size, complexity, etc.

The steps in this process are as follows:

Step 1   Determine the global properties of the project/task, for example:
- Its size
- Type of application
- Major 'functions'
- Development method
- Programming language
- Experience of project team
- Experience of project manager
- Level and quality of support tools
- Physical development environment
- etc.

Note that the size of a project can be calculated using Function Point Analysis (Appendix C).

Step 2   Find one or more past projects/tasks which are similar to the project/task to be undertaken, in terms of its global properties. It is desirable but not essential that past projects/tasks used a similar programming language and development method.

Step 3   The effort for a similar previous project/task is taken as the base estimate for the new project.

A word of warning. Care needs to be taken to determine how much of the effort on the chosen project was attributable to unnecessary work which may have been due to open-ended requirements, poor management procedures, teething troubles with new technologies, etc. This is why it is very important to document all the problems encountered during development. A pointer for checking for this type of situation is to compare the estimated effort made before development commenced and the actual effort.

The analogy method can be enhanced by selecting a similar project/task which is larger in size than the new project/task and a project/task which is smaller in size than the new project/task. Then interpolate between the two projects/tasks to obtain an initial estimate of the effort for the new project/task.

The main strengths of the analogy method are that it:

- Is based on empirical evidence
- Focuses at the system level.

The main weaknesses of the analogy method are that it can be:

- Highly subjective in terms of choosing a similar project/task
- Difficult comparing projects which use different development methods and tools and different work environments, etc.

EFFORT TABLES

For enhancements to an operational system the following method can be used to assess the impact of a change to the code and test cases based on the:

- Number and complexity of modules to be changed/created
- Complexity of the interfaces between modules to be changed
- Number and complexity of test cases to be changed/created.

In order to estimate the effort needed to implement a change we need to:

- Estimate the size of the change in terms of how many modules will need to be changed/developed
- Estimate the complexity of the change to the code.

To illustrate this method we now provide an overview of how to estimate the effort needed to change a module. The complexity of a module (difficulty in making changes to it) depends on a variety of factors, such as:

- Its size
- Its control structure
- Its data structures
- The number of modules it interfaces to
- The level and quality of the available supporting documentation
- etc.

Let us categorize the complexity of a module using the following three categories:

- Complex
- Average
- Simple.

Checklists should be used to help assess the complexity of a module.

Let us categorize the scope of a change to a module using the following three categories:

- Major (equivalent to writing a new module)
- Average
- Minor.

For each system, a table should be produced depicting the effort needed to change a module based on its complexity and the scope of the change in terms of percentage of code to be changed. Figure 32.1 provides an example of such a table. For example, for system X the effort to make an average size change to a complex module is 5 days.

It should be noted that the values in the table in Fig. 32.1 are only examples. The initial values should be supplied by staff familiar with the system. Then, as validated historical data becomes available, it can be used to calibrate the initial values.

Typical characteristics of a module that need to be considered in order to assess the complexity of a module are:

- Control structure
  - the number of paths through the code
  - the number of loops
  - the nesting of loops
  - for each loop, the number of entries and exits
  - etc.

System X	Scope of change		
	Major	Average	Minor
Complexity of module			
complex	10 days	5 days	2 days
average	5 days	4 days	1.5 days
simple	4 days	2 days	1 day

Figure 32.1 Look-up table for assessing the impact of a change to a module.

- Data structures
- Design constraints on timing
- Interrelationship between modules
- Effort needed to test the module
- Level of comments, supporting documentation
- Number of defects found in operational use
- Number of changes implemented.

Characteristics of modules and test cases

To support this method, the following tables should be produced for each system:

- A table of modules depicting their interrelationships, namely the direct and indirect interfaces between modules
- A table defining the number of changes made to each module
- For each module, a table of its associated documents and their characteristics
- A table of system test cases depicting their characteristics such as duration of test, expected behaviour of the system when running the system test, input data and expected output data
- For each system test case, a table of its associated documents and their characteristics.

33

CAPTURING INFORMATION

In this chapter we discuss ways to improve the capture of information relating to a change to an operational system.

The information contained in a change request may lack sufficient detail to enable estimates to be produced that management have confidence in. On the other hand, because of the timescales involved in waiting for a requirement specification to be produced, it may be unacceptable to wait for estimates that are produced from a requirements specification. Therefore, the change request form should contain sufficient information to help ensure that estimates of effort are not based on open-ended requirements. In particular:

- A change request should be classified using the following classification scheme:
  - functional change to solve a problem
  - functional change to improve efficiency
  - functional change to allow interoperability of systems
  - correction of a fault
  - planned enhancement
  - non-functional change (infrastructure, etc.)
  - documentation change
  - project requirement.

This classification scheme will help to identify which of the WBS tasks will need to be undertaken during its implementation.

- A change request should include a set of questions that estimators want answers to in order to estimate effort and timescales, such as:

  - What is wanted (e.g. functional requirements) and how well should it do what is wanted (e.g. quality requirements)?
  - Why is it wanted? (To solve a problem, to increase response rate, to increase functionality, etc.)

- What will be the benefits?
- What will be the drawbacks?
- What will be the consequences of the change?
- What will be the consequences if it is not implemented or there is a delay in its implementation?
- Who will receive or be affected by the benefits and drawbacks?
- When is the change needed by?
- What is its priority?
    urgent (needed now)
    needed by next version
    low priority (within three years)
    If it is urgent, the reasons why it is urgent should be stated.
- Each question on the change request form should be classified as mandatory (meaning it must be completed) or optional (meaning it is up to the instigator as to whether they can provide information).
- The change request form needs to request sufficient information while at the same time not falling into the trap of requesting unnecessary detail which may result in:
  - people being reluctant to supply such detail
  - people inadvertently providing misleading information because they did not understand fully what information was required.
  The change request form needs to request enough information so that the requirement is not open ended and it is possible to:
  - determine the impact of a change request on the current system and the workload of the groups who will be tasked with its implementation
  - determine whether the change request is feasible in terms of timescale and effort
  - make an initial assessment of the effort needed to implement the change request which management have confidence in
  - produce estimates of effort within the timescales imposed by management planning activities.
- It may be necessary to provide two types of change request form, namely:
  - a short form version for simple changes which are straightforward
  - a detailed version for changes that are non-trivial which requires the instigator to supply detailed information.
- The change request form(s) should, where possible, provide lists of possible answers so that the instigator of a change may only need to tick the boxes appropriate to their change. This both reduces the workload of the instigator on many occasions and encourages the provision of all the relevant information.

GENERAL RULE

Estimates should not be produced from open-ended change requests. However, it is not realistic to assume that a change request form will provide the right level of detail at the first attempt. It is a subjective judgement as to whether a change request is open ended. The approach is to improve the change request form as the estimation process becomes more mature. One way to reduce open-ended change requests is to devise requests for information on the change request form that require quantitative answers, but this will require a high degree of sophistication from the instigator of the change request, which in the short term may not be realistic.

34

ASSESSING THE QUALITY OF AN ESTIMATION PROCESS

In this chapter we provide a technique for measuring the effectiveness of an estimating process in terms of how well the estimates converge to the actual value. The idea is taken from DeMarco (1982).

The goal of the estimation team is not to provide targets for the development team to strive towards nor to state what they should do, but rather to provide a reasonable planning projection of what they will do.

The quality of an estimate is only a function of how quickly it converges to the actual result. A way to measure the quality of an estimate (defined as the midpoint between the lower bound of the estimation interval and the upper bound of the estimation interval) is to divide the shaded area in Fig. 34.1 into the area under the actual effort, which is

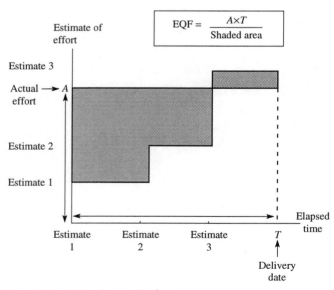

$$EQF = \frac{A \times T}{\text{Shaded area}}$$

Figure 34.1 Estimating quality factor.

denoted the estimating quality factor (EQF). This gives a unitless number between 0 and infinity. High numbers characterize good estimates. Note that the EQF is independent of the units of measure used. That is, the EQF is the same whether effort, which is represented on the vertical axis, is measured in days, weeks, months, etc. or whether elapsed time, represented on the horizontal axis, is measured in hours, days, weeks, etc.

The EQF can only be calculated when the actual effort is known. DeMarco suggests that estimators should aim to achieve values of 8 and above for the EQF.

With such incentives estimators are encouraged to re-estimate when changes occur to the requirements or it is suspected that the estimates are inaccurate. There is no tendency to stick with a bad estimate until the estimator sees a politically appropriate moment late on in the project to change it.

NOTE

The quality of an estimate should not be judged in isolation. The accuracy of an estimate needs to be viewed in relation to productivity achieved by the development teams. For example, the accuracy of the estimates produced may be within 5 per cent of the actual values in all cases, simply because a large contingency was included with the result that productivity was very low.

35

ESTIMATING TIMESCALES

In this chapter we discuss techniques to help in determining unrealistic timescales.

PEOPLE AGAINST TIME TRADE-OFFS

Having determined the effort needed to complete the project we now need to determine the timescales. Managers need to use the estimates of effort to determine the timescales, which cannot be produced in isolation as they are dependent on a variety of factors, such as:

- The priorities of other projects
- Impact of other projects being developed
- Long-term planning priorities
- Time available to carry out system tests
- Availability of staff, etc.

Sadly there is no simple formula of the form:

$$\text{Timescale} = \frac{\text{effort}}{\text{number of staff}}$$

The productivity of twelve people working for one month will not be the same as one person working for twelve months. When the customer needs the system much earlier than originally planned, you cannot simply double the staff on the project and expect to complete it in half the time.

In general, the productivity of project teams decreases as the size of a project team increases (Fig. 35.1). There are a variety of reasons for this, one of the main ones being the communications overhead. Experience has shown that trying to estimate the communications overhead can be exceptionally difficult.

However, there is a trade-off between the size of a project team and the elapsed time required (ETR). This leads to the question of how much work can be squeezed into a set

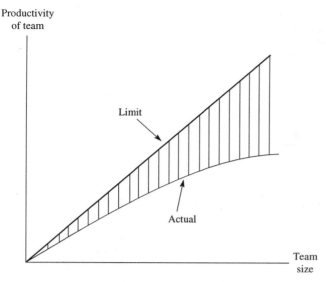

Figure 35.1   Relationship between productivity and team size.

period of time. Trading off people against time is only feasible within certain limits. We now discuss these limits.

Empirical evidence should be gathered to produce a set of base formulas for determining how much time it takes to use the estimated effort effectively for various categories of projects. Projects should be categorized according to factors such as:

- Size of team
- Peak staff loading
- Number of tasks
- Interdependencies between tasks
- Internal interdependencies of tasks (interdependence of subtasks for a task)
- Etc.

Figure 35.2 provides an example look-up table of the increase in the idealized duration for a task corresponding to:

- The size of a team
- The interdependencies between the subtasks carried out by the staff working on the task. Note that it is assumed that tasks have been broken down into packages of work that require no more than a team size of eight.

Note that idealized duration is defined as:

$$\frac{\text{effort}}{\text{number of staff working on the task}}$$

where the number of staff are assumed to be working full time for the duration of the task.

Size of team	Level of interdependence	% increase to idealized duration
n staff	None	0
	Minimum	n × 5
	Low	n × 25
	Average	n × 50
	Extensive	n × 75
	Full	n × 100

Figure 35.2 Look-up table for increasing idealized duration.

Note that the categories for the level of interdependence correspond to the following:

- *None* corresponds to the situation where all team members can work in parallel
- *Minimum* corresponds to the situation where all team members can almost work in parallel
- *Low* corresponds to the situation where all team members can for the most part, work in parallel
- *Average* corresponds to the situation where either team members are partially dependent on other team members or some team members need to work in sequence while others can work independently
- *Extensive* corresponds to the situation where all team members need for the most part to work in sequence
- *Full* corresponds to the situation where all team members need to work in sequence.

Boehm (1981) collected empirical data to produce the following generic base formula for a software project linking effort in months to the ETR:

$$\text{ETR} = [2.5 \times (\text{effort in months})^{0.33}]^S$$

where the ETR is stated in months and S is a scaling factor with a value between 0.75 and 1.6 which is dependent on the characteristics of the project under development. Thus a software project produced with inadequate tool support by staff with little experience will have a high factor suggesting a longer timescale. The formula should be calibrated as data on the actual effort and timescale become available. It may be necessary to have a set of equations relating to the different categories of software projects undertaken.

This formula is appropriate for projects with a peak loading of at least five people and requiring at least three months effort.

The formula can be used as a guideline by project managers to deal with customers who want to impose unattainable timescales and to check the feasibility of a contractor's estimate.

Empirical evidence shows that the following bound is a physical limitation on trade-offs between ETR and size of project team:

$$\text{Lower bound on ETR} = 0.7 \times [2.5 \times (\text{effort in months})^{0.33}]$$

These bounds will need to be adjusted to take account of particular approaches such as using a package solution.

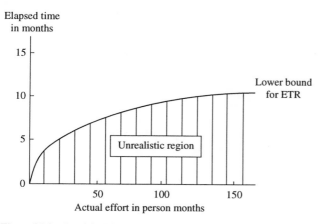

Figure 35.3 Empirical bounds for ETR.

The advice is always to compare proposed timescales to implement a project to the lower bound on the ETR, before committing to deadlines. Figure 35.3 depicts this lower bound for achievable timescales.

DEADLINES

If a deadline is imposed and the:

$$\text{available time is less than } 0.7 \times [2.5 \times (\text{effort in months})^{0.33}]$$

the following options should be considered:

- Reducing functionality
- Phasing delivery
- Opting for package solutions.

Then re-estimates should be made to reflect any proposed changes.

CONSTRAINTS

When estimating timescales, the figures shown in Figure 35.4 need to be considered.

Therefore, it should be assumed that staff are available to work 210 days per year out of a possible 260 (52×5); in other words, 17.5 days per month.

	Days
Annual leave	25
Public holidays	8
Training	7
Sick leave	8
Departmental meetings	2
Total	**50**

Figure 35.4   Unavailability of staff.

36

SUMMARY

There is no magic wand to wave to produce an accurate estimate. The best way to produce accurate estimates of effort for software projects is to base your method on using validated historical data.

The main points concerning estimating are:

- Estimates should be expressed as four numbers:
  - the most likely value
  - an upper bound
  - a lower bound (sometimes referred to as the base estimate)
  - a confidence value, expressed as a percentage, that quantifies the chance that the actual value will be within the bounds.
- The earlier an estimate is produced in the development process, the greater the inaccuracy.
- Estimates must incorporate the uncertainty in the information used to produce the estimate.
- Estimates are dynamic and should be revised as more information becomes available or when the requirements change.
- The estimation process should use more than one method to derive the base estimates of effort.
- The estimation process should be repeatable and traceable. Thus all the assumptions and calculations used in producing the estimate should be recorded.
- The estimation process should employ a feedback mechanism to help improve the estimation process.

Section 6

Conclusion

*Example is not the main thing in influencing others.
It's the only thing.*

Albert Einstein

Running a Measurement Programme is a continuous process of measuring processes and products, determining trends, analysing data to help determine where improvements are needed and providing feedback to both managers and project teams. Like most things in life, it sounds easy in theory, but the reality can be very different. Many Measurement Programmes which started out with all the right intentions have sunk without trace.

One of the best ways of learning to set up and run a Measurement Programme is by apprenticeship to someone who has a track record in software measurement. For many IS departments, this approach may not be possible. The purpose of this book has been to provide the reader with the next best thing, namely, learning through case studies. This book has shown you how to get started in using measurement as a management tool based upon a case study involving an IS department in a major financial institution. Their short-term goal was to set up a Measurement Programme to monitor their performance with respect to a number of changes that were being made to their software development processes. The book then described how to expand the programme to meet the following long-term goals, which should be common to all IS departments, namely:

- Derive a set of measures that can be used to specify and measure the quality of a software system
- Develop a Measurement Programme to enable defects to be used as a process improvement tool
- Develop a Measurement Programme to support an estimation process.

More often than not, when managers decide to use measurement as a management tool, the first question that they ask is: 'What should I measure?' This type of approach is doomed to failure. Furthermore, this type of approach makes it that much harder to relaunch a Measurement Programme because project teams will be unhappy that their initial contribution was wasted. For example, too often IS departments record information on defects without having a specific purpose for the data. Not surprisingly, this data usually ends up gathering dust in a filing cabinet. The main point here is that you do not just record data on defects to tell you how many you have. You collect the information to support you in pinpointing where improvements are needed. All this may sound like common sense, but common sense is not always common practice in IS departments.

This book has shown you that measurement must have a purpose and that the first question should be: 'How can measurement help our department meet its objectives?' In other words, the goals of a Measurement Programme must be driven by the needs of management, which, in turn, relate to the business goals. Only then can you begin to determine what needs to be measured.

Too often IS departments only use measurement to monitor and control the progress of ongoing projects. It is not enough to use measurement to tell you a software project is over budget and late. Measurement is worthless if all it does is show trends that give management a good feeling. As a manager you should be using measurement as a process improvement tool. In other words, the data needs to be acted upon by management. However, data should not be viewed in isolation, as the following story highlights.

In 1992 the UK National Health Service introduced a number of changes to try and decrease the number of patients waiting to be treated. The changes were aimed at reducing the consultation and treatment time given to each patient. Within eighteen months of implementing the changes the trend in the number of patients being treated was increasing. The improvement programme was hailed as a success. However, on closer examination of the data, it turned out that there was a substantial increase in the number of patients who were having to come back for more treatment because their original treatment was inadequate.

Using measurement as a process improvement tool should be a combination of the following three complementary approaches:

- Learning from mistakes
- Building on what is done well
- Process re-engineering.

Finally, failing to use measurement as a management tool will mean lost opportunities, but you cannot assume your competitors are going to do the same. Where the leaders go, the rest need to follow if they want to stay in business.

Appendix A

GLOSSARY OF ABBREVIATIONS

AFPC	Adjusted Function Point Count
BDR	Breakdown ratio
CASE	Computer-Aided Software Engineering
CMM	Capability Maturity Model
CSF	Critical Success Factor
DET	Data element type
DOD	Department of Defense
EI	External input
EIF	External interface file
EO	External output
EQ	External inquiry
EQF	Estimating quality factor
ESPRIT	European Strategic Programme of Research in Information Technology
ETR	Estimated timescales required
FPA	Function Point Analysis
FPC	Function Point Count
FTR	File types referenced
GQM	Goal–question–metric
GSC	General system characteristic
IBM	International Business Machines
IEEE	Institute of Electrical and Electronic Engineers
ILF	Internal logical file
IS	Information services
ISO	International Standards Organisation
IT	Information technology
KLOC	Thousand lines of code
KPI	Key performance indicator

LOC	Lines of code
LOQUM	Locally defined quality modelling
MP	Measurement Programme
MTTF	Mean time to failure
MUG	Measurement User Group
MUSiC	Measuring Usability of Systems in Context
QA	Quality assurance
RAG	Red–amber–green
RECUP	Repair, enhancement, conversion, user support, prevention
RET	Record element type
SCF	Schedule compression factor
SEI	Software Engineering Institute
SPC	Statistical process control
UFPC	Unadjusted Function Point Count
VAF	Value adjustment factor
WBS	Work breakdown structure

Appendix B

ANALYSIS TECHNIQUES

A science is as mature as its measurement tools.

Louis Pasteur

This appendix provides an overview of the following analysis techniques:

- Box plot
- Pareto diagram
- Fishbone diagram
- Scatterplot
- Trend analysis.

BOX PLOT

A box plot can be used to:

- Detect implausible values in a data set
- Provide information about the centre and spread in a data set
- Provide information about the skewness in a data set.

In order to use a box plot it is necessary to define what is meant by:

- A data set
- Median value of a data set
- Lower and upper fourths of a data set
- Box length of a data set
- Upper and lower tails of a box plot
- Outliers.

A data set is a set of values obtained from a set of related items. For example, the following data set relates to the size of 15 modules where size is measured in lines of code (LOC):

$$25, 34, 44, 45, 57, 67, 92, 105, 120, 123, 166, 205, 234, 266, 480$$

The median value of a data set is the value which divides the data set in half, when the data set is written in ascending order. In our example, the median value is 105.

The lower and upper fourths of the data set are the values that split the data set into quarters, when the data set is written in ascending order. In this example, the lower fourth is the value 45 and the upper fourth is the value 205.

The calculation used in constructing the median value, lower fourth value and upper fourth value for an even number of values in a data set can be found in Devore and Peck (1986).

The box length of a data set is defined as the distance from the lower to the upper fourth. In our example the box length is 160.

The upper and lower tails of the box plot are constructed by multiplying the box length by 1.5 and adding and subtracting from the upper and lower fourths respectively. In our example we have:

- Lower tail of the box plot = −195
- Upper tail of the box plot = 445.

Note that in our example the lower tail can be truncated to zero since negative LOC are not meaningful.

Values outside the upper and lower tails of the box plot are termed 'outliers' (implausible values). In this example, the value 480 is an outlier.

Figure B.1 depicts the box plot for our example. The box plot shows the skewness of the data set by the position of the median in the box. If the data set is symmetric the median value of the data set will be positioned in the centre of the box, whereas if the data set is skewed the median value will be offset from the centre of the box. In our example, the data set is skewed to the left.

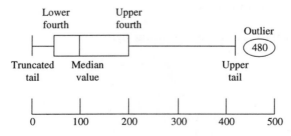

Figure B.1 Box plot for LOC example.

PARETO DIAGRAM

A Pareto diagram can be used to help indicate which type of problems should be solved first. We will show how to use a Pareto diagram via the following example. There are many aspects of software development that can be improved by using the information generated from analysing the data relating to defects. The difficulty is knowing where to begin. For example, suppose we have categorized defects into a set of types, such as shown in Fig. B.2.

Now we wish to try and eliminate those types of defects that occur most often in a particular class of systems. The purpose of the graph in Fig. B.3 is to depict the frequency of the various types of defects found during operational use in a sample of 'similar' projects.

The horizontal axis of the graph in Fig. B.3 lists the type of defects with the most frequent one on the left and progressing through frequency to the least frequent on the extreme right. This type of graph is called a Pareto diagram.

According to Fig. B.3, unclear instructions should be tackled first. Pareto diagrams appear very simple, yet they are very effective at highlighting the priority areas and focusing people's attention on the key issues.

Type of defect	Description of defect	Code
Computational	Incorrect operand in logical expression	C1
Computational	Division by zero	C2
Input/output	Input file not opened before use	D1
Input/output	Input read from incorrect data file	D2
Interface	Incorrect interface protocols	I1
Interface	Unclear instructions	I2
Logical	Logical activities out of sequence	L1
Logical	Non-termination of a loop	L2

Figure B.2 Example types of software defects.

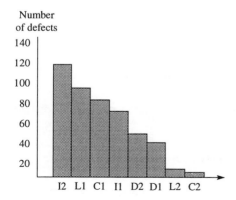

Figure B.3 Pareto analysis of software defects.

FISHBONE DIAGRAM

The fishbone diagram analysis technique can be used to help identify the causes of an effect. The technique consists of the following steps:

Step 1   Choose the effect to be studied and define it in objective terms; for example, delays in delivery and faults during operational use.

Step 2   Produce a list of major categories of possible causes. For example, some of the factors to be considered in determining the cause of a software defect are communications, experience of staff and development tools.

Step 3   Hold a meeting and brainstorm possible causes within major categories to produce a list of causes and subcauses for each category. Typical questions to consider are:
- Is there any record of this cause?
- Does the category interact with other factors?

Step 4   Represent effect, categories and causes and subcauses in a diagrammatic form to assist in developing intercausal relationships, as depicted in Fig. B.4.

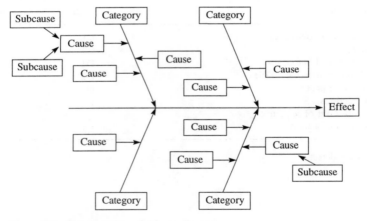

Figure B.4   Template for a fishbone diagram.

Step 5   Analyse each cause to focus on more and more specific causes.

Step 6   Check the diagram to make sure all the known causes are included on the diagram.

Step 7   Identify and mark up on the diagram the likely root causes.

Step 8   Gather data to verify the most likely root causes. A Pareto diagram is a good way to display this data.

SCATTERPLOT

Scatterplot diagrams are a useful way of examining the relationship between two variables, for example the number of defects detected in a module and the size of a module. If the value of one variable appears to affect the value of the other variable, the variables are said to be correlated. If an increase in one variable results in an increase in the other variable then there is said to be a positive correlation. If an increase in one variable results in a decrease in the other variable there is said to be a negative correlation.

A correlation may be detected by plotting the two sets of values against each other, forming a scatterplot. It is important to realize that even though a scatterplot may indicate a relationship between two variables, changes in one variable may not lead to changes in the other variable, This can occur when there is no cause and effect relationship between the two variables themselves, but when there is a third factor which can cause changes in both elements simultaneously.

Figure B.5 provides an example of a scatterplot to show the relationship between the effort required to produce a module and the size of a module (measured in lines of code) for a software project. The scatterplot shows that unsurprisingly the effort required to produce a module tends to increase with the size of a module. In our example in Fig. B.5 it is possible to draw an informal relationship line simply by looking at the scatterplot that demonstrates the relationship. Statistical techniques exist to calculate the exact position of the relationship line and can be found in Devore and Peck (1986).

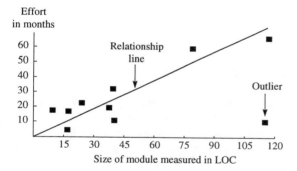

Figure B.5 Example of a scatterplot.

The cause of the outlier in Fig. B.5 could have been due to a variety of reasons, such as modifying an existing module (reuse).

TREND ANALYSIS

A common problem when analysing data is to determine trends. There are a variety of ways to finding a trend (if one exists) in a data set. We will describe how to use the technique of *moving average* by using it on the data set depicted in Fig. B.6. The moving average technique smoothes out the irregularities in the original data.

The technique is best described by considering the calculation of a 'two-point' moving average. In Fig. B.7 the average value of each pair of successive points (the 1st and 2nd,

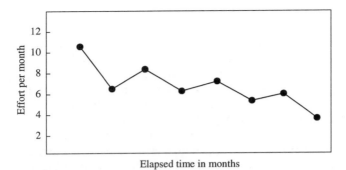

Figure B.6   Effort spent on corrective maintenance.

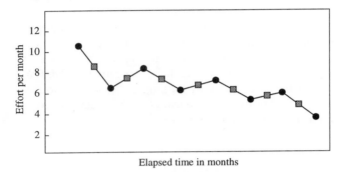

Figure B.7   Calculating a two-point moving average.

the 2nd and 3rd, the 3rd and 4th, etc.) has been calculated and plotted midway between them on the horizontal scale.

Figure B.8, which shows only the moving averages, gives a smoother graph than the original data, enabling a trend line to be drawn more easily through the points.

Figure B.9 represents the original series of data points plotted as a 'four-point' moving average. The 'four-point' moving average is drawn by plotting the average of each successive group of four values (the 1st, 2nd, 3rd and 4th, the 2nd, 3rd, 4th and 5th, etc.). The four-point moving average is smoother than the two-point moving average.

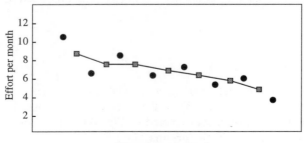

Figure B.8   The two-point moving average smoothes the data.

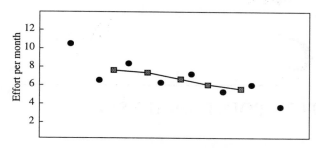

Figure B.9   The four-point moving average.

Appendix C

OVERVIEW OF FUNCTION POINT ANALYSIS

In this appendix we provide a step-by-step guide to using Function Point Analysis (FPA) to size a software system.

FPA can be viewed as a technique to measure the size of a software system which:

- Is best suited for transaction processing systems
- Can be used for sizing a system to be developed from scratch and sizing a change to an existing system
- Can be calculated from the high-level design
- Is independent of the programming language used
- Emphasizes the user's view of the system rather than the implementation used to satisfy the requirements
- Has been shown to work for the IT industry.

FPA was invented by Alan Albrecht (Albrecht, 1979) at IBM in the late 1970s and has evolved into a standard technique which has been adopted by organizations throughout Europe, USA and Australia. This appendix will concentrate on describing Albrecht's version of FPA. Another description can be found in Dreger (1989).

BASIC CONCEPT OF FPA

The basic concept behind FPA is that it is possible to measure the size of a system in terms of the functions it delivers to the user. FPA can be viewed as an equation (Fig. C.1) whose variables correspond to information about the system in terms of:

- Inputs to the system
- Outputs from the system to the users and other systems

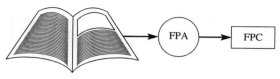

System description

Figure C.1 Overview of FPA.

- User inquiries
- Data files updated by the system
- Interfaces to other systems.

The equation generates a unitless number which is known as the Function Point Count (FPC) for the system.

MISCONCEPTIONS

Many misconceptions exist about FPA, so the first thing to do is to establish three basic ideas that should be appreciated by anyone before they start to use FPA, namely:

- FPA is not a de-skilled activity and is not a simple count of specific characteristics of a software system.
- FPA produces a unitless number. This means that strictly speaking there is no such thing as a 'function point'.
- The FPC produced by FPA is a measure of system size. It is not an estimating technique nor is it a device for measuring productivity. However, size is a component in cost estimates and productivity measures. FPCs can be used to show trends, to compare productivity of projects or project teams and to aid in the identification of factors that have an effect on productivity.

REASONS FOR USING FPA

Organizations who have introduced FPA tend to use it to help to:

- Measure what the user requested and received
- Measure the service a department provides
- Estimate the effort needed to develop a software system
- Measure productivity trends
- Evaluate the size and complexity of a software package that is under consideration to be purchased (does it offer more than other packages, would it be cheaper to produce it in-house, etc.)
- Determine the defect density of a software system
- Provide quantifiable information for discarding less profitable projects
- Provide a normalization factor for software comparison

- Prove that projects are being properly managed
- Determine if projects overran on effort and or timescales because they delivered more functionality than was originally asked for.

WHAT PROPERTIES SHOULD A SIZE MEASURE POSSESS?

We now discuss the main characteristics that are required of a software size measure.

Traditionally software size was measured using lines of code (LOC). The main disadvantages of using LOC are that they are:

- Not language independent
- Not available early on during development
- Not meaningful to the user.

The experience of using LOC as a size measure led to the following requirements of a software size measure.

Relationship with effort

The effort to perform a task should be proportional to the size measure. However, the relationship should be significant rather than perfect.

Technology independent

The measure should be independent of implementation decisions such as choice of the development method, design notations, and the programming language. Productivity gains should be expected when new technologies are introduced such as a fourth generation language, but these gains come from reduced effort not increased size.

Objective

The result of the measurement should be independent of the person carrying it out.

Normalization factor for comparison

A size measure should be applicable across projects and across organizations to enable comparison. This approach is a very common management requirement but it can cause serious problems. There is one golden rule to remember when comparing parts of the same organization: there is no such thing as good and bad productivity, only higher and lower.

Early availability

If a size measure is used for estimation then it needs to be available as early as possible, certainly at the end of high-level design.

Meaningful to the user

If used in estimation then the size measure should be meaningful to users and customers so that it can facilitate negotiation.

Does FPA meet all these requirements? The remainder of this appendix will show that the answer is an emphatic yes.

TYPES OF COUNT

There are three types of count that can be performed depending upon the type of FPA exercise that is being carried out.

Design count

This is performed for a new system being developed. In this case, the FPC is calculated from a description of the system such as the high-level design.

System count

This encompasses the whole system, and this type of FPC is done at the end of a development project.

Enhancement count

This situation arises where a system exists and further releases are made of that system. In this case, added, changed and deleted functionality is considered rather than the totality of the system. However, do not fall into the trap of counting the total system before enhancement, then after the enhancements have been implemented and subtracting one total from the other. This is not a valid approach.

OVERVIEW OF HOW TO PERFORM AN FPC

We now provide an overview of how to perform an FPC. There are seven main steps to calculating an FPC, namely:

Step 1 Define the scope of the system to be measured.

Step 2 Identify the occurrences of inputs, outputs, inquiries, files and interfaces to other systems.

Step 3 Classify the complexity of each occurrence of a function type.

Step 4 Apply weightings to the function types to reflect the value to the customer.

Step 5   Calculate the unadjusted FPC by summing over all the occurrences of the function types.

Step 6   Derive the value adjustment factor (VAF) which makes allowances for overall system characteristics.

Step 7   Finally apply the VAF to the unadjusted FPC to give the adjusted FPC.

STEP 1 — ESTABLISH THE SYSTEM BOUNDARY

The concept of a system boundary is an important aspect for FPA. It is where data enters or leaves the system. The boundary is used to limit the scope of the sizing exercise and to help identify and classify the function types. Changing the system boundary will, in general, change the FPC.

It may be argued that FPA can never be totally automated because there will always be a subjective element in determining where to fix the system boundary. Beyond the boundary there may be users, operators, interfaces to equipment which the software monitors or controls and other software systems. Figure C.2 provides an example of a system boundary.

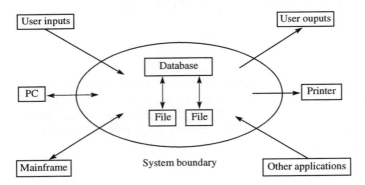

Figure C.2   Example of a system boundary.

STEP 2 — IDENTIFY THE FUNCTION TYPES

FPA considers a system from the user's point of view by looking at external features, namely the functionality it provides to the user. It does this by identifying the occurrences of five basic function types (also known as components and parameters) which are now described.

Internal logical files (ILFs)

Informally, internal logical files can be thought of as files held within the system (lies within the system boundary) and maintained by the system, or files that belong to another system but are maintained by the system being sized. Maintained here means files that are added to, changed or deleted. Formally, an ILF is a collection of data held within the system that is:

- Used and/or maintained by the system
- Regarded by the user as a file.

An ILF is taken from the user's viewpoint, not the implementor's. From the user viewpoint an ILF is how the user would view or group the data, rather than the storage technology such as tables, paths, etc.

Examples of ILFs are:

- User-maintained file (such as list of employees with their address and telephone number)
- Databases
- Help message file
- Security file.

Examples of internal files that are not ILFs are work files and sort files. These do not correspond to a specific user requirement. They are part of the how, not what; in other words they are implementation specific.

External interface files (EIFs)

Informally, external interface files can be thought of as files that are held on other systems and read by the system being sized. Formally an EIF is data that is:

- Used by the system
- Stored outside the system
- Maintained by another system.

Examples of EIFs are:

- Data file received from the user that the system is going to use
- Files received from another system
- Databases maintained by other systems.

The following are not EIFs:

- Data received from another system that adds, changes or deletes an ILF (this is counted as an external input)
- Data formatted and processed for another system (this is counted as an external output).

External inputs (EI)

Informally, external inputs can be thought of as inputs from the user that maintain files. Formally, an EI is an input to the system that crosses the system boundary and maintains an ILF.

An example of an EI is:

- A data screen input (such as a staff number to enable the system to create a new staff file).

The following are not EIs:

- Menu screens
- External data used by the system, but not maintained on ILFs.

External outputs (EO)

Informally, external outputs can be thought of as outputs which provide the user with data generated by the system. Formally, an EO is an output, in the form of a report or message, from the system that crosses the system boundary and is sent to a user, other systems, peripherals such as printers, etc.

Examples of EOs are:

- File transfer to another system
- Printed documents (reports, customer invoice, wage slip, etc.)
- Screen reports
- Error messages on a screen.

The following are not EOs:

- Identical reports which have the same format and processing logic; for example, two reports that contain customers' names, the first having customers' names beginning A to L and the second having customers' names beginning M to Z
- A printed report that was triggered by a request from a user which only required collating the information from different sources, not maintaining any ILFs.

External inquiries (EQ)

Informally, external inquiries can be thought of as interactive inputs requiring a response. The concept of an EQ sometimes causes confusion. The question often asked is: why go to all the bother, why not just count the input and output part separately? The answer is that, as no data within the system boundary changes, the value of an external inquiry is less than an input and output.

Examples of EQs are:

- Retrieval of data
- Help request from a user followed by a help message displayed on the user's screen.

An example of an inquiry that is not an EQ is an error/confirmation message.

Guidelines for identifying function types

The main guidelines for identifying the function types are:

- Determine the occurrences of function types from the user's viewpoint.
- Only one function type can be assigned to each dataflow and datafile.
- Do not waste time splitting hairs in deciding whether a function type is an EO or a EIF, etc. Consistency is more important than precise categorization.

STEP 3 — CLASSIFY COMPLEXITY

Having identified the occurrences of the various function types identified in the system, the next step is to assign a complexity rating to each one. The complexity of each occurrence of a function type is rated on a simple three-point scale as:

- Low
- Average
- High.

The complexity is based on the number of fields and record types occurring in files and interfaces, and the number of fields and files occurring in inputs, outputs and inquiries. Further on in this appendix we describe how to determine the complexity of a function type.

STEP 4 — APPLY WEIGHTINGS

Having assigned a complexity rating to each occurrence of the various function types identified in the system, the next step is to weight them (Fig. C.3).

For example, an external input which is rated as having a low complexity is assigned a weighting of 3. Informally, this can be thought of as 3 function points.

These weightings were derived from empirical analysis of historical data from IBM projects within one specific environment. The work was performed by Alan Albrecht. The analysis used relatively simple statistical analysis techniques, and looked at the relative

Function type	Low	Average	High
Internal logical files	7	10	15
External interface files	5	7	10
External inputs	3	4	6
External outputs	4	5	7
External inquiries	3	4	6

Figure C.3   Weighting of complexity ratings of the function types.

effort to develop different function types. It should be noted that the weights are a part of FPA and that FPA, in general, provides a good correlation with effort in homogeneous environments; hence, pragmatically they appear to have some validity.

Great play has been made about the fact that these weights can be tailored or calibrated to specific environments, However, no organization has reported significantly better FPA to effort or cost relationships using their own weights as opposed to these 'industry standards'.

It may be that in the future their contribution will be seen as less important than it is today and organizations will start to use unweighted counts of the basic function types. However, few organizations have so far adopted this approach.

STEP 5 — CALCULATE UNADJUSTED FPC

The next step is to calculate the unadjusted FPC which attempts to measure the pure information handling capacity of the system as seen by the user. This is done by multiplying the occurrence of each variety of function type by its weighting and then summing over all of them. For example, if there are two occurrences of a low complexity internal logical file, then this will contribute a count of 14 to the overall unadjusted FPC. Figure C.4 provides an example of an unadjusted FPC.

It should be noted that due to the weightings there can be approximately 100 per cent difference between:

- an unadjusted FPC having all the occurrences of its various function types rated low complexity
- an unadjusted FPC having all the occurrences of its various function types rated high complexity.

Function type	Complexity	Occurs	Weight	Count
Internal logical file	Low	2	7	14
	Average	1	10	10
	High	0	15	0
External interface file	Low	0	5	0
	Average	3	7	21
	High	1	10	10
External input	Low	1	3	3
	Average	2	4	8
	High	0	6	0
External output	Low	3	4	12
	Average	1	5	5
	High	0	7	0
External inquiry	Low	2	3	6
	Average	1	4	4
	High	1	6	6
			Unadjusted FPC	99

Figure C.4 Example of an unadjusted FPC.

STEP 6 — DERIVE VALUE ADJUSTMENT FACTOR

Having calculated the unadjusted FPC the next step is to calculate the value adjustment factor (VAF) which will be applied to the unadjusted FPC to derive the FPC. The VAF is an adjustment of the unadjusted FPC to take account of the processing characteristics of the system.

To transform the unadjusted FPC into a size measure which is more closely related to the size of the work to be performed by the development team, the unadjusted FPC is multiplied by a VAF which reflects the *degree of influence* of the following 14 general system characteristics (GSCs):

Data communications System data and control information are sent or received over communication facilities. Terminals connected locally to a control unit are considered to use communication facilities.

Distributed data processing Distributed data or processing functions are part of the system.

Performance System performance objectives, in throughput or response time, influence the design, implementation and maintenance of the system.

Heavy use of configuration The user wants to run the system on equipment that will be heavily used.

Transaction rate The transaction rate is high and influences the design, implementation, and maintenance of the system.

On-line data entry Support for on-line data entry and control functions.

End-user efficiency The on-line functions emphasize user efficiency.

On-line update The system provides on-line update for ILFs.

Complex processing Processing involves many control interactions and decision points, or extensive logical and mathematical equations.

Reusability The system and the code will be designed, developed and supported for reusability in other systems.

Installation ease Conversion and installation ease.

Operational ease Back-up, start-up and recovery procedures provided.

Multiple Sites The system will be specifically designed, implemented and maintained to be installed at multiple sites for multiple organizations.

Facilitate change System designed to support change. For example, the provision of a flexible query capability.

To calculate the VAF first assess the degree of influence of each of the 14 GSCs using an integer scale between zero and five:

0   not present, or no influence
1   insignificant influence
2   moderate influence
3   average influence
4   significant influence
5   strong influence throughout

The scores for each GSC are then summed to derive the VAF using the formula:

$$\text{VAF} = 0.65 + 0.01 \times \sum C(i) \qquad 1 \le i \le 14$$

where $C(i)$ is an integer between 0 and 5 which corresponds to the degree of influence associated with the ith GSC.

STEP 7 — CALCULATE THE FPC

The final step in calculating the FPC for a system is simply to multiply the unadjusted FPC by the VAF to give:

$$\text{FPC} = \text{unadjusted FPC} \times \text{VAF}$$

The VAF can scale the unadjusted FPC by ± 35 per cent.

ASSESSING THE COMPLEXITY OF THE FUNCTION TYPES

We now describe how to assign a complexity rating of Low, Average or High to each occurrence of the various function types identified in the system.

In order to assign a complexity rating it is necessary to define three terms used in the assessment.

Record element type (RET)

A record element type is a unique record format within an ILF or EIF. Informally, a RET can be thought of as a group of similar records within a file.

RETs are user-recognizable categories of data in an ILF. For example, a customer file may consist of *wholesale customers* and *retail customers*. This file would be viewed as having 2 RETs. Similarly a personnel file that consists of male employees and female employees would be viewed as having 2 RETs.

Data element type (DET)

A data element type is a unique occurrence of data, also referred to as a data element, variable or field. DETs are user-recognizable, non-recursive fields and can be present within all functional types.

Informally, a DET can be thought of as a group of similar fields within a record. For example, if a date is stored as three separate fields (day, month, year) for implementation reasons rather than to meet any customer requirement then the three fields should be viewed as one DET.

To further illustrate the concept, consider an external output that prints out:

- Staff name using two fields (1 for forename, 1 for surname)
- Staff address using 4 fields
- Hours worked during the month
- Tax code.

Then this external output may be viewed as 4 DETs.

File types referenced (FTR)

File types referenced refers to the number of ILFs or EIFs read, created or updated by a function type. Informally, an FTR can be thought of as references to a group of similar files. To illustrate this concept, consider for reasons of size a file of customer names and addresses split into a file that stores names beginning A to L and another file that stores names beginning with M to Z. Then these two files would be viewed as one FTR.

Complexity of ILFs and EIFs

For ILFs and EIFs calculate the following pair of numbers:

- Number of distinct records in the file — record element type (RET)
- Number of distinct fields in the file — data element type (DET).

Distinct means as viewed by the user. For example a file of customers' names could consist of two distinct records, retail customers and wholesale customers. Then use the following complexity matrix to assign a complexity rating:

To illustrate the use of the table consider the following two examples:

RETs	1–19	DETs 20–50	51+
1	L	L	A
2–5	L	A	H
6+	A	H	H

- An ILF having 25 DETs and 6 RETs is assigned a complexity rating of High.
- An EIF having 12 DETs and 1 RET is assigned a complexity rating of Low.

Complexity of EIs

For inputs (EIs), calculate the following pair of numbers for each occurrence of an EI:

- Number of files referenced — file types referenced (FTR)
- Number of distinct fields in the input — data element type (DET).

Then use the following complexity matrix for EIs to assign a complexity rating:

FTR	DETs 1–4	5–15	16+
0–1	L	L	A
2	L	A	H
3+	A	H	H

To illustrate the use of the table consider the following two examples:

- An EI having 12 DETs and 15 FTR is assigned a complexity rating of High.
- An EI having 3 DETs and 10 FTR is assigned a complexity rating of Average.

Complexity of EOs

For outputs (EOs), calculate the following pair of numbers for each occurrence of an EO:

- Number of files referenced — file types referenced (FTR)
- Number of distinct fields in the output — data element type (DET).

Then use the following complexity matrix for EOs to assign a complexity rating.

FTR	DETs 1–5	6–19	20+
0–1	L	L	A
2–3	L	A	H
4+	A	H	H

To illustrate the use of the table consider the following two examples:

- An EO having 29 DETs and 0 FTR is assigned a complexity rating of Average.
- An EO having 4 DETs and 2 FTR is assigned a complexity rating of Low.

Complexity of EQs

The complexity of external inquiries is performed by assessing the complexity of the input and output components separately and assigning the 'higher' complexity rating to the EQ.

The notion 'higher' should be interpreted as: High is regarded as 'higher' than Average and Low and Average is regarded as 'higher' than Low.

As an illustration, consider a request to print a report (regarded as an external inquiry) that has to collate the information for the report from six files. Furthermore, suppose the report has seven fields as viewed by the user. Then the output is regarded as having High complexity.

APPLYING FPA TO AN ENHANCEMENT

To calculate the FPC for an enhancement project, the following formula should be used:

$$FPC = (ADD + CHGA) \times VAFA + DEL \times VABF$$

where:

ADD is the unadjusted FPC of those functions that were added to the system by the enhancement project.

CHGA is the unadjusted FPC of those functions that were modified by the enhancement project. This number reflects the enhancements after the modifications.

DEL is the unadjusted FPC of those functions that were deleted by the enhancement project.

VAFA is the VAF of the system after the enhancement project.

VAFB is the VAF of the system before the enhancement project.

FPC FOR AN ENHANCED SYSTEM

To calculate the FPC of a system after it has been enhanced by a project, the following formula should be used:

$$FPC = [(UFPB + ADD + CHGA) - (CHGB + DEL)] \times VAFA$$

where:

UFPB is the system's unadjusted FPC before the enhancement project.

ADD is the unadjusted FPC of those functions that were added to the system by the enhancement project.

CHGA is the unadjusted FPC of those functions that were modified by the enhancement project. This number reflects the enhancements after the modifications.

CHGB is the unadjusted FPC of those functions that were modified by the enhancement project before the modification.

DEL is the unadjusted FPC of those functions that were deleted by the enhancement project.

VAFA is the VAF of the system after the enhancement project.

In most cases, a good approximation can be obtained by using the formula:

$$FPC = (UFPB + ADD - DEL) \times VAF$$

YOUR QUESTIONS ANSWERED

We now provide answers to typical questions that are likely to be asked about FPA.

What is Mark II FPA?
It is a variation of Albrecht's version of FPA.

Are the FPCs obtained from using Albrecht's FPA compatible with the FPCs obtained from Mark II FPA?
One of the concerns, justified or not, that led to the development of Mark II FPA was that the original Albrecht form of FPA 'underscored' large database applications (systems greater than 400 FPCs). In the light of this, Mark II was specifically designed so that the FPCs for smaller systems (less than 200 FPCs) would be very similar to the FPC one would obtain using the Albrecht variant. As systems or application size grows (over 400 FPCs) one should expect to see a divergence between the scores obtained for the two techniques with Mark II FPCs being higher.

How much training is needed to perform an FPC?
Between two and five days: one day of theory and the rest doing practical exercises under the guidance of an expert counter. At this point a person should be able to perform an FPC. However, only with experience gained in producing FPCs on a variety of systems will the counter become proficient.

How much time does an FPC take?
In general, it varies from 0.05 to 0.2 per cent of the total project effort. The time will depend on a variety of factors such as quality of the supporting documentation, whether the count is being performed on the high-level design or the code itself, etc. Empirical evidence has shown that as a project gets larger, the amount of time (relative to the size of a project) needed to carry out an FPC decreases. The reasons for this finding are still not clear.

An efficient and quick approach is to use an expert counter working together with system developers.

What confidence can I place in the accuracy of an FPC?
The accuracy will depend on two things, namely:

- The experience of the counters
- The stage in the development process that the FPC was performed at.

An FPC produced from the high-level design will be more accurate than an FPC produced from a requirements specification. One way to access the accuracy of the counters is to periodically ask them to produce an FPC from a standard example that has been sized by an expert counter and to compare the results. Standard examples can be found in textbooks on FPA or can be devised by expert counters.

It is more important that the FPC be obtained with a defined and consistent process, than that it be precisely accurate.

I've heard that there can be a difference of up to 500 per cent between an FPC produced from a requirements specification and produced when the development of the system has been completed. What are the reasons?
There are many reasons, such as:

- The introduction of additional functionality that was not part of the original specification
- The level of detail exhibited in a specification is coarser than the implementation, therefore the number and complexity of the function types will be underestimated in a specification.

How do you guarantee consistency in counting?
As with any measurement, the measure is only as good as the numbers. An organization using FPA should:

- Provide training for its staff
- When starting up have an expert counter to assist projects and as project staff become more experienced decentralize the role of the expert counter
- Provide guidelines and checklists to help a counter determine the occurrences of function types, assess the complexity of function types and assess the impact of the 14 general system characteristics
- Establish internal guidelines to determine if the FPC is consistent.

If all the 14 general system characteristics which are used to compute the value adjustment factor are rated as average will the VAF = 1?
No. The VAF = 1.07. This is due to the problem of the chosen scale. It should be noted that Albrecht described the value 3 as the average on a scale of 0 to 5. This in itself is curious because it is not the median value. However, if the value 2.5 was chosen as the average value (which is not allowed) then the VAF = 1.

What is the average and best productivity rates in terms of FPCs per person month for a software development team?
Let us define productivity as:

$$\text{Productivity} = \frac{\text{FPC for the system}}{\text{effort to produce system}}$$

Then an average productivity rate for the software industry is between an FPC of 10 and an FPC of 20 per person month. A very good productivity rate is an FPC of 70 per person month. This has been achieved using a CASE environment and utilizing reusable code.

Having said this, it should be stressed that FPA should not be used to decide whether productivity is good or bad; rather it should be used to assess changes in productivity rates.

Can FPA be used to measure the productivity of an individual?
FPA is not suitable for measuring an individual's productivity. FPA should be used to measure the productivity of a team rather than an individual.

Is FPA a cost estimation tool?
FPA is not a cost estimation tool. It is a technique to measure the size of a software system from a description of the system (requirements specification, high level design, etc.). However, most cost models use system size as a parameter.

If an FPC is used as a size measure for input into a cost model which has similar adjustment factors to FPA, won't certain adjustments be made twice?
In theory, yes. Therefore, care needs to be taken to avoid this situation.

It has been said the FPA can be used to support estimating and assessing productivity. Does this create a conflict in the requirements of such a measure? Productivity requires a measure that is technology independent (at least language independent) while estimating requires a measure that is technology dependent.
This conflict has been resolved in the past by using technology-dependent multipliers, such as LOC per FPC, to convert from the more technology-independent 'user function' measures to the technology-dependent size or effort measures of the target system.

Can FPA be applied to help measure the effort needed for a particular phase of a project?
In general, no. However, if historical data is available, it should be possible to use the ratio method to measure the effort of a project phase. For example, a rule of thumb in software development is that effort for the three main activities design, code and test, and integration are usually in the ratio 20:50:30. This rule of thumb could be calibrated using historical data from 'similar' past projects.

Can FPA be used to size software deliverables, such as user's guides and maintenance manuals.
Empirical observations have discovered characteristic relationships between FPCs and software deliverables. For example:

$$\frac{\text{number of A4 pages of a maintenance manual}}{\text{FPC for the system}}$$

lies in the range [0.6, 1]. These types of relationships can be calculated by an organization using historical data.

Is there a relationship between the average number of pages of A4 documentation associated with a project and its FPC? Here documentation means all the associated documents such as requirements specification, design specifications, review reports, test reports, user manuals, etc., but excluding code listings.
A rule of thumb is to use the following equation:

$$\text{Number of A4 pages} = 20 \times \text{FPC}$$

Can FPA be used for sizing maintenance activities?
Yes, when the maintenance activity results in added functionality. However, considerable effort may go into software modifications that do not significantly alter the functionality of the system as perceived by the user. For example, performing preventive maintenance. In such cases FPA would not appear to be appropriate. A possible solution to this situation is to use maintenance data from historical operational systems having a similar FPC.

Can the formula:

$$\text{Defect density} = \frac{\text{number of defects}}{\text{FPC for the system}}$$

be used to compare the reliability of operational systems, where for instance the number of defects refers to the defects detected during the first six months of operational use?
The first thing to say is that the formula defines defect density. The second thing to say is that it is not the number of defects but the severity of defects that is important; that is their impact on the user. Some defects may cause a minor inconvenience to the user while others are classed as catastrophic by the user. Having said all this, the answer to the question is a guarded yes.

Is the probability of a software developer making a mistake independent of the FPC for a system? In other words is the defect density on larger projects greater than the defect density on smaller projects?
The first thing to say is that not all defects that are detected during operational use are due to the developers. For example, the defect may be due to ambiguous or conflicting requirements on the part of the user. Secondly, developers working on systems having a high FPC due to their 'complexity' (in terms of the way function types are categorized in FPA) are likely to make more mistakes than developers working on similar sized systems that are less 'complex'.

Can FPA be used to help choose a software package?
Yes. Get the vendor to supply a FPC for the package you are considering. This will give you a feel for the size and complexity of the system.

Can the coarse categorization of the complexity of function types into either low, average or high lead to an inappropriate weighting for very 'complex' function types.
This has been a criticism of Albrecht's FPA. Mark II FPA has tried to address this problem.

Were the choice of weights for the pairs (function type, complexity) derived objectively?
The choice of weights were derived empirically. Some people would say the choice of weights was determined subjectively from IBM experience and this has led some people to assert that they may be inappropriate elsewhere.

Should the weights be calibrated to particular organizations?
Theoretically the answer should be yes. However, to perform a calibration means that validation historical data from at least 30 projects needs to be collected or available (note that there are 15 choices: 5 function types each having a choice of 3 complexity ratings). For most organizations this data is not available. Remember also that changing the weights introduces problems when one wishes to compare productivity across organizations.

Besides measuring the size of a system, does FPA measure the 'complexity' of a system?
First, we need to define what we mean by 'complexity'. In qualitative terms 'complexity' is a comparative term. For example, suppose we have two distinct systems having the same FPC, implemented by the same development team in the same development environment, taking the same amount of time to develop, in the same programming language. Furthermore, suppose one system has twice as many lines of code as the other. Then intuitively we would say that the system with fewer lines of code was more complex.

The value adjustment factor (VAF) partially measures the complexity of a system, so in that sense you could say that FPA also partially measures the complexity of a system.

Does the VAF take into account the effect of different working methods, use of CASE tools, staff experience?
No. However, FPA used in productivity measures should demonstrate that projects that use modern development methodologies and CASE tools are more productive than projects developed using older technologies.

Can the VAF explain the difference in productivity between development teams?
In general, no. The VAF can only increase or decrease the unadjusted FPC by 35 per cent. The total absence or total presence of one of the 14 general system characteristics that go to make up the VAF makes only a very small percentage difference in the count. Furthermore, the VAF operates at a system level, not at the development environment.

Can FPA be applied to systems based on object-oriented analysis and design techniques?
The key point to remember is that object-oriented techniques are one mechanism by which the requirements for a system can be derived and the components of that system can be designed. While there is no formal mapping between the two approaches it is generally possible to apply FPA to object-oriented requirements specifications and designs.

Why is FPA not applied to 'real-time' environments?
The main concern is that, as FPA was specifically developed for data processing environments, the technique does not account for the complex processing of scientific algorithms usually associated with 'real-time' applications.

What type of systems can FPA be used on?

FPA is best suited to data processing systems, typically large file-based systems produced by banks, insurance companies and retail organizations. The technique was developed for use on transaction-oriented business application systems, either on-line or batch, which manipulate data stored in files or databases. In general it is not suitable for:

- Systems that primarily involve computing mathematical algorithms
- Embedded systems
- Operating systems
- Compilers
- Command and control systems.

Does the following relationship hold? Let S1 and S2 be two systems developed in the same language. Then:

$$FPC(S1) > FPC(S2) \text{ if and only if } LOC(S1) > LOC(S2)$$

In general, empirical evidence has supported this hypothesis. However, there are special cases where the relationship does not hold.

It would not be difficult to design two systems S1 and S2 having the same FPC and implemented in the same programming language and satisfying the following relationships:

- Each user function in S1 can be implemented in less than 20 LOC.
- Each user function in S2 requires more than 40 LOC.

Another example. Consider two systems S1 and S2 such that:

$$FPC(S1) = FPC(S2).$$

Furthermore, let S1 consist solely of 'low complexity' function types and S2 consist solely of 'high complexity' function types. Then the following relationship holds:

- S1 will have many more occurrences of function types than S2.

In such a situation it is not difficult to construct examples where the relationship $LOC(S1) > LOC(S2)$ holds.

Is it possible to relate FPCs to LOC, that is can you transform an FPC into LOC for a particular programming language?
Some work has been done in this area, most notably by Behrens (1983) and Jones (1985). They have independently produced tables that relate FPCs to LOC for certain programming languages. These tables can be used as a rough guide to checking an FPC when a development project is complete. At this point, the number of LOC will be known and using one of the conversion tables you can convert it into FPCs. However, Jones (1985) reports the accuracy as being in the range ±20 per cent. A sample from a Behrens table is:

Language	LOC per FPC
Assembler	320
C	150
Cobol	106
Fortran	106
PL/1	80

An FPC for a system is supposed to measure the 'functionality' of the system from the user viewpoint. If it is a well-defined measure then it needs to satisfy, among other things, the relation:

- *For two requirements specifications RS1 and RS2, if RS1 has more 'functionality' than RS2 then*

$$FPA(RS1) > FPA(RS2)$$

where FPA(RS) denotes an FPC.

The question is, does this relation hold?
Nobody has ever attempted to validate FPA in this way. On the other hand no one has identified a valid alternative functionality measure.

If you partition a system S into two subsystems S1 and S2 does the following relation hold:

$$FPA(S) = FPA(S1) + FPA(S2)$$

In general, no.

Are the function types of FPA that were defined by Albrecht in the late 1970s and early 1980s still appropriate to many of today's interactive data-centred business systems?
The glib answer is, 'Show me a better method'. Albrecht's view was that FPA should be an evolutionary technique. It is hoped that FPA will evolve to address this type of criticism. For the present, where difficulties arise, FPCs may need to be adjusted to take account of systems having such characteristics. One way would be to use historical data from similar systems.

When should an FPC be undertaken?
There is no one answer. When FPA is used for estimating purposes it can be used when the feasibility study has been completed or when the requirements specification is complete.

Does an FPC take into account the level and quality of the support documentation (user manuals, etc.) that needs to be produced for a system?
Albrecht's FPA does not take this into account.

What is the maximum variation between an unadjusted FPC and an adjusted FPC?
±35 per cent.

What is the maximum variation between weighting every occurrence of all the function types as Low and at the other extreme weighting every occurrence of all the function types as High?
Approximately 100 per cent.

Is a spreadsheet suitable for assisting an organization in performing an FPC?
Yes.

Can FPA be automated?
This question usually stems from experience with sizing a system using LOC. In new development environments, calculating the LOC automatically is a trivial task. It is interesting to note that there has been much less success in automating LOC in the maintenance environments where LOC are added, deleted and changed. It can be done but the algorithm is more complex.

For FPA, provided that designs, and eventually requirements, are held electronically and in formats amenable to analysis, there is no reason why major elements of FPA should not be automated. If you look at a tool such as TEAMWORK and the SASD notation it uses, you will realize that most of the information necessary for the function type analysis part of FPA is present. It is only a question of setting up the necessary routines with the TEAMWORK library.

SUMMARY

You will face problems as you implement FPA within the organization. Face these problems pragmatically and with the view that problems are there to be solved and you will soon establish FPA as a beneficial technique.

The main points to remember about FPA are:

- An FPC is a measure of system size, it is not a measure of effort.
- Albrecht's version of FPA is suitable for transaction-based systems, and, in general, it is not suitable for systems where most of the time the system is busy processing mathematical algorithms.
- When calculating an FPC determine the functionality of the system being sized from the user's viewpoint.
- Consistency is the key word in performing an FPC.
- Albrecht has always stated that FPA is an evolutionary technique. It is not, nor should it, be seen as cast in stone.

Appendix D

SEI CAPABILITY MATURITY MODEL

In this appendix we provide an overview of the Capability Maturity Model (CMM) developed by the Software Engineering Institute (SEI) of Carnegie Mellon University by answering the following questions:

- What is it?
- What is the detailed structure of the model?
- How does it work?
- What is the output from an assessment?
- What are the basic principles?
- What are its strengths and weaknesses?
- What is its relationship to process benchmarking?

Before answering these questions we will start by providing some background information.

BACKGROUND

Up to the mid-1980s The US Department of Defense selection process for choosing defence contractors emphasized price and timescales as the critical factors. Because this approach produced unsatisfactory results, the US Air Force sought an orderly and public method that it could use to identify the most capable software contractors. In 1986 the US Air Force sponsored the SEI of Carnegie Mellon University of Pittsburgh to set up a Software Capability Evaluation project.

Another project initiated at the SEI around this time was concerned with process assessment. This focused on helping contractors to improve their capabilities and was based on work done at IBM.

Thus the two projects can be seen to complement each other. In fact, it could be argued that evaluating the capability of a contractor only has a very limited value. What was needed was something that would raise the standards of all defence contractors to meet the needs of the US Department of Defense.

The work at the SEI was driven by Humphrey and his co-workers. A major output of their work is the CMM, which we will now discuss.

WHAT IS IT?

The SEI CMM can be thought of as a tool to help:

- Identify weaknesses and strengths in a software development process
- Support process improvement initiatives
- Procurers evaluate the capability of software vendors.

The SEI CMM (Fig. D.1) is a five-level model which can be used to describe the effectiveness of a software development process:

Level 1   This is known as the initial process level and represents a process that is unstable and disorganized, in terms of both quality assurance and development practices. For example, change control is lax, and there is little senior management exposure or understanding of the problems. They may have quality manuals but they usually remain unopened.

Level 2   This is known as the repeatable process level and represents a stable process with a repeatable level of statistical control by initiating rigorous control of costs, timescales and changes. A company at the repeatable level is characterized by

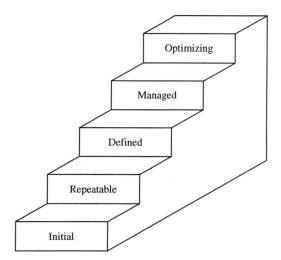

Figure D.1   The five levels of the SEI CMM model.

projects that produce plans which are usually adhered to until a spanner is thrown into the works when a customer requests a major change to the requirements midway through a project.

Level 3   This is known as the defined process level and represents a process that has been defined to help ensure a consistent implementation and acts as a basis for continuing progress. For example, a project team faced with a crisis will continue to use the defined process.

Level 4   This is known as the managed process level and represents a process that gathers process data to understand, control and improve each process. In other words it uses measurement to quantify the quality of its work.

Level 5   This is known as the optimizing process level and represents a process where measurement is an integral part of the process and is used to continually improve and optimize the process. Much of the measurement data will be collected automatically.

In general, these levels are popular because they:

- Reasonably represent the actual historical phases of evolutionary improvement of many organizations
- Suggest interim improvement goals and progress measures
- Make obvious a set of immediate improvement priorities, once an organization's status in this framework is known.

In general, the levels represent the steps an organization needs to go through as it improves quality practices with the goal of becoming the best of the best. An organization cannot miss out a step as each step builds on the previous steps. In other words a company cannot move onto the next level until it has addressed and controlled the problems of the lower levels. This mistake is often made by companies who have good intentions about improving their development process but go about it the wrong way and end up demotivating people; for example, collecting data without having first defined what you want to use the data for and collecting sophisticated data about an *ad hoc* development process.

WHAT IS THE DETAILED STRUCTURE OF THE MODEL?

As we have said the SEI CMM consists of five levels. Each level of the CMM is divided into a set of *key process areas* (Fig. D.2) which identify the goals that must be reached before an organization can say it has achieved a certain level.

Each key process area is then refined into *key practices* (343 in total) which are the procedures and activities that most contribute to achieving the goals of the key process areas. The key practices are evidence that the goals have been attained. Finally, each key practice has one or more *key indicators* which help to determine whether the goals have been satisfied.

Level	Key process areas
5 Optimizing	Defect prevention
	Process improvement
4 Managed	Quality management
	Process measurement and analysis
3 Defined	Training programme
	Interfaces
	Requirements analysis
	Design
	Test
	Peer reviews
2 Repeatable	Subcontract management
	Quality assurance
	Configuration management
	Project planning
	Project management

Figure D.2 Key process areas for SEI CMM.

Key indicators then form the basis of the SEI questionnaire (Fig. D.3), which is used to help certified assessment teams trained by the SEI to either perform process assessments or evaluate a contractor's capability. There are approximately 120 questions (40 for Level 2, 40 for Level 3, 20 for Level 4 and 20 for Level 5). The questionnaire when used in process

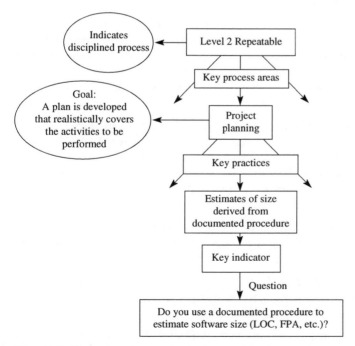

Figure D.3 Derivation of a question in the questionnaire.

assessment will indicate what an organization should focus on to improve its software process in order to move to the next level.

HOW DOES IT WORK?

There are three components to using the CMM:

- The model itself
- A questionnaire to help assessment teams perform process assessment or to evaluate a contractor's capability
- Assessment teams.

We now discuss the steps in using the CMM for process assessments and capability evaluations:

Step 1   Select the assessment team. It should be appreciated that all comparisons require consistency in the interpretation of the questions and the resulting evaluations. This is emphasized by the SEI who require that trained teams are necessary to undertake or monitor the initial results before these are used as a result of applying their method.

Step 2   Obtain answers to the questionnaire and analyse the answers to estimate the maturity level which is calculated as follows:

Level 2   Determine the percentage of affirmative answers for the project to all Level 2 questions and to the critical success factor (CSF) questions for Level 2. If the percentage of affirmative answers to all questions is at least 80 per cent and the percentage of affirmative answers to CSF questions is at least 90 per cent, the project has qualified at Level 2; otherwise, it is at Level 1. If Level 2 is achieved, go on to the next step.

Level 3   Determine the percentage of affirmative answers to all Level 2 and 3 questions combined and to the CSF questions for Level 2 and 3 combined. Again, if the percentage of affirmative answers to all questions is at least 80 per cent and the percentage of affirmative answers to CSF questions is at least 90 per cent, the project qualifies at Level 3; otherwise, it is at Level 2.

Level 4   If the project qualifies at Level 3, this procedure is repeated, combining Level 2, 3 and 4 answers, again requiring 80 per cent for all questions and 90 per cent CSF questions.

Level 5   If the project qualifies at Level 4, the evaluation for Level 5 combines Level 2, 3, 4 and 5 answers, again using 80 per cent and 90 per cent as the criteria.

From the above calculations, a position relative to Levels 1–5 can be estimated for each project.

Step 3   Conduct an on-site visit.

Step 4   Produce a key process area profile.

WHAT IS THE OUTPUT FROM AN ASSESSMENT?

The output from an assessment is a key process area profile detailing the strengths and weaknesses of an organisation in relation to the key process areas. The key process area profile rates each key process area on a three-point scale as:

- Fully satisfied
- Partially satisfied
- Not satisfied.

An organization's maturity level is set at the highest level at which it satisfies all key process areas on a continuing basis.

WHAT ARE THE BASIC PRINCIPLES?

The SEI CMM is based on the principles originally put forward by Shewart (1939) at the Bell Telephone Laboratories in the 1930s, and further championed by Edwards Deming (1986) and Juran in their process improvement work in Japan and the USA from the late 1940s onwards. It is also based on the more recent work of Crosby (1984).

The basic principles of the SEI CMM are:

- Capability is increased and risks are reduced through the increased understanding, definition and standardization of processes.
- Process improvement is not based solely on what changes you introduce but also on the sequence in which you perform the changes.
- Save costs and improve the quality of your products by preventing problems, not just reacting to them. For example:
  - using historical data to predict effort and timescales of projects
  - using defect analysis to help prevent defects occurring.

WHAT ARE ITS STRENGTHS AND WEAKNESSES?

The main strengths of the SEI CMM are:

- It is based on quality principles that have been widely proven in both engineering and manufacturing and are now being demonstrated as equally effective for software.
- It uses widely recognized and proven statistical techniques.
- Key indicators have been identified to measure the effectiveness of key process areas. Final selection of these indicators will be based on their empirical performance determined during pilot testing, through assessments and evaluations and through

extensive reviews with industry and government working groups.

- It provides a coherent path that a company can follow in its quest to become the best.
- It can be used to assess projects, departments or whole organizations.
- It is applicable for process assessment, capability evaluation and in process monitoring.
- It is in the public domain.
- It is backed up by a considerable experience of use.
- It has credibility from its sponsorship by the US Department of Defense, the largest software procurer in the world.
- It is internationally recognized.
- It continues to be evolved by the Software Engineering Institute of Carnegie Mellon University.
- It is used as a basis for business process improvement purposes and is in wide use, often in amended form, by procurers and software engineering organizations internationally.

The main weaknesses of the SEI CMM are:

- It is based on a synthetic benchmark because at the time of its inception in 1987 it was not known whether there were any organisations at Level 4 or 5. However, due to its evolutionary nature this weakness is being eradicated.
- It does not provide quantifiable measures that a company should attain when it is at a certain level. For example, it would be very helpful for a company to know:
  - what the accuracy of their estimates of effort and timescales should be when they are at a certain level
  - what their defect density of their systems should be during operational use when they are at a particular level.
- It focuses only on good practices. A highly bureaucratic organization may be very high on the SEI CMM but might perform poorly because of inefficiency and slow communication.
- Its origin and focus on large-scale software developments make it of limited use for small organizations.
- Terminology and lifecycle concepts are biased towards the US Department of Defense.
- The level of subjectivity, which is being addressed by improving the questionnaire and providing training programmes for the assessors.
- It provides too coarse an evaluation.
- Its process coverage is deficient in some areas compared with ISO 9001, particularly with respect to:
  - evaluating maintenance and service support activities
  - delivery and installation.
- It is an expensive process to apply (Humphrey, 1989), but on the other hand the benefits far outweigh the costs.

WHAT IS ITS RELATIONSHIP TO PROCESS BENCHMARKING?

We now address the issue of determining the fundamental difference between using the SEI CMM and process benchmarking to support process improvement. First, we need to clarify the terminology. Associated to using process benchmarking as a tool for process improvement is a set of critical success factors and associated to the SEI CMM is a set of key process areas. The concepts underlying critical success factors and key process areas are essentially the same.

The key differences are that:

- When using process benchmarking as a vehicle for process improvement, the critical success factors are not fixed, but are generated from the business objectives.
- When using the SEI CMM as a vehicle for process improvement, the key process areas are predefined.

This raises the question as to whether there are any critical success factors that are not covered by the key process areas. The answer is yes; for example, delivery and installation.

It should be noted that the SEI CMM can be used to help prioritize the critical success factors. For example, suppose three critical success factors have been identified. Then if these factors map onto the key process areas or key practices then it may be possible to use the priority rating imposed by the five levels of the SEI CMM to impose a priority on the factors. For example, a factor mapped onto to a lower level than another factor will take priority, because according to the SEI CMM you cannot progress from a lower level to a higher level until you have addressed the problems of the lower level.

GENERAL QUESTIONS ON THE SEI CMM

To conclude our discussion of the SEI CMM we answer some general questions:

Does an assessment cover the whole organization?
No, an assessment covers a project, a set of projects or a site.

What is the role of the questionnaire?
It is only the starting point for gathering information. The primary concern is whether an organization obtains the goals for a given maturity level. The questionnaire samples the key process areas for each level of the SEI CMM and identifies those areas that require further investigation. It is the starting point for the assessment team when they visit the company and provides guidance for them to focus on the initial maturity level estimated from the analysis of the questionnaire.

Are questionnaire scores used to evaluate a contractor?
There is a common misconception that questionnaire scores alone are used to evaluate the capability of a software developer. This is not the case. The questionnaire is used as a framework for evaluation, but the evaluators are trained to assess an organization's strengths and weaknesses in a number of key areas, including:

- Project planning
- Project management
- Configuration management
- Quality assurance
- Standards and procedures

- Training
- Process focus
- Peer reviews and testing.

These strengths and weaknesses are then used to determine the risks associated with awarding a contract to a vendor. These risks are then considered in conjunction with other factors such as price and the proposed personnel.

Does an SEI CMM assessment provide a numerical score?
The original SEI model was associated with giving a numerical score between 1 and 5 when it was used to assess a software development process or evaluate a software contractor. The 1991 version of the model tries to play down the use of numbers in assessments and evaluations and provides a key process area profile instead.

Does a high rating guarantee quality products?
Attaining a higher level on the SEI CMM is a necessary but not a sufficient condition for achieving the goal of producing 'high quality' software products more efficiently than your competitors.

Are non-SEI assessments accurate?
The SEI would prefer that the team conducting the assessment has been trained by the SEI. But the demand for assessment has outstripped SEI's resources. Therefore, the SEI has licensed several organizations to train the trainers so that these people can assist companies in conducting self-assessments. A self-assessment shows an organization how to improve to the level it desires. The accuracy of the assessment depends very much on following the SEI's extensively tested assessment process.

Does the SEI CMM assess an organization's application expertise and use of technology?
No.

Does the SEI CMM assess an organization's ability to motivate and retain staff?
No, but this may be part of a later version.

How does a capability evaluation differ from a process assessment?
The two differ in:

- Purpose
- Motivation
- Objective
- Ownership of results
- Interview techniques
- Scope of inquiry
- Formulation of outcome
- Training of assessment teams.

Could a vendor customize their evaluation responses to achieve an artificially high rating?

This concern results from a misconception that the questionnaire is the sole vehicle for evaluating the capability of a vendor. The SEI's experience demonstrates that the SEI's method makes this strategy impractical. When trained evaluators look for evidence of process practices based on well-defined engineering principles, they have no difficulty identifying organizations with poor software capability. Well-run software projects leave a clear document trail that less competent organizations are incapable of emulating. For example, an organization that manages software change control has change review procedures, formal approval forms and documented minutes. In other words an audit trail. Organizations that do not do this are incapable of pretending that they have.

How do organizations measure up when assessed?
The SEI has produced a state-of-the-practice report concerning assessments carried out by the SEI up to April 1991. The data was derived from 59 assessments on 27 sites and 296 projects and revealed that:

- 81 per cent of the sites are at Level 1
- 12 per cent of the sites are at Level 2
- 7 per cent of the sites are at Level 3
- 88 per cent of the projects are at Level 1
- 5 per cent of the projects are at Level 2
- 5 per cent of the projects are at Level 3
- 2 per cent of the projects are at Level 5.

Is the level of an organization determined by averaging projects evaluated?
While the SEI's CMM method determines the level for the organization as a whole by averaging the levels of the projects evaluated, many practitioners do not consider that a true picture can be obtained by simple aggregation of project-centred analysis. To achieve an understanding of these wider processes, success factors identified as organization-wide are selected as representing this wider picture. Such factors as those related to training, human resources and the environment are used and have found wide acceptance.

Appendix E

DATA COLLECTION FORMS

In this appendix we provide the following data collection forms to support the Measurement Programme described in Section 1, namely:

- Defect Data Form for a Review
- Summary Defect Data Form for Testing
- Individual Defect Data Form for Testing
- Summary Defect Data Form for Operational Failures
- Individual Defect Data Form for Operational Failures
- Reasons for Variations Between Estimates and Actuals
- Reasons for Variations Between Baseline and Actual Productivity.

Defect Data Form For A Review

Name of person completing the form		Project name	Date
Name of document being reviewed			

Type of review	Inspection	Walkthrough	Other (please specify)
Defects found			
Defects corrected			
Defects introduced in analysis			
Defects introduced in design			
Defects introduced in code and unit test			
Not known where defect introduced			
Defects introduced due to bad fixes			

Guidelines for completion

It is mandatory for the form to be completed.

It is the responsibility of the moderator of the review to get the form completed.

Each item of data to be recorded should be an integer.

The form should be completed once the review has finished and the actions from the review completed.

On completion of the form, it should be returned to the measurement team.

Summary Defect Data Form For Testing

Name of person completing the form		Project name	Date
	System test	User acceptance test	Regression test
Defects found			
Defects corrected			
Defects introduced in analysis			
Defects introduced in design			
Defects introduced in code and unit test			
Defects introduced during testing			
Not known where defect introduced			
Defects introduced due to bad fixes			

Guidelines for completion

It is mandatory for the form to be completed.

It is the responsibility of the project leader to get the form completed, who may delegate this responsibility.

Each item of data to be recorded should be an integer.

The form should be completed within one month of the finish of testing.

On completion of the form, it should be returned to the measurement team.

Individual Defect Data Form For Testing

Purpose	
The purpose of this data form is to record information relating to a defect found during testing (System testing, User acceptance testing and Regression testing).	
Name of person completing the form	Date
Project name	Defect reference number

What activity detected the defect?

System test ☐   Acceptance test ☐   Regression test ☐

Was the defect corrected?   Yes ☐   No ☐

In which phase of development was the defect introduced?

Analysis ☐   Design ☐   Code and Unit test ☐   Testing ☐   Don't know ☐

Was the cause of the defect due to correcting another defect?

Yes ☐   No ☐   Don't know ☐

Guidelines for completion

It is not mandatory for the form to be completed. The form can be used to support the project leader gathering the data to complete the form entitled *Summary Defect Data Form For Testing*.

If the form is used, it is the responsibility of the project leader to get the form completed, who may delegate this responsibility.

If the form is used then it should be completed when the defect is corrected and signed off.

The form is internal to the project and does not need to be returned to the measurement team.

Summary Defect Data Form For Operational Failures

Name of person completing the form						Project name	Date
How often is the system run?							
Daily	Weekly	4 weekly	Monthly	Quarterly	6 monthly	Yearly	On request
Has the system run during the period covered by this form?						Yes	No

	First two months in production
Defects found	
Defects corrected	
Defects introduced in analysis	
Defects introduced in design	
Defects introduced in code and unit test	
Defects introduced during testing	
Not known where defect introduced	
Defects that caused a system crash	
Defects introduced due to bad fixes	

Guidelines for completion

It is mandatory for the form to be completed.

It is the responsibility of the corrective maintenance team to get the form completed.

Each item of data to be recorded should be an integer.

The form should be completed after two months of operational use.

On completion of the form, it should be returned to the measurement team.

Individual Defect Data Form For Operational Failures

Purpose			
The purpose of this data form is to record information relating to a defect found during operational use.			

	Date
Name of person completing the form	

Project name	Defect reference number

Was the defect corrected?				
Yes	No			

In which phase of development was the defect introduced?				
Analysis	Design	Code and unit test	Testing	Don't know

Did the defect cause a system crash?				
Yes	No			

Was the cause of the defect due to correcting another defect?				
Yes	No	Don't know		

Guidelines for completion

It is not mandatory for the form to be completed. The form can be used to support the project leader in gathering the data to complete the form entitled *Summary Defect Data Form For Operational Failures*.

If the form is used, it is the responsibility of the project leader to get the form completed, who may delegate this responsibility.

If the form is used then it should be completed when the defect is corrected and signed off.

The form is internal to the project and does not need to be returned to the measurement team.

Reasons For Variations Between Estimates and Actuals

Purpose		
The purpose of this data form is to record the reasons for a variation of more than 15% between the estimated effort and actual effort for a project.		

Name of the person completing the form	Date	
Project name		

Was the estimate above or below the actual effort?	Above	Below

What were the reasons for the variation? Please mark the appropriate boxes with a + or − to signify a positive or negative effect on the variation.

Project timescales		Miscalculation of risks	
Productivity rate of project team		Novelty of project	
Amount of rework		Size of project team	
Estimated size of project (FPC)		Experience of project team	
Complexity of project		Experience of project manager	
Time spent system testing		Use of new methods/tools	
Premature loss of key staff		Strategic/political decisions	
Misunderstanding of requirements		Experience of estimator	
Unplanned changes to requirements		Incorrect formula/assumptions	
Others (please specify)		Don't know	

Guidelines for completion

It is the responsibility of the project manager to get the form completed.

The form should be completed within one week of the project being completed.

On completion the form should be returned to the measurement team.

Reasons For Variations Between Baseline and Actual Productivity

Purpose			
The purpose of this data form is to record the reasons for a variation of more than 15% between the productivity achieved by a project and its baseline productivity.			
Name of person completing the form		Date	
Project name			
Was the productivity above or below the baseline?	Above	Below	
What were the reasons for the variation? Please mark the appropriate boxes with a + or − to signify a positive or negative effect on productivity.			

Project timescales		Novelty of project	
Amount of rework		Size of project team	
Size of project (FPC)		Experience of project team	
Complexity of project		Experience of project manager	
Development process		Premature loss of key staff	
Time spent system testing		Use of new methods/tools	
Time spent on analysis and design		Structure of project team	
Unplanned changes to requirements		Don't know	
Others (please specify)			

Guidelines for completion

The form should be completed if there is a variation of more than 15% between the productivity achieved by the project and its associated baseline productivity.

It is the responsibility of the project manager to get the form completed.

The form should be completed within one week of when the project manager is informed of the productivity.

On completion the form should be returned to the measurement team.

Appendix F

YOUR QUESTIONS ANSWERED

In this appendix we provide answers to typical questions that are likely to be asked by a team tasked with setting up and running a Measurement Programme.

EFFECTIVENESS OF REVIEWS

What measures can be used to help identify improvements to the review process?
Reviews should be monitored to determine their cost effectiveness. Typical measures to support the goal of improving the effectiveness of a review are as follows:

- Preparation time
- Size of product being reviewed
- Duration of review
- Cost of review
- Number of attendees at review
- Skill of reviewers
- Skill of moderator
- Number of issues raised
- Number of issues that would have resulted in a defect
- Major issues versus minor issues
- Number of issues open over time.

One way to improve the effectiveness of reviews is to determine the optimal number of people who should attend.

To help ensure reviews are productive, reviewers should be made to feel that the work is worthwhile. One way to do this is to provide them with feedback on the results, such as

Number of inspections	27
Effort spent on inspections	290
Number of issues raised	840
Number of issues which were defects	456
Average effort in hours to detect a defect during an inspection	0.6
Average effort in hours to find and fix in testing	8.1

Figure F.1   Example data relating to inspections.

quantifying the money saved by conducting reviews. Figure F.1 provides an example of the way feedback could be given to the reviewers on inspections.

PROGRESS MONITORING

What is the RAG technique?
The RAG (red–amber–green) technique is a very simple and effective way to present senior management with a status report on the progress of projects. Each project is assigned one of three colours (green, amber or red) where:

- Green means the project is on budget, to schedule and will meet its requirements
- Amber means the project is experiencing some problems and plans have been implemented or are being drawn up to rectify the problems
- Red means major action required.

Each month project managers are required to answer a set of questions regarding the progress of their project. For example:

- What percentage of the requirements will be met?
- What percentage of milestones due have been achieved?

The answers are then used to assign the project a colour.

To be successful, the RAG approach needs to be operated in conjunction with a culture that encourages project managers and their staff to report problems early on.

The RAG approach can be enhanced in the following way. First, expand the three categories budget, schedule and requirements against which progress is monitored. Then for each category classify it as:

- Critical
- Unsatisfactory
- Satisfactory
- Excellent.

Checklists should be developed to support this classification. Finally, each category should be further classified as stable, getting better or getting worse.

TASK ALLOCATION

When recording effort is there a problem with apportioning time to the various phases of development?
When collecting data relating to effort spent on various development activities, it can be difficult apportioning time. Sometimes it is not clear where one activity ends and another activity starts. For example, it is not always easy to determine where development ends and corrective maintenance begins. It may be the case that during the implementation of a change, an inherent defect was found in a module. This creates the problem of where to allocate the time spent on its correction. Another example is where to book the effort spent attending meetings (design reviews, progress meetings, etc.).

To minimize the risk of incorrectly allocating time to a task, the following should be done. First, have a well-defined work breakdown structure which is used consistently by the whole IS department. Secondly, educate staff on the importance of recording their time to particular activities.

HISTORICAL DATA

What are the problems associated with using historical data?
Some organizations have historical data which has not been collected with a particular purpose in mind; for example, the collection of defect data without any goals of how the data is going to be used. Historical data can be hazardous if the data:

- Has not been validated
- Is used for a different purpose than originally planned
- Uses non-standard measures (for example, 8.5 hours for a working day).

The solution is to record:

- Why the data was collected
- Who collected it
- How it was collected
- How it was validated
- Where it was collected from
- When it was collected
- Etc.

DATA COMPARISON

What are the dangers of using data to compare the performance of project teams?
It can be difficult comparing data. For example, it may be the case that one project required less effort to implement than another similar project because of the difference in the experience and skills of the development teams.

Also, it is dangerous and can be misleading to compare productivity and effort data with other companies and against industrial norms without knowing the definitions used and rules for collection. The percentage of time spent in each development phase is also difficult to compare unless it is known what activities are included in each phase. Furthermore, projects using a prototype approach to development usually find it difficult to distinguish between design and implementation.

The solution is to try to normalize the attributes of a project that affect what is trying to be compared.

SUBJECTIVE DATA

Should we be collecting subjective data?
In the long term, requests for subjective data shall be avoided wherever possible. However, where validated historical data is unavailable, it may be necessary to use subjective data.

Where subjective data is requested, it should be categorised into ideally three categories but never more than five categories. For example, estimators should use one of the following three categories to estimate the chance of underestimating the effort needed to implement a software system due to the novelty of the work as:

- Very likely
- Likely
- Unlikely.

The subjectivity of choosing a category can be minimized by providing checklists to help determine the most appropriate category.

UNPAID OVERTIME

Should we record the effort of staff who work unpaid overtime?
Many staff work unpaid overtime. This may create a dilemma for management who realize that if they start recording all the hours their staff work then they may have to start paying them for the overtime they do.

The solution is to try to produce realistic plans based on quantifiable information, so that staff are not required to work overtime to meet unrealistic schedules. Sadly, life is never that simple. Where staff work overtime, this effort needs to be recorded to provide an accurate picture of how long a task took. Otherwise estimates based on historical data will be inaccurate.

DATA ANALYSIS

What should be done with outliers?
Whether outliers are included in the data set or not, all outliers should be investigated to determine their cause.

PRODUCTIVITY

How do we deal with the variations in staff productivity?
It is not uncommon to find variations in the productivity of individual developers to be in the ratio of 4:1. The reasons for this are many and varied; for example, the differences in the experience of individuals, the level of tool support, etc.

   Experiments have shown that the differences cancel each other out for project teams of seven or more people.

QUALITY OF ESTIMATION PROCESS

How can we assess the accuracy of our estimation process when all the projects that have been estimated by the process will not be completed for at least one year?
If historical data is not available, one possible way to assess the accuracy of an estimation process is to use it to estimate the effort of projects that have already been completed, then compare estimates with the actual values.

USE OF EXPERT ESTIMATOR

Who should perform the estimates?
There are three main choices, namely:

- Allow projects to perform their own estimates
- Appoint a principal estimator who will be responsible for advising projects and auditing their estimates
- Set up an estimation group who will be responsible for producing all the estimates, collecting data on estimating and improving the estimation process.

Using a principal estimator or estimation group will help to ensure that estimators will improve their skills at estimating.

DATA COLLECTION

Is accuracy the most important aspect of data collection?
Consistency, accuracy and validation are the key elements in data collection. However, in the short term consistency is more important than trying to attain one hundred per cent accuracy. In the long term as project teams become more experienced at data collection the accuracy should improve.

How can we ensure that data will be provided by the project teams?
Draw up a schedule of when projects should be providing data based on their project plans, so that you know what data should be provided during the year; for example, when projects should be producing estimates, defect data relating to system testing, etc. Then, if this data is not provided, investigate the reasons why.

TESTING

How can measurement help in testing?
It is always possible to conduct more testing. Measurement provides the data that is necessary to understand the costs and benefits of performing tests. For example, part of the strategy for the NASA Space Shuttle software involves using measurement to identify the most defect-prone modules and allocating more effort to test these modules. Another example is where measurement shows that the defect detection rate is increasing during testing. In such a case, the product should not be released to the customer.

When testing the code, should targets be set for the number of defects to be detected?
This could be dangerous. What do you do in the case where your tests discover very few defects? Does this imply that the code is highly reliable or does it suggest that the tests were poor in the sense that they did not adequately exercise the code? If you have set a target for the number of defects to be removed during testing, it needs to be qualified by the number and quality of the tests it took to detect the defects. If it took only a small amount of testing to uncover the defects then this may indicate 'poor' reliability. A measure relating to system testing is the percentage of system tests that were successfully executed (did not detect a defect). However, this measure must be viewed in relation to the quality of the test scripts.

Targets should be set to indicate when system testing should be abandoned. That is when the defect-detection rate exceeds a threshold value.

MAINTENANCE

What is RECUP?
RECUP stands for: Repair, Enhancement, Conversion, User support, Prevention.

Maintenance effort should be broken down into RECUP categories to help provide an indication of where there may be a problem. For example, if a significant portion of time is expended in user support, the time spent in improving user support facilities (documentation, on-line help facilities, etc.) should result in less demand for support and hence improved maintenance productivity.

REACTION OF PROJECT TEAMS TO MEASUREMENT

Will project teams react badly to being measured?
Not if the objectives of the Measurement Programme are explained to the project teams and it is explained to them that management have been trained in what they can and cannot do with the data. Project teams do have a fear of being judged against arbitrary measures, such as unrealistic schedules; for example, underbidding the competition by promising to meet unrealistic timescales at a cost that is based on fantasy rather than fact.

MEASURING INDIVIDUALS

Should individuals be measured?
Your objective should be to measure processes to identify areas for improvement. It should not be to measure individuals to determine whether they are to blame for the low productivity being achieved on a project. Measuring processes will involve collecting data on individuals, such as duration and effort spent on a task. However, this data should not be used against individuals. For example, defect data should not be used to target individuals. Good managers do not need measurement to know which of their staff are good and which of their staff need additional training. Measurement should be used to assess the impact of training programmes.

The following story illustrates the negative impact measuring individuals can have. It was told by a presenter at the Applications of Software Measurement annual conference held in Orlando in November 1993. Sadly, it shows what can happen when an organization goes about introducing a Measurement Programme in the wrong way.

A presenter at the conference was explaining how her company had 'successfully' implemented a Measurement Programme and told the following story of how it had been accepted and supported by even the most reluctant staff. The presenter explained there was one particular software maintenance engineer who was cynical and uncooperative towards the Measurement Programme. One day this maintenance engineer overheard two managers talking about his performance in the corridor. He heard one manger say to the other that his productivity was very low. (We were never told how this productivity was measured.) The maintenance engineer went away and thought about this. He then realized that his productivity was low because he was booking all his time to corrective maintenance, whereas in fact he was doing many other things, such as preventive maintenance (re-engineering old code, etc.). From then on the maintenance engineer booked his time to all the activities he undertook and this was reflected in an immediate increase in his productivity. The presenter then went on to say how the maintenance engineer became supportive of the Measurement Programme through this episode.

This story sadly illustrates three fundamental mistakes. First, not explaining the purpose of the Measurement Programme to the staff. Secondly, using data to measure individuals. Thirdly, not training people to collect data properly and not training managers on what they can and cannot do with the data. For example, not talking about an individual's performance in a corridor.

MISUSE OF DATA

How do you stop data being misused?
The best way to stop data being misused is by training. Do not collect data to try and confirm incorrect beliefs. Staff need to be trained to evaluate the data collected and when it is in conflict with their beliefs, to investigate the reasons why.

Do not fall into the trap of jumping to the wrong conclusions by collecting too little data or ignoring certain data values simply because they do not fit in with your intuitive beliefs. This is nicely illustrated by the joke mathematicians like telling about physicists:

A physicist's proof that all integers divide 72 goes like this. One divides 72, two divides 72, three divides 72. Hey, this is looking good, let's jump a couple of numbers. Six divides

72, seven is an experimental error, eight divides 72, nine divides 72. Therefore we can conclude that all numbers divide 72.

ROUNDING ERRORS

How should we avoid rounding errors?
To help to reduce errors caused by stating measures in fractions of their associated units, measures should, in general, be requested in whole numbers. Where necessary, numbers should be rounded to the nearest whole number using the following formula:

- Rounded down if the fraction is greater than zero and less than half
- Rounded up if the fraction is greater than or equal to half.

For example, the lowest unit of effort for a particular task should be recorded in hours using whole numbers and not using decimal points. Effort should not be stated as 6.3 hours but as 6 hours.

GENERAL

What is the Baldridge award?
The Baldridge award is a national quality award for US companies. It was established to achieve two primary objectives, namely:

- To raise the consciousness of US business leaders regarding the issue of quality
- To provide a framework for measuring the quality efforts undertaken by US businesses.

What is the difference between assessment and evaluation?
Assessment in the UK means using a formal process to perform an assessment. Assessment in the USA means using an informal process to perform an assessment.

Evaluation in the UK means using an informal process. Evaluation in the USA means using a formal process.

Are published industry statistics useful?
Care needs to be taken when using industry statistics. In general, they are not broken down across industries.

BIBLIOGRAPHY

Albrecht, A. J. (1979) 'Measuring Application Development Productivity' in *Proceedings Joint SHARE/GUIDE/ IBM Application Development Symposium*.

Amory, W. and Clapp, J. A. (1973) *A Software Error Classification Methodology*, MTR-2648, Volume VII, Mitre Corporation, Bedford, MA.

Ashley, N. (1989) *Classification System For Software Defects*, Technical Report For European Space Agency.

Ashley, N. *Principles of Function Point Analysis — METKIT Module*, BRAMEUR Ltd, Aldershot, UK.

Ashley, N. (1993) 'Introduction to METKIT', *Information And Software Technology*, **35** (2), February 1993.

Ashley, N. and Bush, M. (1993) *METKIT: Toolkit For Metrics Education*, IEEE Software, Piscataway, NJ.

Basili, V. and Rombach, D. (1988) The TAME Project: Towards Improvement-Oriented Software Environments', *IEEE Transactions On Software Engineering*, **14**.

Basili, V. and Selby, R. (1987) 'Comparing The Effectiveness Of Software Testing Strategies', *IEEE Transactions On Software Engineering*, **SE-13** (12).

Behrens, C. (1983) 'Measuring The Productivity Of Computer System Development Activities With Function Points', *IEEE Transactions On Software Engineering*, November 1983, 648–52.

Boehm, B. (1981) *Software Engineering Economics*, Prentice-Hall, Englewood Cliffs, NJ.

Bowen, J. (1980) *Standard Error Classification To Support Software Reliability Assessment*, National Computer Conference, USA.

British Deming Association (1989) *Profound Knowledge*, SPC Press, UK.

Collofello, J. and Balcom, B. (1985) *A Proposed Causative Software Error Classification Scheme*, National Computer Conference, USA.

Crosby, P. (1984) *Quality Without Tears*, Plume, USA.

Crosby, P. (1986) *Quality Is Free*, McGraw-Hill, New York, USA.

Currit, A., Dyer, M. and Mills, H. D. (1986) 'Certifying The Reliability Of Software', *IEEE Transactions On Software Engineering*, **SE-12** (1), January 1986.

DeMarco, T. (1982) *Controlling Software Projects*, Yourdon Press, USA.

Devore, J. and Peck, R. (1986) *Statistics — The Exploitation and Analysis Of Data*, West Publishing Company, USA.

Dreger, B. (1989) *Function Point Analysis*, Prentice-Hall, Englewood Cliffs, NJ.

Edwards Deming, W. (1986) *Out Of The Crisis*, Cambridge University Press, Cambridge, MA.

Fenton, N. E. (1991) *Software Metrics — A Rigorous Approach*, Chapman and Hall, London.

Gillies, A. (1992) *Software Quality — Theory and Management*, Chapman and Hall, London.

Goodman, P. (1993) *Practical Implementation Of Software Metrics*, McGraw-Hill, London.

Grady, R. B. and Caswell, D. L. (1987) *Software Metrics: Establishing A Company Wide Program*, Prentice-Hall, Englewood Cliffs, NJ.

Hennell, M. (1989) *TESTBED — Technical Description*, Program Analysers Ltd, UK.

Hollocker, C. (1990) *Software Reviews and Audits Handbook*, Wiley, USA.

Humphrey, W. S. (1989) *Managing The Software Process*, Addison-Wesley, Wokingham, UK.

Ishikawa, K. (1987) *Guide To Quality Control*, Asian Productivity Organization, Japan.

Jones, C. (1985) 'A Process Integrated Approach To Defect Prevention', *IBM System Journal*, **24** (2).

Juran, J. (1979) *Quality Control Handbook*, McGraw-Hill, USA.

Kirakowski, J., Porteous, M. and Corbett, M. (1992) 'How To Use The Software Usability Measurement Inventory: The User's View of Software Quality', *Proceedings 3rd European Conference On Software Quality*.

McCall, J., Richards, P. and Walters, G. (1977) *Factors In Software Quality*, US Rome Air Development Report NTIS AD-A049-014, 015, 055.

Ostrand, T. and Weyuker, E. (1984) 'Collecting and Categorizing Software Error Data In An Industrial Environment', *Journal Of Systems and Software*, **4**, 289–300.

Parnas, D. (1972) 'On Criteria To Be Used In Decomposing Systems Into Modules', *CACM*, **14** (1), 221–27.

Pirsig, R. M. (1974) *Zen And The Art Of Motorcycle Maintenance*, Corgi, London.

Sartre, J. -P. (1943) *Being And Nothingness*, Gallimard, Paris.

Shewart, W. (1980) *Economic Control of Quality of Manufactured Product*, American Society for Quality Control.

Shewart, W. (1986; original publication 1939) *Statistical Method From The Viewpoint Of Quality Control*, Dover Publications, USA.

Watts, R. (1987) *Measuring Software Quality*, National Computing Centre, Manchester, UK.

Weinberg, G. (1992) *Quality Software Management: Volume 1. Systems Thinking*, Dorset House Publishing, USA.

Wheeler, D. and Chambers, D. (1986) *Understanding Statistical Process Control*, SPC Press, USA.

Wirth, N. (1974) 'Program Development By Stepwise Refinement', *ACM Computing Surveys*, **6**, 247–259.

Yasuda, K. (1989) 'Software Quality Activities in Japan' in *Japanese Perspectives in Software Engineering*, Addison Wesley.

INDEX